HOUGHTON MIFFLIN BOOKS
IN AMERICAN HISTORY

Under the editorship of
GEORGE E. MOWRY

Americans in Conflict

The Civil War and Reconstruction

David Lindsey
California State University
Los Angeles

Houghton Mifflin Company · Boston
Atlanta Dallas Geneva, Illinois
Hopewell, New Jersey Palo Alto London

To Avery O. Craven,
William T. Hutchinson, and Walter Johnson

The photograph on the cover shows Pvt. Edwin Francis Jennison of a Georgia regiment. Pvt. Jennison was killed at Malvern Hill, shortly after this picture was taken. (The Bettman Archive)

Printed in the U.S.A.

Library of Congress Catalog Card Number: 73–8077

ISBN: 0–395–14068–4

Contents

Maps

Editorial Foreword

This is one of a number of brief volumes being prepared to cover and give attention to significant events and time periods in our history. Each is written by an authority in the period or topic, and each will seek to give both the student and the general reader an understanding of the dominant personalities and the major forces that have given direction to American experience down through the years.

Since there have been many such projects in the past, the question may be asked—why still another? In explaining why societies change, Ralph Waldo Emerson commented that new times virtually demand "new measures and new men." He might also have added to his imperatives, new history. For just as men search the past to understand better the present, the ever-changing present continues to throw new light on the past. From the changing perspectives of each new cluster of years come new interpretations of the past, and from such interpretations, new insights into the present and the future. To that extent no history has ever been definitive; all are to a degree mythic. And like myth, history needs to be changed to encompass both the past and the present to make them understandable.

For some time, there has not been a new brief volume covering the period from 1840 to 1877. But since the celebration of the Civil War Centennial during the sixties, numerous studies have appeared on practically every aspect of these years. Professor Lindsey has dutifully incorporated both the new findings and the subsequent interpretations of this literature. Yet, at the same time, he has maintained an objective viewpoint, seeking to set down the truth as nearly as it can be recorded by one man. One of the most satisfying qualities of this volume is its ample presentation of the black man's contributions to the Civil War, a story of achievements heretofore slighted at best and at worst ignored. In short, this volume is signally successful in using the sensibilities of the present to illuminate the past and the successes and the failures of the past to invigorate those of the present.

George E. Mowry
Chapel Hill, North Carolina

Preface

Since the guns fell silent at Appomattox, successive generations of Americans have exhibited an enduring fascination with their Civil War. Understandably so, for that conflict stands as a unique, intensely American experience, searing the consciousness of a people and sending repercussions through more than a century to today's generation. The war's action and adventure, courage and color are hard to match even in the most suspense-filled fiction. But beyond its pageantry, the Civil War, more than all other American wars, holds a deep meaning for Americans. Its outcome not only determined the survival of the nation but changed the economic face of the country and revitalized long-held American ideals of freedom and human dignity.

In this book I seek to present briefly the story of how and why Americans went to war, how the Union military success was won, and what immediate consequences the war produced. The volume treats concisely those aspects of American development from the 1840's to the late 1870's that bear on the coming of the war, its prosecution, and its results. But the prime focus is American politics, reflecting my own interests and my conviction that social and economic issues in a democratic society ultimately push their way into politics, demanding a political resolution. Covered, too, is the story of the black Americans, who at the time comprised one-eighth of the American population. As ante-bellum slaves, they were active participants in prewar American society. They were not only subjects of wartime policy but active contributors to Union military success and central figures in the postwar Reconstruction.

This largely narrative presentation is designed to provide the reader with a basic introduction to the American Civil War and to serve as a framework for further study. Those seeking the interpretations of other historians and details of military campaigns and engagements may consult the extensive bibliography.

This volume has been a long time in the making, and many persons have given me aid and encouragement, knowingly or otherwise, in its molding. The three scholars to whom it is dedicated did much during my years at the University of Chicago to pique my curiosity and spur my inquiry into the American experience. Countless students during my twenty-seven years of college and university teaching in Ohio, California, Athens, and Madrid contributed more than they knew to stimulating my thinking. Colleagues and fellow historians have generously provided the benefit of their counsel in planning this work, notably Don Fehrenbacher of Stanford, Robert Cruden of Lewis and Clark, Harris Dante of Kent State, and Samuel McSeveney of Vanderbilt. Even more concretely, I am indebted to Harold Hyman of Rice University, who scrutinized the full manuscript and provided helpful criticism; to George Mowry of the University of North Carolina for useful comments on the entire work; and to James Sefton of California State University, Northridge, John Niven of Claremont Graduate School, Irving Ahlquist and David Williams of California State University, Long Beach, each of whom read selected chapters and unsparingly offered constructive suggestions. Finally, my wife Suzanne cheerfully rendered material assistance in the early stages and with affectionate patience gave moral support during the latter stages making possible the completion of the book.

David Lindsey
Belmont Shore, California

PART I

The Coming of the War, 1830–1860

The Civil War was the most fateful struggle in the history of the United States. It looms as a giant landmark in our historical development. Its coming flowed from many streams of America's previous experience. Its fighting cost the lives of over 600,000 young men, more than *all* other American wars combined. Starting as the last gentlemen's war, it became the world's first modern, total war by the time it ended. On its outcome hinged the survival of the nation. From it arose, in essence, a new country as the American people moved away from the old agrarian-rural past toward the industrial-urban society of twentieth-century America. The war outlawed Negro slavery and generated renewed efforts to give the American dream of the Declaration of Independence full meaning in reality.

From its birth in the American Revolution the United States had been a dream and an experiment. To believe that "government rests upon the consent of the governed," that "all men are created equal," and that men are capable of governing themselves seemed fantasy enough in 1776. But to construct a government upon such foundations and to expect it to survive and function seemed sheer delusion. Yet Americans of the Revolutionary generation boldly launched the experiment, giving it practical form in the Constitution of 1787. In time, Americans of the mid-nineteenth century would kill and be killed to determine whether that experiment, "conceived in liberty and dedicated to the proposition" of equality could "long endure."

The story of the coming of the Civil War spans the half century from 1812 to 1861. It is the story of a vigorous people bursting with energy, rushing to possess the land, clear its forests, plant and harvest its yield, unearth its minerals, all the while pushing westward to the continent's limits. It is the story of men of ingenuity and enterprise making mines and mills produce a flood of goods, building roads and rails to the far reaches of the land, and sailing merchant ships to distant shores. It is the story, too, of newcomers fleeing the Old World's restraints for the promise of a better life in the New. The promise, although usually viewed as material gain, carried with it a strain of idealism. Many old and new Americans, believing man to be essentially good by nature, strove to root out social injustices, chief among them slavery, and to mold a society where human liberty and decency would flourish. It is the story also of a struggle for political and economic power, of a battle between human greed and altruism that would climax in an "irrepressible conflict" whose results would reshape the fate and face of the nation.

1

A Nation of Sections

1. Shaping America's Growth

In the years from 1812 to the Civil War, powerful forces played upon and shaped America and its people. The forces that touch men's minds and hearts are difficult to discern, impossible to measure, yet they are potent in effect. One such force was the growing nationalist pride with which men called themselves Americans, as, for example, in the elation they felt when news of Andrew Jackson's smashing victory in 1815 over the British at New Orleans flashed across the land. Enthusiasm roused by that triumph stirred other feelings. Believing that the nation should be made strong and should command the allegiance of all its citizens, Americans after 1815 rallied in support of proposals to buttress the nation with a network of roads, canals, and coastal forts, a tariff to stimulate domestic manufacturing, and a stable banking-currency system. They strove to make the country secure against foreign threats, foster internal growth, lessen divisive forces within, and encourage national unity. Movements like New England's separatist drive of 1814–15 were condemned for weakening the nation's fiber. Even political unity seemed at hand when James Monroe's second election as President in 1820 was hailed as ushering in an "era of good feelings." Nationalism in America was on the move. In the four decades ahead it would have an increasing appeal to men's feelings.

While nationalism drew men's loyalty toward the nation, another force, a kind of micro-nationalism, pulled in the opposite direction. The attachment men felt for local community was a more tangible feeling, since home, family, neighbors, and place were visible and real, while the nation remained an abstraction. The country's sheer physical immensity, diverse geographic sections, differences in habits, ways of living and speaking engendered sectional feelings as men identified themselves as Westerners, Easterners, or Southerners. As Alexis de Tocqueville observed in the 1830's, "what is going on in the United States" resembles a wide river with "two distinct currents flowing in contrary directions in the same channel." Sectionalism pulled in one direction; nationalism, in another—each generating its own growing support. Eventually, their conflicting demands on men's loyalty would propel Americans into a tragic "brothers' war."

While national and sectional attachments grew side by side, democratic and humanitarian impulses mingled with them in moving men to action. Men's dream of a society where liberty, equality, and decency prevailed began to arouse Americans' thinking and feeling. In the constant struggle for wealth and position, some men rose to the top and others were pushed down; a seemingly privileged aristocracy appeared, taking advantage of less fortunate men. Protests arose that American ideals were being subverted. A progressively improving social order seemed out of reach as ruthless, ambitious men brushed aside the weak and handicapped, leaving them even more deprived in the face of odds they could not hope to overcome.

Inherent in the American dream was a belief that the individual himself was perfectible and that his self-improvement bettered society. All that was needed was the will, desire, and impulse. Vigorous Christian evangelism during the 1830's stirred a host of social-economic reform movements. In "freedom's ferment" vocal advocates championed many causes: free public education, international peace, women's rights, decent treatment of paupers, criminals, the mentally ill, the deaf, the dumb, the blind, and those held in bondage, whether wage slaves of the North or chattel slaves of the South. Inevitably reformers collided with entrenched interests that resisted change. But what reformers lacked in practicality they made up in zeal and righteousness. Conflict between reformers and status-quo advocates pushed Americans toward battling in pursuit of or in defense of what they believed right and just, democratic and humane. At length nationalism, cloaked in reforming idealism, would clash with sectionalism, wrapped in a sincere defense of the established social order.

Beyond the arena of moral crusading, the nation's relentless drive westward across the continent brought annexation of new lands that raised questions requiring policy decisions. Which policies men espoused varied with their economic and sectional interests and their moral and political convictions. Which should prevail: the Declaration of Independence with its emphasis on human rights, or the Constitution with its stress on property rights? Were not these two basic documents contradictory when it came to making policy to govern the possible extension of slavery into new western territories? Was it true, as Abraham Lincoln argued, that the Founding Fathers had placed "slavery in the course of ultimate extinction"? Or did they intend, as Jefferson Davis held, that Western Federal territories, "being the common property of the States," were to be open equally to all, including those who might migrate there taking slaves with them?

Meanwhile, other factors were producing "a cement of union," which tended to counteract the centrifugal forces. By 1850, interstate migration carried over 6 million of the nation's 19 million people from the state of their birth to residence in another state. Keeping in touch with friends and relatives at home tended to lessen sectional parochialism. From 1820 to 1860 sweeping changes in transportation—canals, turnpikes, steamboats, railroads—sliced through the barrier of distance spectacularly, while the electric telegraph (commercially established in 1844 by Samuel F. B. Morse from scientist Joseph Henry's work with electricity) gave instant communication over a 500,000-mile network of wires by mid-century. And the nationalist pronouncements of John Marshall in law and John Quincy Adams in diplomacy proved dynamic offsets to sectional tendencies.

But sectionalism still persisted. In Congress, where each section feared others might gain at its expense, debates were heated over tariff and land policy. Federal aid for transportation, too, touched off sectional rows, punctuated by appeals to the Constitution, strictly construed, and to state rights. Whether one argued in a nationalist or sectionalist vein on these matters often depended on who was in power and who was out of power at the moment.

In the four decades preceding 1860 these forces—nationalism, sectionalism, democratic-humanitarian reform, the westward thrust—served to generate an atmosphere of growing sensitiveness, tension, suspicion, rigidity, and ultimate hostility. Difference of opinion came to be magnified into conflict of principle. Rising emotions made calm, rational discussion of issues ever more difficult. The democratic process of free, open airing of issues producing workable accommodations of conflicting interests ran into mounting obstacles as the moral issue of slavery pushed into politics in the 1840's and demanded attention. Men of the various sections, who in the 1820's had felt and thought in much the same way, found themselves in the 1850's growing increasingly tense, rigid, and doctrinaire. Each section, conjuring up an ugly stereotype of its adversary, grew more and more convinced that its way of living and its own security were in jeopardy. Out of this tangle of emotion, idealism, conviction, and economic interest came the Civil War. How did it happen?

2. The Sections Take Shape: Northeast, Northwest, South

A look first at how the sections took shape will help in understanding how the war came. As of 1830 three distinct geographic sections were discernible. Although they shared many similarities, each had sufficiently clear features to set it apart form the others as an identifiable section.

The *Northeast*, lying between Lake Erie and the Atlantic Ocean and extending from the Canadian border in the north to Pennsylvania's southern border, encompassed two subsections—New England and the Middle Atlantic states.

New England's six states, squeezed between the Atlantic to the east, Canada to the north, and the Lake Champlain-Hudson valley to the west, were largely covered by hills like the Berkshires in the south and mountains like the Green, White, and Maine ranges in the north. The rugged, heavily indented coastline stretched for a thousand miles from "down east" Maine southward past Cape Cod's hooked point and Narragansett Bay to Connecticut's shore, sheltered from the open sea by outlying Long Island. Hundreds of protected bays and inlets offered splendid harbors for small craft and larger ocean vessels. While the mountains touched the sea on Maine's "rockbound coast," farther south a narrow coastal plain spread across eastern Massachusetts, Rhode Island, and Connecticut. Rivers flowed mostly from north to south. The Connecticut, the longest, flowed 300 miles from the Canadian border to Long Island Sound. The fall line of New England's many swiftly flowing streams lay close to the sea, providing power for industry, with natural transportation nearby.

By the 1830's New England boasted 200-year-old cities at Boston, Providence, New London, and other points. For two centuries residents had come almost exclusively from the British Isles, making a homogenous population exceeding two million by 1830. During the next three decades French Canadians filtered into northern New England to work as lumbermen in the forests and sawmills. At the same time a wave of Irish immigrants came into southern New England making Boston soon become the largest Irish city outside of Dublin.

As immigrants poured in, natives deserted the area by the tens of thousands. Chiefly farmers unable to make a living, they fled seeking new opportunities in seaboard cities or on fertile lands bordering the Great Lakes. Some pushed farther west to Iowa, Oregon, or California. A few even struck out for, and some found, the main chance—plantations or cotton brokerages—in the South.

Consequently, New England's native population suffered sharp attrition, 1.5 million leaving between 1790 and 1830, and another half a million by 1850. But their places were so quickly filled by the oncoming rush of immigrants that by 1850 the section's population had reached 2.7 million. As new arrivals settled, hostility flared between native Protestants and the resented Irish Catholic newcomers with their strange brogue and "papish practices." In Massachusetts a rampaging mob burned a Catholic convent to the ground. Newcomers at first found the going tough, with only the roughest, most unskilled jobs being open to them.

The chief economic pursuit for most New Englanders, as for most other Americans of the time, was traditionally agriculture. But the difficulties of farming stony hills soon turned men's energies to other pursuits. The section's indented coast, with its good harbors and abundance of fish, drew men to the sea. Indeed, the codfish had long been enshrined as the state symbol of Massachusetts. Forests lying close to the sea had led naturally to the building of all manner of ships for many years. By 1840 ship builders were turning out that masterpiece of marine beauty and sailing efficiency, the swift Yankee clipper which outran anything that sailed the seas. Trading in the West Indies, Europe, the Mediterranean, the China coast, wherever opportunity challenged Yankee shrewdness and bargaining skill, brought the rise of well-to-do merchants in seaports scattered from Portland to Salem, Boston, and New London.

But the section's economy was also undergoing the shock of change brought on by new technology and the increased demands of a growing population. The 1807 Embargo Act, followed by the War of 1812, had driven Yankee vessels off the seas. Distressed merchants, anxious to keep their stymied capital turning a profit, sought other outlets. As the war shut off British supplies, merchants found that textile manufacturing offered attractive returns. Raw material was readily at hand from wool-bearing sheep raised on abandoned farms now converted to pasture. Technical know-how had been available since Samuel Slater put together his mill at Pawtucket in 1793. Water power to turn the wheels that drive the machines for spinning and weaving was available for harnessing in the area's many streams. Cheap labor was in large supply as farmers' daughters welcomed a few years in town tending textile mills to earn dowry money. And the humid, maritime atmosphere provided a special advantage in twisting fibers into textile yarns and threads.

In 1814 three Salem merchants, Francis Lowell, Nathan Appleton, and Patrick Jackson, established the Boston Manufacturing Company plant at Waltham. For the first time in America the entire process from spinning fiber into thread to weaving thread into cloth was operated continuously on power-driven machinery under a single roof. Soon other textile mills blossomed along the rivers at places like Lowell, Lawrence, Manchester, and other towns. Here the mill dominated the town. Across the main street from the mill stood the company's dormitory where female operatives, fresh from the country, got room, board, and company-sponsored protection. Working hours at the mill ran from dawn to dusk six days a week; wages were $1.50 to $2.00 a week. As Irish immigrants increased in numbers, mill owners welcomed them as even cheaper, permanent replacements for the girls who usually stayed only a few years at most.

All the ingredients of the industrial revolution were here—capital, raw materials, labor supply, management, machines, and power to drive them. Although contemporaries did not fully realize it, the model for the industrial-urban America of the future was in the making here.

By 1830 New England was in transition in other ways as well. Traditionally the Calvinist spirit undergirded the New England Puritan's concern for his own salvation and his hope that he was among God's elect, predestined to eternal glory. It was also tied to his desire to make a good communtiy while here on earth. The Puritan ethic—work hard, save one's earnings, be productive, avoid showiness and extravagance—was to do God's will. It also happily reinforced New England Yankee traits—hard driving energy, shrewd bargaining, using one's wits to one's own advantage and profit. The older Puritan harsh view was already softening before the industrial revolution emerged. The old conception of a stern Jehovah, meting out just punishment to sinners, was yielding to the new, warmer view of a God of love and kindness. Unitarianism, called the "religion of the arrived," ushered in a new nineteenth century belief in the oneness of mankind, brotherly love, social consciousness, and social justice. While the sterner Puritan Congregationalism persisted in the countryside, it gave way rapidly in the cities to the warmer, more humane religion that exhorted men to "social usefulness" in attacking society's ills and rooting out injustices in order to build a better society. This influence, too, would go far toward molding a new America.

The *Middle Atlantic* area, lying west and south of New England, stretching over New York, New Jersey, and Pennsylvania as far south as the Mason-Dixon line that formed Pennsylvania's southern boundary, completed the *Northeast*. This area's most striking feature was its diversity. Topography varied from southern New Jersey's flat, sandy pine barrens to the high, green Adirondacks of upper New York, from Pennsylvania's seven-ranged Allegheny Mountains to upstate New York's Finger Lakes country, from Lake Champlain's waters to the rich farm fields of southeast Pennsylvania. The Hudson and Delaware Rivers, flowing southward for hundreds of miles, formed respectively the East coast's best deep-water harbor at New York and a fine anchorage at Philadelphia. Via these river estuaries, ocean ships could penetrate inland to Albany and almost to Trenton.

From colonial times this area's population was the most mixed and cosmopolitan in America. Dutchmen and Swedes in the Hudson and Delaware valleys were joined by English and Welsh and later by numerous Germans and Scotch-Irish. Each group brought its own mores, language, and religion. Here Scotch Presbyterians jostled pietistic Germans, Dutch Reformed, Lutherans, Episcopalians, Quakers, Mennonites, Amishmen, Jews, and Huguenots, each group establishing its own houses of worship and schools. As the nineteenth century advanced, additional Germans, British, and Irish joined older settlers, making a relatively easy transition in the expanding cities of New York and Philadelphia and their satellites. Population grew steadily to almost 6 million in 1850, when, including New England, four out of every ten Americans resided in the Northeast.

The diversity that marked the land and the people was reflected also in the region's economy. Swaths of fertile soil provided the basis for productive farms—Pennsylvania ranking high among the country's wheat-growing states, New York in dairy products, and New Jersey in truck farm vegetable growing. Rich and readily accessible deposits of iron and coal in Pennsylvania brought iron foundries into operation and the beginnings of a steel industry. Coal provided fuel for power to supplement that of the waterfalls for the rapidly developing mills of the Passaic, Delaware, and Lehigh valleys.

Transportation, already good on the broad, deep rivers, improved still more in 1825 when New York under Governor DeWitt Clinton's guidance completed its 363-mile Erie Canal connecting the Hudson at Albany with Lake Erie at Buffalo. In consequence, New York with its magnificent harbor tapped the vast hinterland extending more than a thousand miles into the Great Lakes heartland of the country. Goods and passengers flowed in a rising tide in both directions over the Hudson-Erie Canal route. Pennsylvania tried valiantly but vainly to catch up by constructing a road-canal system from Philadelphia to Pittsburgh 300 miles west on the Ohio River—only to abandon the inefficient scheme and sell the whole works to the Pennsylvania Railroad in 1846.

Here, as in New England, the Middle Atlantic states bore the stamp of what would become twentieth century America—in the broad diversity of people, folkways, and economic pursuits, in the thriving commerce, finance, and banking, and in the rich production of its mines and mills, farms and forests.

Farther west beyond the Appalachians sprawled the fertile lands of the *Old Northwest*. An area richly endowed by nature, ranging west from Pennsylvania's western border, stretching between the Ohio River and the Great Lakes, and spilling across the Mississippi, the Northwest was far from uniform in land, people, and development. Its southern area, touching on the Ohio and extending northward through the southern one-third of Ohio, Indiana, and Illinois, untouched by the ancient ice glaciers, remained hilly, rough, and heavily wooded. Across the northern segments of these states and across Michigan, Wisconsin, Minnesota, and Iowa, the glacier had long ago leveled and smoothed the land, leaving a thick blanket of incredibly fertile soil. Here the broad prairies rolled unbroken westward as far as the eye could see, a farmer's paradise destined to develop as the granary of America and the world.

Settlers, attracted by the good soil and climate, came to occupy the area in four major streams. The earliest, beginning in the 1790's, were upland Southerners from Virginia and Kentucky who occupied the bottomlands of the Muskingum, Scioto, Great and Little Miamis, Whitewater, and Wabash valleys. Most of them stayed in the lower tier of counties closest to the Ohio River, edging as far north as Chillicothe and Lancaster, Richmond and Terre Haute, Vandalia and Springfield. Like most pioneers, they came seeking better farm land; they liked what they found—plenty of big trees meant to them abundant water and good soil.

Following the first settlers, a bit farther north came Pennsylvanians and Jersey men, settling in central Ohio, Indiana, and Illinois. Even today settlements made by Pennsylvania Mennonites and Amish more than a century and a half ago dot the landscape of Ohio's Holmes County and the region just west of Toledo and the Elkhart-Manchester enclave in Indiana. Farther north still, filling the counties along Lake Erie, came New England Yankees and York Staters (many of the latter themselves simply transplanted New Englanders). In Ohio's northeast corner, still called today the Western

Reserve, where Connecticut retained legal title to the land while yielding formal jurisdiction to the United States, the New England imprint remains sharply etched. Yankee towns like Hudson and Oberlin cluster around the central town commons flanked by school and church right out of the Connecticut valley. Town names repeat such New England names as Boston, New Haven, Deerfield, Andover, Salem, Amherst, Norwalk, Bristol, Plymouth, and Marblehead. Farther west Yankees generally avoided Indiana, preferring Michigan's oak grove lands and the prairie lands of northern Illinois, southern Wisconsin, and Iowa.

In addition to the native migration, newcomers from abroad poured into the region also in the nineteenth century, especially after the Erie Canal opened. Germans came in the largest numbers, filling large sections of emerging cities like Cincinnati, Cleveland, Chicago, Milwaukee, and St. Louis. Irish, too, followed by Canadians and Scandinavians, came taking up jobs as laborers on the rising internal improvements or as farmers.

Each migrating family wanted land, and the federal government met their demands generously. To ease the strain of large farm purchases (initially set at 640 acres), a liberalized federal Land Act of 1820 allowed a buyer to purchase 80 acres at $1.25 per acre making a total purchase price of $100 cash. Such an easy land policy, linked with the opening of the Erie Canal, soon made the Old Northwest the fastest-growing section. Its population spurted from 1.5 million in 1830 to almost 5 million by 1850.

At the outset, new settlers cut trees from a few acres, built a cabin, planted corn, and let their pigs wander freely through the woods. But the frontier moved swiftly across the Northwest. By the 1830's farming emerged from primitive, subsistence conditions. The broad, flat prairie lands, under the impact of the newly developed steel moldboard plow, Cyrus McCormick's grain reaper, and a host of planting, cultivating, and threshing machines, soon burgeoned with abundant harvests. In wheat, corn, hogs, and other livestock, the Old Northwest became the dominant provider of America's food supply—and much of the Old World's, too. Other economic pursuits soon took hold. Michigan and Wisconsin became major producers of lumber and forest products. Mining yielded coal in Ohio and Indiana, lead in Illinois and Wisconsin, copper in upper Michigan, and later iron ore in the Lake Superior area.

Transportation facilities were already set by nature. The major rivers, most of them flowing south to the Ohio or southwest to the Mississippi, naturally funneled much of the section's trade southward to New Orleans and the Gulf. But by the 1840's the trade pattern was gradually shifting as the Great Lakes region filled with inhabitants who sent tons of goods flowing eastward via the Great Lakes–Erie Canal pipeline to New York and to Europe beyond. Internally, each state sought to improve transportation facilities by building canals during the 1820's and 1830's. Poorly planned and financed, most of these plans collapsed under the impact of the Panic of 1837. In the economic revival of the 1840's a web of railroads came to crisscross the section. By the 1850's when railroads from the East coast penetrated all the way to Chicago, the highly significant shift in normal trade patterns became even more visible. The section's natural trade orientation southward via the Mississippi–New Orleans route weakened markedly, while strengthening commercial ties pulled the Northwest and the Northeast closer together, with important consequences for the nation's destiny.

The third section of the country, the *South*, might more accurately be pluralized and termed the "Souths," since its immense physical size gave it extraordinary variety and diversity. Sprawling from Maryland south to the Florida Keys and west to Arkansas and the Texas plains, the South spanned a geographic area larger than the Northeast and the Northwest combined. Far from being a uniform physical entity, the section displayed incongruities ranging from Virginia's Dismal Swamp cypress woods to the cloud-shrouded peaks of the Great Smokies on the North Carolina–Tennessee border, from Kentucky's rolling Blue Grass country to Georgia's red-hill piedmont, from Florida's sandy stretches to the Missouri Ozarks, from the miasmic bayous of Louisiana to the fertile Alabama-Mississippi Black Belt. Great physical differences marked the South in its soils, topography, and flora, and in the stamp of its lands. Even ordinary speech echoed with sharp contrasts, as the Kentucky mountaineer had to listen closely to catch the drift of the Georgia "cracker's" soft drawl.

If the South did form something resembling a single section, it had become such perhaps as the result of climate and physical phenomena and a sharing of certain mental attitudes that had arisen from many generations of occupation. Clearly the weather gave the South a certain distinctness of its own. Long, hot summers were both its "blessing and curse." "Ninety degrees in the shade," reflecting fact as well as catch phrase, tempered men's outlook on life and living. And with the heat came high humidity and heavy rains. Downpours crashed suddenly from a summer sky, clear and innocent at one moment, only to jettison a deluge of water at the next. Creeks, brooks, streams were everywhere, coursing down from the red hills, cutting through the coastal plain—"flowing through the lives as well as the lands" of the Southern people, as one observer aptly put it. Big, broad, sluggish rivers ranged from the Potomac on the north, southward through the Rappahannock, York, James, Santee, Pedee, Savannah to the Chatahoochee, Alabama, Tombigbee, Pearl, Perdido, and those master rivers the Tennessee and the Cumberland, flowing westward to rendezvous with the Ohio and the Mississippi. And from farther west came the Missouri, Arkansas, Red, Brazos, Colorado (of Texas), and the Rio Grande.

For people who lived close to the land, weather and water molded the lives of Southerners. The long, hot summers, combined with plentiful rainfall, provided an enviably lengthy growing season. Vegetation of all sorts flourished. With nature herself providing such lavish advantages, farming became the natural pursuit by which Southerners made a living.

The growing season ranged from six months in the upper South to a virtually frost-free year in lower Louisiana, Florida, and Texas. Practically every plant, crop, and vegetable could be grown easily and well in the section. But physical advantages could abruptly turn to dangers. Growing open row crops left the soil exposed to the elements all year round. With no saving winter's frost, like that in the North, to hold the soil tight in winter, heavy rains spelled disastrous erosion, carving gullies that grew to almost canyon size through open cotton fields, for example. Without the protection of modern soil conservation practices, much of the crucial eight to ten inches of the earth's topsoil, in broad areas of the lower South especially, washed off the land to clog the slow-moving brown streams with mud and silt, thereby increasing the risk of periodic floods.

While climate conditioned the South to concentrate on farming and gave it something of a surface unity, the presence of large numbers of Negroes also had a strong effect. By 1860 blacks in the South numbered close to 4 million, meaning that roughly one in three Southerners was a Negro. Since more than 90 per cent of the blacks were held in bondage, Southern whites associating color with social position, developed a mental attitude that placed a special value on the color—or rather colorlessness—of a man's skin, regardless of what the skin covered inside the man. This attitude consciously or subconsciously underlay much of the thinking, feeling, and response of Southern whites—a feeling that whiteness gave superiority in aptitude, ability, and social position, and a bias that blackness consigned a man to society's "mudsill" to perform the menial, manual labor tasks of the society. Negro bondage, as it became a crucial element of intersectional contention, is discussed at length in the next chapter.

Besides racial prejudice and bias, other attitudes affected those who lived in the South and contributed to giving the section some sense of unity. Imported from England in the seventeenth century came the notion that the ideal way of life was that of a country gentleman. Owner of a landed estate with many workers to handle field work and household services, the country squire needed only to supervise his manor. But more than that—since he received much, much was also expected of him. *Noblesse oblige* required that he give his time and energy to his community's affairs, as church warden, militia officer, justice of the peace, or county or state official if called upon. He was assumed to have acquired education, social breeding, refinement, perhaps a liking for books. But he was also expected to follow an active life—riding, hunting, dueling (when the code of honor required), cultivating the social graces that went with being a gentleman. In short, he was looked to as a leader in his community, even as Washington, Jefferson, the Lees, Harrisons, Carters, and Byrds were in theirs. Only a tiny fraction of Southerners ever rose to be country gentlemen. But countless men on the make sought to climb to the estate of country gentlemen. The influence of the ideal was immeasurably potent in Southern society.

Other attitudes—a sensitivity to real and fancied insults to personal honor, a tendency to militance and violence, as frequent duels in the area attest—were apparent along with a haughty scorn for engaging in grubby business matters. But also a feeling of friendly, warm social exchange pervaded the relaxed conversations, the easy give and take of country living. A strong sense of attachment for local place existed, a feeling for the land, for the special place of one's birth and upbringing. If a man moved away from his birthplace and childhood home, it was still home for him—the place to which he looked back fondly and to which he hoped to return. Here was an attitude perhaps typical of a rural, farming society where land, especially that unique piece of land from which came one's livelihood, was special and precious. From this attitude arose a sense of stability, of belonging, of permanence that was peculiarly Southern.

There was, too, a curious paradox and contradiction in other attitudes as well. The sense of personal integrity made the honor system of student examinations operate effectively at Southern universities long after Northern institutions had been forced to abandon it. Yet honesty, courtesy, special deference to women (if they were white), consideration for the feelings of others clashed inexplicably with those recurring traits of oversensitiveness, narrowminded bigotry, disregard for and even violence toward inferiors upon occasion. How could all this be squared with the sunnier side, represented in the adage that the way to tell a Southerner from a Yankee was that the former would stop and chat with you just to pass the time of day, while the Yankee would talk only if he figured he could make a fast buck from you?

As suggested above, favorable physical conditions turned Southerners to farming. But in farming the differences were marked, for example, between the small subsistence farm of the Arkansas frontier and the medium-sized general farm of the Shenandoah valley of Virginia as opposed to the giant cotton plantation of the Alabama Black Belt or the sweeping acres of a central Tennessee livestock spread. But whatever the farm's size, the livelihood of most Southerners came from farming and related occupations.

Types of farming varied widely from one area to another. The old tobacco world of long-settled tidewater Virginia-Maryland had in colonial times set the pattern later copied elsewhere in much of the South: the large estate with endless rows of tobacco tended by bent-over black slaves supervised by overseer and master. Carolina's rice-raising region with its unique methods and problems was almost as old as the tobacco-growing area and formed a distinct, colorful region. The "sugar bowl" area of southern Louisiana, too, formed a special subsection with its frost-free, year-round operations that proved highly profitable when well managed. Farther north, the fertile pastures of central Kentucky-Tennessee spawned livestock raising that bred not only sleek race horses but also the stolid mule, which served as the ubiquitous, formidable work animal of the deep South where high temperatures ruled out the horse.

But far and away the reigning crop was cotton. It had not always been so. Indeed, until the late eighteenth century only a minute cotton crop was raised in America, and that a special type known as Sea Island or long-staple cotton. It was a type that would grow only under the benign, maritime influence of the Georgia-Carolina coast (and offshore islands) and was in great demand for its strong, 2½-inch long fibers. Only after 1794 when Connecticut Yankee Eli Whitney, serving as a tutor on a Georgia plantation, contrived the cotton gin that effectively separated the small, black cotton seeds from the fibers in the boll did cotton growing spread over the face of the South. The cotton gin in fact propelled a revolution in both agriculture and industry. Its impact shook the nation.

Its immediate effect in the South stimulated the raising of Upland or short-staple cotton, called the "the most democratic of plants" since it grew on almost any type of soil under almost any conditions wherever a 200-day frost-free growing season prevailed. By 1800 Georgia-Carolina farmers raised 30 million pounds of cotton, then doubled that by 1810. Rapidly others rushed into cotton production, spreading it over the vast, untilled acres that General Andrew Jackson had seized from the Creek Indians in central Alabama-Mississippi. Land-hungry settlers surged into the region by the tens of thousands. Cotton output rose sharply. By the 1840's an immense "cotton kingdom" blossomed in a giant, white crescent extending from Virginia through the Carolinas and Georgia across Alabama, Mississippi, Louisiana, then north into Arkansas and Tennessee with spurs jutting off into Florida and Texas. In 1834 the south Atlantic coastal states marketed 150 million pounds; the newer South, 297 million pounds. Dixie, which in 1820 supplied half of Britain's cotton import needs, provided 82 percent of Britain's needs and 75 per cent of Europe's by 1840. In 1850 cotton comprised two-thirds of the total value of American exports. Understandably Southern men cried, "Cotton is King!" At home Northern mills absorbed 78 million pounds in 1831 and eight times that amount in 1850. The Northeast's industrial revolution came to depend much more on cotton than on wool.

By the late 1850's the population of the South was composed roughly one-third of Africans whose seventeenth-and eighteenth-century forebears had been kidnapped in western Africa and forcibly transported to America and two-thirds of people drawn almost exclusively from the British Isles during the same centuries. In the first four decades of the nineteenth century Southerners, pushing swiftly westward, filled the lower Mississippi valley

Slaves in the land of cotton. (Brown Brothers)

and the broad Gulf plain as far west as Texas. The population makeup remained essentially unchanged as new European immigrants persistently avoided settling in the South. Indeed, in those years some Southerners, as noted earlier, migrated north across the Ohio River (as did Abraham Lincoln's family in 1816) seeking new land to avoid competing with slave labor.

In the newer South of the Gulf Plain and lower Mississippi valley, men pushed harder to seize better lands, get ahead quicker and make money faster. Slaves there were often worked harder than in older parts of the South in order to produce bigger cotton crops. In the newer South, too, religious groups changed under the impact of frontier evangelist camp meetings, emotional conversions, and the ever-present circuit rider. Methodists and Baptists, adapting readily to new conditions, easily won the largest followings, trailed by the less flamboyant Presbyterians, while the more sedate Episcopalians remained strongly rooted in the seaboard South. French, and some Spanish, influences were most visible in New Orleans and the "Cajun" country of the Louisiana bayou region where French speech, law, terminology, and customs lingered firmly.

By the 1830's, then, the South exhibited diversity and variety. But the rise of the cotton kingdom with the accompanying spread of Negro bondage was beginning to give an appearance of sectional unity and coherence to the section. During the next two decades a growing insistence upon orthodox conformity in upholding the Southern social system with its "peculiar institution" would render the section even more close-knit.

2

Dilemmas of Democracy on the Move

During the second quarter of the nineteenth century the United States was growing with startling speed. Agriculture, industry, and commerce expanded swiftly to ever higher levels of output and activity. So, too, did America's population expand. And its territory spread westward from the Mississippi watershed to absorb the immense area from Texas to California and the vast desert-mountain area in between.

While territory and material production swelled, Americans became increasingly aware of shortcomings in putting into full practice the ideals they had long professed. Liberty, equality, and justice were loudly proclaimed every Fourth of July. But inconsistencies, limitations, and failures to implement these ideals were widely evident. In the Jacksonian era a start was made in broadening the suffrage, ending imprisonment for debt, launching free common schools, and tackling the problems posed by society's unfortunates and oppressed. The continued existence of slavery—at the very least an embarrassment in a self-proclaimed free, democratic, Christian society—troubled the consciences of many men. In time, social reforming efforts would combine in a concentrated drive to eradicate slavery.

At the same time, the westward drive, seemingly unrelated to the slavery issue as it first appeared, would at length focus the country's attention on the dilemma inherent in spreading slavery into newly-gained territories won in the name of extending freedom. By midcentury, acquisition of a large chunk of Mexican land would force political leaders into making a decision on the issue of slavery in the new territories—a decision many had hoped to evade. But the question would not down—and persisted to torment America's leaders throughout the 1850's.

1. Slavery Casts a Dark Shadow

Slavery took root in the South during colonial times when Africans were imported to do the hard labor of clearing the forests, plowing, planting, and harvesting crops in Britain's North American colonies. Since slavery was unknown in English common law, Negroes were initially treated as indentured servants, held in the same manner as poor English and Scotch-Irish immigrants, bound to labor for a master for a term of four to seven years, thereby reimbursing the latter who had paid for the cost of the transatlantic passage. Gradually the term of the African immigrant's indenture was extended to life. Then it was passed to his children, and chattel slavery became a fact. British colonial subsidies for American staple crops such as tobacco, which required large numbers of laborers for planting and harvesting, helped fix slavery as a labor system from Maryland-Virginia south to Georgia.

By 1808 when Congress finally outlawed the brutally vicious African slave trade, Negro bondsmen in the South numbered 1,160,000. The total grew to 2 million by the 1830's and to 3.8 million in 1860 (when approximately 250,000 free Negroes also lived in the South). Distribution of the slave population was extremely uneven, varying from a few in the Appalachians and other areas unsuited to staple crops to heavy concentrations in tidewater Virginia, the coastal Carolinas and Georgia, and the cotton belt running west from Georgia. In some counties slaves formed two-thirds to three-fourths of the total population. Although slavery generally occupied the best farm lands of Dixie, by 1860 more than 500,000 slaves also lived in Southern towns and cities, working as servants, mechanics, laborers in construction, manufacturing, cabinet making, iron working, and barbering.

Ownership of slaves was also uneven. The 1850 census showed that one-half of the 347,525 slaveholders held fewer than four slaves each, while another 135,000 had fewer than twenty each. Of large slaveholders, 35,900 owned between twenty and ninety-nine, and 1,700 others held more than 100 each. Overall, approximately one-fourth of the South's white population was directly connected with "the peculiar institution" as part of a slaveholding family. However, to say that the other three-fourths of the white people had no immediate concern with slavery is misleading, for they were often closely tied to and much influenced by slaveowning families. Large slaveowners, especially, exercised in Southern affairs, political, social, and cultural, an influence proportionately far greater than their numbers warranted. Furthermore, nonslaveholders usually aspired to become slaveowning planters; hence, they deferred to the latter, whose social status, prestige, and influence they hoped one day to acquire themselves. Often they were far more tenacious in defending slavery than were owners themselves.

By 1850 the Black Belt of the Gulf States, running from Georgia west to Louisiana, held the heaviest concentration of slaves. Here cotton plantations ran to hundreds and sometimes thousands of acres tended by scores and even hundreds of laboring slaves. Slavery was primarily a labor system. A large plantation was operated somewhat in the fashion of a large-scale factory, with the same economic advantages of close supervision, specialization, and division of labor. Besides the field hands, other slaves worked as carpenters, mechanics, masons, leather workers, coopers, metal workers, cooks, and house domestics. To carry out the plantation's main objective—cotton production—the owner often assigned to his overseer the supervising of day-to-day operations. The overseer usually organized workers into gangs under drivers, who were themselves slaves. Gangs did the plowing, "chopping" (hoeing), thinning, and finally the picking and ginning of the cotton. Other gangs tended the livestock, corn, peanuts, and vegetables in an effort to make the plantation self-sufficient. To stimulate increased production some planters offered incentives and rewards like a shortened workday if a specific task was done quickly, special holidays, extra rations of food and clothing. For the most part workdays differed little from those of other farm workers of the time—work from sunup to sundown with a two-hour midday break; hard, physical labor for the field hands; Sundays off and a two-week Christmas holiday. Living conditions were generally primitive, food rough and coarse, shoes and clothing usually sturdy and adequate. Even vehement antislavery men conceded that slaves were normally adequately fed, clothed, and housed.

Generalizing about slavery is risky. Practices varied widely, depending on many factors: age and sex of the slave; type of work (sugar harvesting was intense and prostrating); region of the South (generally work was less harsh in older, stable areas like Virginia, more rigorous in newer lands like Mississippi); size of plantation or farm (where the owner himself worked along with a few slaves, they were usually better treated); personality, temperament, and conscience of the master (some were kindly; some, cruel and sadistic); personality and temperament of the slave (some were amenable and cooperative; others, balky and rebellious).

Yet the business of owning and being owned imposed certain demands upon both the owner and the owned. Restriction and limitation accompanied benefit and advantage. From the owner's standpoint, tight control over his labor force gave him the benefits of division and specialization of labor. If births exceeded deaths on the plantation, his labor force increased. He was untroubled by labor turnover, strikes, walkouts. He could plan ahead, knowing how many workers he would have from one year to the next and how much production he could expect.

But his disadvantages were also large, larger than he usually recognized. Disease and epidemics could cripple his work force. A slave escaping was always a risk. But even more serious was the economic rigidity that straightjacketed him; much of his capital was tied up in his labor. He could not adjust production to changing market conditions. His costs remained fixed. If cotton prices sagged, he could not, as the Yankee manufacturer could, lay off some workers (or all) until prices recovered. True, he could sell slaves, but doing so meant reduced production for years ahead, even though crop prices might rebound in a year or two. Although he paid no wages, he bore costs of food, shelter, clothing, medical and certain social services, all of which he must cover out of his production.

To suggest that slaves enjoyed advantages would seem patent nonsense. Yet in the sense that prison provides perfect social security, slavery too offered that condition. All the slave's physical needs were met—food, housing, clothes, child care, health care, old age security. He was relieved of uncertainty about job or unemployment, sickness or lost time on the job; his job was always there. He had no need, therefore, to worry or hurry. He need not worry about bad weather, drought, flood, insects, and blight, nor about market conditions or falling prices. The morrow would take care of itself.

But the very fact that the slave was exempt from such worries robbed him of his individuality, his dignity as a human being. To eliminate the stimulus of worry stole from him all responsibility for his own affairs, his family, his life. Physical freedom had already been torn from him. He could make no choices on his own, no decisions about employer, job, home, way of living. He was subject to the humiliation of physical punishment at the hands of another man. He had no civil rights or privileges and was not a citizen. He could be bought and sold as a chattel, a thing, without his consent. His family could be broken up involuntarily. A chance for education, even for religious worship, was severely limited. But most degrading was to be robbed of the spur of worry and the incentives of free choice and responsibility to determine his own course.

The environment of slavery bred an atmosphere of mutual fear and dread that sometimes exploded into violence. Although it was said that the owner's property was in "the slave's labor," the owner did in fact exercise total control over his slave's existence. Even the kindest master on occasion resorted to physical punishment, and if a slave escaped, his master resorted to hunting him down. The time might arise when economic necessity forced him to sell or buy part of a Negro family. Antislavery propaganda sometimes exaggerated, but brandings, floggings, mutilations, even murder occurred within the system. Slaves who rebelled or fought back against unfair treatment were brutally punished, as numerous records testify. If an owner killed a slave, he often got off scot-free since a black's testimony was not admitted in court.

To believe that Negro slaves adjusted readily to their lot because of a carefree nature is sheer delusion. True, some house servants responded to kind treatment with loyal and devoted service. But field hands did not relish working day after day in the broiling sun for another man's gain. They employed many self-protecting devices against overwork and abuse: slowdown in the field, pretended illness, self-mutilation, and at times open defiance. Slave revolts were frequent enough to keep Southerners defensive and edgy. The Gabriel Prosser revolt in Richmond (1800) and the more serious slave conspiracy planned by free Negro Denmark Vesey in South Carolina (1822) brought severe reprisals. The Virginia uprising led by the remarkable Nat Turner (1831), who believed himself divinely appointed, dealt death to 57 whites, but 100 Negroes died in retribution. Rumors of "Negro plots" spread panic through parts of the South often between 1830 and 1860. Controls grew tighter: fewer passes to leave the plantation, night patrols in the countryside, more police in the cities.

The atrocity that was slavery exposed its most horrid brutality in the slave markets, scattered from Washington to New Orleans. To be "sold down the river" struck a Virginia slave with terror, the nightmare of being shackled by the slave dealer in a coffle of bondsmen headed for certain extermination by overwork or malaria in the miasmic Louisiana sugar fields. As Lincoln said in 1854, even Southerners were revulsed by that "sneaking individual . . . the SLAVE-DEALER." The slave trader often took advantage of upper South planters in distress, buying their slaves cheap and selling at high prices in the deep South. By 1850 the price per slave ran about $800, at times up to $1,500 for a "No. 1 field hand" and $1,300 for "best grown girls." The domestic slave trade carried 180,000 slaves from upper to lower South between 1840 and 1850, 230,000 in the next decade. Profits were enormous, one dealer making $500,000 in a few years.

Whether slavery itself was profitable has long been debated. The answer is not easily calculated, for it involves technical accounting questions, as for example whether the loss of interest on a planter's capital invested in slaves should be charged as a cost of doing business. But several points are clear. The $100,000 investment in slaves required for large plantation operation would have yielded a better return if put into manufacturing or commercial enterprise. However, this is perhaps another way of saying that agriculture itself is seldom profitable. What gave Southern planting the appearance and illusion of profitability was the steady rise in land prices, which somewhat concealed the widening margins between production costs and market price of product.

To avoid complete reliance on agriculture, some Southern spokesmen like William Gregg urged diversification into manufacturing. Others like James D. B. DeBow called for commerce to be managed by Southern men. Little came of either proposal. By 1860 the South produced less than 10 per cent of the nation's total manufactures; industrial employment in the preceding decade grew modestly from 165,000 to 190,000. The Southerner's distaste for business cost him heavily. To market his crop the planter engaged commission merchants or "factors." The factor, residing in a commercial town or port, arranged for warehousing and shipping of crops, securing insurance, loans, equipment, and supplies, finding buyers for cotton, and purchasing slaves. Most factors were Yankees, who collected fat brokerage fees of 2½ to 10 per cent. About forty cents of every dollar paid for cotton went to New York merchants or their agents in the South. Planters complained of constant indebtedness to factors, who often dictated the kind and amount of crop acceptable on consignment to meet the planters' debts. Clearly the South did not take full economic advantage of its immense cotton harvests, allowing peripheral profits to be siphoned off into other hands.

Why, then, did Southerners cling so tenaciously and so long to their "peculiar institution" of slavery, which brought doubtful gains and exacted heavy economic toll? The answer lay in Southern social attitudes and self-delusions. For one, being an owner of a large plantation was viewed as the highest pursuit a man could engage in, conferring social position and prestige, regardless of how marginally profitable the pursuit might be in hard reality. Being a plantation master with many persons to do his bidding and with many dependent upon him brought the planter certain psychic rewards of self-importance and self-esteem, immeasurable in terms of dollars and cents. Further, the fear that emancipating slaves, especially in the deep South where Negroes were most numerous, might generate racial warfare and plunge whites into the position of a minority reinforced a notion that blacks were not qualified to enjoy freedom. These factors compounded the anti-Negro feelings of white nonslaveholders, who fearing black economic competition wished to keep blacks in bondage. Small farmers aspiring to be planters joined in a vigorous effort to maintain slavery as a means of saving what little social status they enjoyed, even though slavery brought them no direct economic benefits.

Would slavery have died out in time, as lands suitable for growing staples became fully exploited? Some contended that this would occur by the late 1800's. But considerable evidence suggests a contrary conclusion. Much usable land in the South had not been occupied even by 1860, as substantial expansion of Southern agriculture from 1865 to 1914 indicates. Besides, surplus slaves could have been transferred from farming to urban industry as the century advanced. And, clearly, neither contemporary Northern opponents nor Southern defenders of the day believed that slavery was about to wither and die, as the torrid disputes in the 1850's over slavery's extension vividly testify.

So black bondage stamped its harsh, vicious imprint on the section that proclaimed its benefits—indeed on the entire society of the nation that professed to be democratic. It did much harm, physical and psychic, to the Negro. The injury it inflicted on the slaveowners, and indirectly on their defenders, in exercising life-and-death control over other human beings was less obvious though nonetheless large. Often the worst and most inhuman traits were brought to the surface, even among the most well-intentioned of slaveholders. The barbaric injustice and viciousness of the institution bequeathed complex racial problems of discrimination and hostility, which nineteenth century generations evaded or refused to recognize. Even the immediate economic consequence of Negro slavery was to plunge the Cotton Kingdom itself into economic bondage to Northern and British masters of capital and industry. And this situation existed in an age when Jacksonian Democracy touted free economic enterprise as the great liberating force in an age when it was hoped that liberty, equality, and justice were to be attained.

2. *Jacksonian Democracy at Work*

When General Andrew Jackson stormed out of Tennessee, riding the wave of his smashing 1828 Presidential victory, and moved into Washington,

Senator Daniel Webster observed, "nobody knows what he will do"; "my own opinion is that he will bring a breeze with him." Little did Webster suspect that Jackson's breeze would shortly become a gale which would thrust America full speed toward its "manifest destiny" and set the wheels of political and social change spinning for a generation to come. Nor could anyone predict in 1830 that Jacksonian policies and reform drives would set the stage for civil war a generation later.

"The age of Jackson" during the second quarter of the nineteenth century spurred efforts to invigorate popular self-government and democratic ideals. Jacksonians held certain political, economic, and social beliefs, and often spoke in terms of ideals voiced by the Founders of the republic. In general terms, the Jacksonians believed that each individual should be free to develop his own talents and to express his views. They also held that the people, as the sovereign authority, should determine political decisions by majority vote. Equality of opportunity, they argued, should become fact as well as a slogan. The twin doctrines of the free individual and equality of opportunity should operate in the economic as well as in the political sphere.

Politically, voting restrictions were already disappearing. By 1840 universal white suffrage, unrestricted, prevailed in all but three states. By a curious twist of prejudice and intolerance, the invigorated democratic spirit failed to carry over to two significant groups—free Negroes and women. Indeed, former Negro voters lost the franchise during the Jacksonian era almost everywhere except in New England; and no new states joining the Union between 1820 and 1860 authorized Negro suffrage. In fact, during these years Northern states increased the limitations upon free black residents.

Nevertheless, popular sovereignty became the rallying cry of the day. The Jacksonian tenet that the people (at least the whites) were the source of political authority and the ultimate sovereign came to be implemented not only by a broadened suffrage but also by wider direct popular participation in the political process. Where an earlier generation had believed that officeholding was best reserved for the qualified elite and that the unruly mob must be checked by built-in restraints, the older restrictions now fell rapidly before the new democratic upsurge. The people's nominating convention now came to replace the old, suspect legislative caucus in choosing candidates for President and for most lesser offices as well. Election of Presidential electors, formerly done by state legislatures, yielded to direct voting on electors by the electorate; so did choosing governors and even state court judges. Property and other similar qualifications for holding office were swiftly swept aside.

Broader public participation spurred what Jacksonians called "rotation of office," meaning executive appointment of loyal partisans to fill public jobs for a limited term. Denounced by opponents as a vicious "spoils system," it was staunchly defended by Jackson himself, who maintained that public office was not "a species of property" to be retained for a long time for "promoting private interests." Rather, he said, the principle of equality of opportunity required open access to Federal jobs by all citizens. That appointees should be drawn from the party victorious at the polls was only right because such partisans reflected the will of the majority. And rule by the majority was a fundamental democratic principle.

Jackson also underscored the doctrine of equality of opportunity in the economic field in his "war" against the second Bank of the United States, which culminated in his veto of the Bank recharter bill in 1832 and his subsequent withdrawal of Federal deposits from the Bank. The "Monster" Bank must be destroyed, he vowed, because as a financial monopoly enjoying special privilege, it denied others equal opportunity in the banking field. Jackson's Chief Justice, Roger B. Taney, reinforced this doctrine in his celebrated *Charles River Bridge* decision (1837), which attacked special privilege and insisted on equal opportunity for private corporations to compete on their own merits. This decision opened the door for states to adopt general incorporation acts that enabled hosts of entrepreneurs to plunge eagerly into a multitude of economic undertakings on a free and equal basis. Government, its functions held to a minimum, would preserve order and serve simply as umpire in the "race of life" among free individuals. Curiously, the leveling, egalitarian influence, much noted in Jackson's day, generated the ironic paradox that freedom to pursue one's economic interests unrestrained often increased economic inequality among individuals.

The Presidency itself received a vital strengthening through Jackson's own efforts. He insisted that only the President serve as the spokesman-leader for all the people of the United States and that the President must function independently of Congress's attempted domination.

His efforts at redefining the role of the central government ignited controversies that extended to the Civil War and beyond. For example, in 1832 Congress reinforced the protective tariff and Jackson approved the bill. In response, South Carolina not only protested but also adopted an ordinance nullifying the Federal tariff law. Nullification was rationalized on the basis of John C. Calhoun's theory that in the American Federal system sovereignty lay with the people of each state. According to Calhoun's theory, since the states had granted specified, limited powers to the Congress through the Constitution of the United States, a sovereign state could properly determine the limits of such powers. If Congress adopted an act exceeding the granted powers, the people of each state. could properly exercise its sovereign authority and nullify such an act.

Some nullifiers went further to assert that a state could also secede from the Union. Jackson promptly rejected South Carolina's nullification effort, thundering that "the power to annul a law of the United States' assumed by one state "is incompatible with the existence of the Union" and borders on treason. He threatened to use military force, if needed, to compel obedience to Federal law by South Carolinians. His strong nationalist affirmation won support on all sides and forced South Carolina to back down, a move that could be taken gracefully in view of the compromise tariff of 1833, which reduced duties. But the controversy remained essentially unresolved—whether a state alone or with other states could reject Federal authority. Three decades later the issue would reappear when seven Southern states, again claiming state sovereignty, would withdraw from the Union. The then President, Abraham Lincoln, knowing well Jackson's 1832 position, would take the same nationalist stand as Jackson. The result would be Civil War.

Despite his nationalist stance in the nullification crisis of 1832, Jackson's attachment to strict constructionist views tightly limiting national power led him to negate efforts for an active Federal government. To Henry Clay's sweeping "American System" proposals for Federal action to stimulate the nation's economic well-being and self-sufficiency, Jackson interposed vetoes. Clay envisoned a balanced national economy: manufacturing fostered by a Federal protective tariff to supplement an already thriving agriculture; commerce encouraged by Federal construction of roads to speed the interchange of eastward flowing farm goods and westward flowing manufactured products, plus a stable monetary-credit system nurtured by the Bank of the United States, a semi-government corporation. In such an "American System," said Clay, all economic interests—manufacturing, farming, trade, finance—would flourish, assuring national security and prosperity. Jackson rejected every Clay-sponsored measure. But the Clay program would not be put down. A generation later it was revived in the hands of a dynamic Republican party that gained political power on the eve of the Civil War.

In the Jacksonian era the desire to make the American dream a reality whipped up a whirlwind of social reform movements. Often inspired by evangelical Christianity, reformers called for an end to war, to imprisonment for debt, and to mistreatment of paupers, orphans, and insane persons. They worked for improved prison conditions and rehabilitation of criminals and for humane treatment of society's misfits and the disadvantaged. Schemes for utopian communities dotted the landscape at Brook Farm, Oneida, New Harmony, and at Fourierist settlements spread from New Jersey to Illinois. Each of these communities claimed to show the way as a model for the good society. Emerson commented that one could scarcely walk down the street in Concord without encountering a man who had plans in his pocket for reforming society. Female militants demanding equal rights for women in 1848 gathered in a national convention at Seneca Falls, New York. Led by Lucretia Mott and Elizabeth Cady Stanton, the resulting Women's Rights Association issued a ringing Declaration of Rights, a model for all subsequent women's liberation drives. Dr. Samuel Gridley Howe, returning from six years of bloody fighting for Greek independence, established a school for deaf-mutes at Boston. The workingmen's movement, originating in Philadelphia in 1828, demanded better treatment for labor, universal free education, and a host of other political and social reforms.

The drive for universal schooling made rapid strides in the 1830's. In the Jeffersonian tradition, education was looked upon as the key to success for a democratic society—an educated, informed citizenry making enlightened decisions on matters of public policy. Following the pioneer work of establishing statewide public school systems, which was done by Horace Mann in Massachusetts and Henry Barnard in Connecticut, other states moved swiftly to create tax-supported common schools. Thaddeus Stevens led the fight in Pennsylvania, which by 1852 had enrolled 492,000 public school students, a figure exceeded only by New York's 862,000.

The increasing rise in literacy, brought on by schooling, stimulated demand for the penny newspapers that first appeared in New York in the 1830's; within twenty years papers like James Gordon Bennett's sensationalizing *Herald*, Horace Greeley's crusading *Tribune*, and the more sedate *Post* under William Cullen Bryant and *Times* under Henry J. Raymond boasted large circulations. An enlarged reading public increased the demand for books, especially those of writers like James Fenimore Cooper, Washington Irving, Edgar Allen Poe, Henry Wadsworth Longfellow, and Herman Melville; and those remarkable historians Francis Parkman, William H. Prescott, and George Bancroft, whose works enjoyed a wide popularity.

The other major reform movement that surged forward rapidly in the Jackson years was the antislavery drive. By the forties it had absorbed the energies of many social reformers who earlier had labored in other causes. The antislavery drive forms the substance of the next chapter. By a curious, ironic paradox, while sympathy for the slave was aroused by the reformers, few showed concern for free Negroes, North or South, or endeavored to include them under the umbrella of democratic ideals.

3. *Free Negroes as Society's Orphans*

The nonslave Negro population of the country grew from 434,000 in 1850 to 488,000 in 1860, forming 12 per cent and 11 per cent respectively of the nation's blacks. Freedom had been gained in a variety of ways. Some Negroes, back in colonial days, upon completing their terms as indentured servants became free landowners; others won emancipation for service in the American Revolution or the War of 1812. In the post-Revolutionary years Northern states (from Pennsylvania northward) had enacted emancipating legislation. Private manumissions had released some Negroes from bondage; in many cases the freedman was the offspring of a master by a slave mother. The statistics for 1850 revealed 581 mulattoes for every 1,000 free Negroes, in contrast to 83 mulattoes for every 1,000 in the slave population. In some instances, self-purchase secured freedom; most notable cases were those of Lunsford Lane, who accumulated savings out of sales of tobacco he cured in Raleigh, North Carolina, and Lott Carey, foreman of a Richmond tobacco house who later went as a Baptist missionary to Liberia.

In the South, freedmen tended to gravitate to the larger cities, doubtless because the chance of making a living was greater and urban anonymity promised a less exposed, more satisfying personal family and social life than did rural living. In the three decades preceding the Civil War the number of free Negroes in Southern cities increased both proportionately and in absolute numbers. Of Dixie's 250,000 free Negroes in 1860 at least 80,000 lived in cities. They exceeded slaves by 10 to 1 in Baltimore, by 9,200 to 1,700 in Washington; while over 18,000 lived in New Orleans.

Jobs were available to free Negroes in larger proportion in the South than in the North. Often they were employed in manual or domestic work, as farm workers, house servants, stable and livery workers; in heavy labor as laborers—roads, canals, and railroads; as workers in tobacco warehouses and small factories; and as porters, dock workers, and stevedores. In many cities they moved into skilled trades as carpenters, masons, and metal workers. Some became entrepreneurs, managing their own shops as tailors, shoemakers, cabinetmakers, or running hotels and restaurants. In some instances they became independent landowners and farmers. One Virginia county in 1860 showed that one-third of Negro family heads had moved up from agricultural work to become farm owners or renters. In Louisiana wealthy black landowners included in their numbers Thomy Lafon with a half-million dollar fortune and Cyprian Ricaud who in 1851 bought a $225,000 plantation in Iberville Parish with ninety-nine slaves. Other Louisiana blacks also operated plantations using slave labor. But most Negro slaveholders acquired slaves on a temporary, benevolent basis, usually acquiring a friend or relative and not freeing him because to do so would have required the manumitted slave to leave the state.

Free Negroes lived in the South under serious restrictions that limited freedom and opportunity more tightly as the years advanced from 1830 to 1860. Generally the free Negro was resented, the fear being that his very presence threatened the continuation of slavery. It was hoped that he might somehow go away. A free Negro was required to carry with him a certificate of freedom. If he lost his "free papers," he might be jailed as a vagrant, hired out, or even sold as a runaway slave. In border states unscrupulous slave dealers were on constant lookout for unwary free blacks to be sent to Deep South slave markets. Or if he failed to pay his debts, taxes, or fines, he could be reduced to servitude by being hired out until his earnings covered the amount in default.

Political, civil, and social rights were severely limited. The free Negro could not hold office in any Southern state and could not vote, except in North Carolina until 1835 and Tennessee until 1834. He could own property and make contracts in most states, but he could not testify against a white except in Louisiana and Delaware. In many states he was prohibited from possessing firearms and liquor. He had to observe a nightly curfew and could not attend public gatherings except in church. He could not move to another Southern state since state laws prohibited his entry; for illegal entry he could be fined $500, which if unpaid could result in his being sold into slavery. But advantages of free status over slavery were clear: he could marry, have children, enjoy a measure of family life in the privacy of his home without constant surveillance by whites, follow a trade, and enjoy the earnings of his own labor.

That the free Negro made advances in the face of such adverse odds says much for his determination and spirit. In cities throughout the South free Negroes banded together in churches, established schools, cultural societies, and mutual aid associations. Baltimore at one time had thirty-five mutual aid societies. In Charleston the Bonneau Literary Society met weekly to stimulate "Literary Improvement . . . and . . . our Mental Faculties," and in New Orleans the noted masked balls were planned in detail to emulate white society. The Brown Fellowship Society in Charleston operated a school for black children. Some individual Negroes, notably in Louisiana, made impressive contributions: Norbert Rillieux developed in 1846 a vacuum cup that revolutionized sugar refining operations; Victor Sejour contributed verse to an anthology of Negro poets, published in 1845 in New Orleans and later went on to see twenty-one of his plays produced in Paris theaters.

In the North, Negroes, numbering 238,000 by 1860, were of course not subject to legal slavery. But many restrictions hemmed in their exercise of freedom. The prevailing attitude held the Negro to be inferior and hence not entitled to equal rights and opportunities. By 1840 only four states—Massachusetts, New Hampshire, Maine, and Vermont—permitted Negro suffrage; New York allowed voting by Negroes who met the property requirement; Connecticut, Pennsylvania, and New Jersey withdrew the suffrage after once permitting it. In the era from Jackson to Lincoln, when suffrage was being extended broadly, no new entering state provided for Negro suffrage. Many states either prohibited or severely restricted Negro migration into their areas. Ohio law, for example, required an incoming black to produce a court certificate of his freedom and to post a $500 bond as a guarantee of good behavior. Strictly speaking, the Negro was entitled to legal protection and redress of wrongs. But in legal cases, all states but one barred Negroes from jury service; five banned his testimony against whites. By prejudice, custom, and practice in most states, he was segregated in transportation facilities, schools and places of public accommodation, and entertainment.

In making a living, too, the black encountered obstacles. Even if he had learned a trade while he was a slave, employment restrictions often blocked him as a freedman from landing a job as a skilled craftsman or from becoming an apprentice. Opportunities usually were available only as common laborer or domestic servant. After 1840, Negroes faced increasing competition even in these fields because incoming European immigrants flooded the labor market. But despite limitations, some Negroes in the North managed to do well economically. In the 1850's blacks in Cincinnati held property valued at $500,000 while black bank accounts in New York totaled over $200,000. Barber shops, restaurants, and catering services were often run profitably by Negro owners. And some Negro farmers prospered; Rush County, Indiana, showed forty-six families owning a total of 3,000 acres in 1857. Other entrepreneurs included James Forten in sailmaking in Philadelphia, William Whipper in lumber in Columbia, Pennsylvania, Henry Boyd in bed manufacturing in Cincinnati. Farther west, many Negroes worked in the fur trade, some rising to become independent operators.

To ward off adversity and to counter restrictions, Northern Negroes organized various mutual self-help societies. Black lodges of Freemasons, dating from Revolutionary War days, were joined in 1843 by the Order of the Odd Fellows. These secret, fraternal groups, supplemented by non-secret groups like the Free African Society, contributed much to Negro uplift. Negro churches were organized beginning in Philadelphia in the 1790's with Rev. Richard Allen's Bethel African Methodist Episcopal church and Rev. Absalom Jones's St. Thomas Episcopal church. The Bethel group, recognized as a separate branch of Methodism with Allen as bishop and popularly known as the A.M.E., spread its congregations through the North, to be followed closely by New York's African Methodist Episcopal Zion Church under Bishop James Varick and by Baptist congregations. In Northern communities the church served many functions besides worship; it provided a school for black children, a social meeting place, and a center for Negro reform and protest movements. Literary societies, which provided libraries and reading rooms, served to stimulate cultural advance in at least forty-five communities by 1860.

Negro churches were instrumental in spearheading a new drive to highlight obstacles blocking Negro progress and to stimulate social reforms. Under the lead of Bishop James Allen, the first national Negro convention brought together at Bethel Church in Philadelphia in 1830 some forty delegates from eight states to discuss mutual problems and work toward solutions. Subsequent conventions met annually until 1837, then sporadically—in 1843 at Buffalo, 1847 at Troy, 1848 at Cleveland, 1853 at Rochester. The last with 140 delegates meeting under convention president Rev. J. W. C. Pennington discussed means for "the amelioration of the condition of the colored people." Acting on Frederick Douglass's appeal "that in our native land we shall not be treated as strangers," the convention set up committees to establish a school for training skilled craftsmen, to safeguard civil liberties, to widen job opportunities, and to combat defamation. Many convention leaders also took an active part in the antislavery drive.

4. Manifest Destiny Propels America to the Pacific

Nineteenth century Americans exuded a restless, driving energy in all their undertakings, but perhaps nowhere else more clearly than in their relentless, expansionist thrust to the Pacific shore. Andrew Jackson himself had sparked an impetuous invasion of Spanish Florida that led directly to American purchase of that area in 1819. For the next three decades Americans moved rapidly by foot, horse, and ship to occupy lands westward to California, while others strove to expand American shipping in the Pacific.

Although the desire for more land and for increased trade supplied basic motivations for the westward drive, a sense of mission and fate buttressed the rationale of America's "empire for liberty." Ardent boosters of their eighteenth century democratic heritage, nineteenth century Americans conceived it as their historic mission to spread the blessings and advantages of democracy to other areas, which preferably should be brought under American control, especially if they were contiguous territories.

As the *Democratic Review's* editor, John L. O'Sullivan, put it: "we are the nation of human progress, and who will, what can set the limits of our onward march?" It was America's "manifest destiny" to expand and to spread "universality of freedom and equality." Historian George Bancroft, whose multivolume history indicated that a divine hand was guiding the rise of the United States, asserted that the "manifest purpose of Providence" decreed "that the light of democratic freedom should be borne from our fires to the domain beyond the Rocky Mountains."

By the 1840's "Manifest Destiny" had become the popular rallying cry and the catch-all justification for occupying all lands between the Atlantic and Pacific. The most ardent expansionists claimed that the United States was preordained "to roll its resistless waves to the icy barriers" of the Arctic, to the isthmus of Panama on the south, and to dominate the Pacific basin as well. Americans, ran the argument, could not refuse their divinely decreed destiny. Indeed, they should step forward and lend a hand to put their "Manifest Destiny" into effect.

And this they did with boundless enthusiasm. In the 1820's and 1830's with startling speed the government removed the eastern Indian tribes, who were charged with blocking progress in their attempt to stem the advancing white settlement. The eastern Indians were resettled on trans-Mississippi lands that explorer Major Stephen Long had earlier reported as worthless for farming purposes. Private entrepreneurs like the Missouri-based Rocky Mountain Fur Company of Jedidiah Smith and William Ashley and the American Fur Company of John Jacob Astor rapidly pushed fur-gathering operations by trapping and trading deep into the mountains of the Far West. Connecticut Yankee promoters Moses Austin and his son Stephen secured land grants from Mexico, and the latter led the first contingent of American settlers into Texas. By 1830 some 20,000 pioneers, mostly Southerners accompanied by 2,000 slaves, had settled in the fertile east Texas area where the virgin soils produced heavy yields of cotton. In 1836, as a result of an uprising and war, Texas separated from Mexico and requested annexation to the United States. President Andrew Jackson, nearing the close of his second term, failed to take action on the request. His hand-picked successor, Martin Van Buren, refused to support annexation proposals. In consequence the Lone Star Republic remained an independent country until 1844 when the question of adding Texas to the Union resurfaced as an issue in the American political arena.

Meanwhile, other Americans pushed on toward the Pacific. The resourceful "mountain men" of fur trade fame scouted out the passes through the mountains, advised later migrants on the best routes to reach the farther west, and often served as guides to migrating parties. Religious missionaries Jason Lee, Marcus Whitman, and Henry Spalding made the crossing to the Oregon country of the northwest and sent back glowing reports of its alluring attractions. Soon a steady stream of migrants was pushing westward along the Oregon Trail to occupy fertile lands in Oregon's Willamette valley. Before the 1830's ended, some hardy adventurers were drifting into Mexican-held California where entrepreneur John Sutter, living in feudal style, welcomed them to his Sacramento holdings.

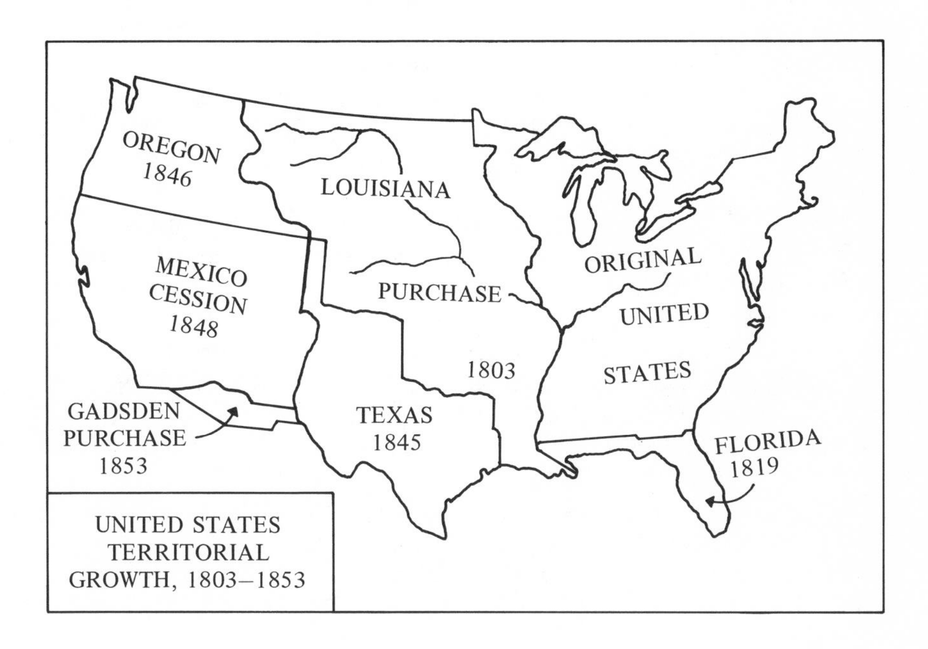

UNITED STATES
TERRITORIAL
GROWTH, 1803–1853

Another group, the Mormons, more formally called the Church of Jesus Christ of the Latter Day Saints, was organized by prophet Joseph Smith in upstate New York. Having been pushed west, the Mormons formed under Smith's lead a community of 10,000 at Nauvoo, Illinois. After Smith was lynched, leadership passed to the more practical Brigham Young who in 1846 led his Mormon followers west to the "new promised land" at the edge of Great Salt Lake. Here they established a thriving farming community that benefited greatly by selling supplies to Oregon-California-bound migrants who passed nearby.

In the 1840's Americans in Oregon multiplied so rapidly that they proceeded to organize a territorial government and called for recognition and support from Washington. The earlier treaty between the United States and England providing for joint occupation by citizens of both nations prevented immediate action by the United States. But many politicians chafed restlessly for a favorable settlement of the issue, some contending that the United States should press for all of Oregon as far north as 54°40′ north latitude.

Along with Oregon, the slumbering Texas question reemerged explosively in 1844 when Secretary of State John C. Calhoun concluded an annexation treaty with the Lone State Republic. When the treaty was defeated in the Senate, where antislavery members resisted it, Texas became an issue in the 1844 Presidential contest, the Democrats calling for immediate acquisition of Texas along with California and Oregon. With the election of Democratic candidate James K. Polk, Congress immediately voted to add Texas to the Union. Polk opened negotiations with England on the Oregon question and with Mexico regarding American purchase of California. Despite chauvinistic campaign cries of "54-40 or fight" (meaning all of Oregon as far as the Southern tip of Alaska), diplomacy produced an Oregon treaty in 1846 splitting the region at the 49th parallel (actually an extension of the United States-Canadian border east of the Continental Divide).

As for California, Mexico refused to negotiate, understandably, since having never recognized the independence of Texas, she protested its annexation by the United States. But Manifest Destiny, with a strong assist from President Polk and his advisers, continued its irresistible drive. While prodding Mexico for payment of long-standing American financial claims, Polk ordered troops under General Zachary Taylor ("Old Rough and Ready" to his soldiers) into a disputed area lying between the Nueces River and the Rio Grande. When a clash with Mexican forces resulted, Polk told Congress that American blood had been shed on what he claimed was American soil. Congress quickly responded by declaring war (40–2 in the Senate, 174–14 in the House).

Taylor's army crossed the Rio Grande and quickly captured Monterey, while Stephen W. Kearny's forces, after seizing Santa Fe, drove on to

California. In California an earlier plan by United States Consul Thomas Larkin for a separatist drive by Spanish-speaking Californians had come to naught. However, American settlers residing north of San Francisco Bay, encouraged by General John C. Frémont whose military force conveniently arrived by the summer of 1846, revolted and proclaimed an independent "Bear Flag Republic." Linked up with Commodore Robert F. Stockton's naval units that reached the California coast about the same time, the combined American forces, including Colonel Stephen W. Kearny's troops, overcame local resistance by January, 1847.

Meanwhile, General Winfield Scott ("Old Fuss and Feathers" to his men) led an expeditionary force that captured Vera Cruz and shouldered its way inland toward the mile-and-a-half-high capital of Mexico City. Scott was soon joined by State Department negotiator Nicholas Trist. When negotiations stalled, Polk ordered Trist to return to Washington. The President was considering proposals for prolonged occupation and possible annexation of all of Mexico. Disregarding orders, Trist remained and, on February 2, 1848, signed with Mexican officials the Treaty of Guadalupe Hidalgo, which secured the Rio Grande as Texas's southern boundary and gained California including the crucial San Diego harbor and all land between Texas and California. In return, the United States would pay $15 million to Mexico and assume $3.25 million of American claims against Mexico. The Senate speedily ratified the treaty 38–14 in March, 1848 (most opposition coming from those "Young America" Senators who wanted to annex all of Mexico). As it was, the treaty added to the American domain an impressive 500,000 square miles whose value would soon become spectacularly apparent. In 1853 the Gadsden Purchase treaty acquired for $10 million a strategic 54,000-square-mile area south of the Gila River.

Like all wars, the war with Mexico spawned results unanticipated at its start. One such unexpected spinoff arose in August, 1846, when Pennsylvania Congressman David Wilmot tacked an amendment to a military appropriation bill that "neither slavery nor involuntary servitude shall exist in any part" of the territory that might be acquired from Mexico. The Wilmot Proviso, repeatedly adopted by the House but defeated by the Senate, launched an angry debate over the westward extension of slavery—a debate that continued for fifteen bitter years. By stirring up sectional animosities, the dispute opened a rift in political party ranks and drove an ever enlarging wedge between increasingly hostile sections. As Emerson had prophesied at the war's outset, "The United States . . . will be as the man who swallows . . . arsenic. . . . Mexico will poison us." By the war's end bitter quarreling was already convulsing the nation's politics. The Republic had spread to the Pacific, as Manifest Destiny decreed, but so had the poison of slavery and its accompanying controversy.

3

The Drive against Slavery

Many Americans, slaveholders among them, had long been troubled over the continuation of slavery. The wave of religious evangelism that swept the land in the second quarter of the nineteenth century roused men's consciences and prodded men to concerned action. Slavery's patent violation of the Christian doctrines of love and human brotherhood was clear for all to see. The Jacksonian ferment of renewed belief in equal rights and opportunities and in social justice forced men to reconsider the anti-democratic barbarity of that "peculiar institution." At first a small band of antislavery critics denounced the vicious evil of human bondage, evoking a defensive response that sought to stifle such "radical agitation."

Abolitionist voices, refusing to be stilled, grew more insistent in the 1840's as they pressed the moral issue of slavery into politics, at first with a small third party. The war with Mexico generated increasing support for the antislavery drive as added adherents insisted that newly acquired lands be preserved for "free soil." Both Democratic and Whig leaders squirmed evasively, and traditional party loyalties began to waver. By mid-century, the slavery issue had grown to crisis proportions and demanded the nation's attention and decision.

1. The Antislavery Crusade Launched

The feeling that slavery was morally wrong was not new among Americans. As early as 1690, Negro bondage was condemned as unchristian by Pennsylvania Quakers, who for the next two centuries urged its abolition. In the wake of the American Revolution, with its proclamation of the natural rights of man, slavery was erased by law in all states from Pennsylvania northward. Although the 1787 Constitutional Convention equivocated, Congress's Northwest Ordinance of the same year expressly banned slavery in the territory north of the Ohio River and set a significant precedent for national action.

After 1815 the new American Colonization Society began urging gradual emancipation and repatriation of blacks from America to Africa. For free Negroes and those to be emancipated by owners, the Society would pay the cost of transportation and settlement in Liberia, a new republic established on Africa's west coast under the Society's auspices. The Society's appeal was greatest in Virginia, Maryland, Kentucky, and Tennessee, which had by 1830 over 100 of the 130 local chapters. Funds from private donors and legislative appropriations proved so small that the Society had sent only 12,000 blacks to Liberia by 1860. Scanty funds, loss of interest, and internal dissension led to the Society's decline before midcentury.

A new sense of urgency was infused into the antislavery drive when Quaker Benjamin Lundy began publishing a paper, *The Genius of Universal Emancipation*. In the late 1820's he employed a young New Englander, William Lloyd Garrison, whose stridency soon landed him in jail. Garrison returned to Boston where in 1831 he inaugurated *The Liberator*, declaring in the first issue: "I do not wish to think or speak or write with moderation. . . . I will not retreat a single inch and *I will be heard*!" Garrison was a curious blend of vegetarian, teetotaler, women's rightist, pacifist, and eccentric, with a sprinkling of humor and wit. His writings grew increasingly vitriolic; slaveholding was not only undemocratic but unchristian and sinful. Slaveholders were "the meanest of thieves and the worst of robbers." When reminded that the Constitution recognized slavery, Garrison labeled it "a covenant with death and an agreement with Hell" and in ceremonious defiance hurled a copy of it into a bonfire on Boston Common. Right was right; wrong, wrong! Slavery must go—immediately!

While Garrison's explosive attacks on "Southern sinners" won much attention, his fanaticism often drove away more Northerners than it attracted to the antislavery crusade. Far more effective work was done by other abolitionists. Of these, Theodore D. Weld (1803–1895) was the most remarkable and significant. As a young, skeptical scoffer at religion in upstate New York, Weld came under the influence of evangelist Charles G. Finney's magnetic revivalist preaching. After wrestling all night with his inner turmoil, Weld experienced a deeply emotional "conversion," "hit the sawdust trail" in a public meeting, and consecrated himself henceforth to labor against sin and slavery. At Cincinnati's Lane Theological Seminary, he roused students to debate the slavery question publicly. When the school's trustees prohibited such student discussions, Weld led a student walkout. The "Lane rebels" enrolled at recently established (1833) Oberlin College, which soon served as a base for his noted "Band of Seventy" students. Devoting weekends, holidays, and vacations to the work, they appeared singly and in groups to preach abolition in churches and public meetings throughout Ohio, Pennsylvania, and New York. Avoiding Garrisonian histrionics, Weld patiently trained his followers in camp meeting techniques to win adherents to abolitionism. Public meetings, followed by persistent organization drives, attracted dedicated members, and local abolitionist societies sprouted throughout the proselyted area.

Weld himself gained enthusiastic support from wealthy New York financiers Arthur and Lewis Tappan, who organized a vigorous New York

Committee and pumped large, crucially-needed funds into the crusade. In addition, Weld convinced many people who later became influential abolitionists—James G. Birney, an Alabama planter who freed his slaves and later ran for President; Ohio attorney Joshua Giddings, soon to become the first full-fledged abolitionist Congressman; Harriet Beecher Stowe, who would write the most effective antislavery novel; Edwin M. Stanton, later to be Lincoln's Secretary of War. In 1837 Weld moved to New York City where his labors at training abolitionist organizers proved so exhausting that he literally wore himself out. Nevertheless, he still managed to shuttle to Washington and supply Congressman John Quincy Adams with ammunition to attack slaveholding. Weld also published a tract, *American Slavery as It Is*, featuring ''A Thousand Witnesses'' to slavery's brutalities. Clearly, Weld's efforts roused the conscience of the North. By 1850 over 2,000 abolitionist societies boasted more than 200,000 members.

Tons of literature—tracts, pamphlets, books, magazines, broadsides—inundated the country. In 1837–38 the American Anti-Slavery Society produced 7,877 bound volumes, 47,236 tracts and pamphlets, 4,100 circulars. Its weekly *Emancipator* reached 217,000 subscribers; its monthly *Human Rights*, 189,000; its youth publication, 131,000.

Theodore Weld in his ninetieth year. (The Sophia Smith Collection, Smith College, Northampton, Massachusetts)

2. Negroes and the Antislavery Drive

Able Negro leaders also labored vigorously for the cause. As early as 1800, Philadelphians Rev. Absalom Jones and James Forten submitted an antislavery petition to Congress. Later when colonization in Africa was proposed, the black response was generally negative. However, prosperous New England Negro shipowner Paul Cuffe, who had earlier taken thirty-eight Negroes at his own expense to a British colonization settlement in west Africa, gave advice to the American Colonization Society. In 1821 the Society established a small contingent of American Negroes at a west African site. Six years later the area took the name Liberia, and in 1841 a Virginia Negro, Joseph J. Roberts, became Liberia's governor and then president, and he succeeded in providing order during the republic's early years.

But many blacks protested against colonization, as did Jones and Forten, declaring that as descendants of "the first successful cultivators" of America they were "entitled to participate in the blessings of her luxuriant soil, which their blood and sweat manured." Other spokesmen asserted: "This is our home . . . our country. . . . Here we were born, and here we will die." In 1827 the first Negro newspaper, *Freedom's Journal*, appeared in New York. Its editors, Presbyterian minister Samuel E. Cornish and John Russwurm, America's first Negro college graduate (Bowdoin, 1826), attacked the Colonization Society for not seeking to eliminate slavery but to eliminate Negroes from the United States.

The newspaper's Boston agent, David Walker (1785–1830), was a free Negro from North Carolina who peddled second-hand clothing and incendiary ideas. In 1829 he published *Walker's Appeal to the Colored Citizens of the World*, a seventy-six -page tract that lashed out at white, slaveholding "devils" for holding blacks in "mean and abject" degradation, condemned colonization, and declared that if emancipation did not come soon in "this Republican land of Liberty" Negroes had a religious duty to rise up, break their "infernal chains," and overthrow their white oppressors in armed rebellion if need be. In that same year Cincinnati mobs attacked Negroes and forced half the city's black population to flee to Canada.

In 1830 the first Negro convention repudiated colonization and urged Negroes no longer able to bear oppression to consider migrating to Canada. It was a year later that Garrison inaugurated his *Liberator*—having read and absorbed *Walker's Appeal* and been impressed by arguments of Forten and his son-in-law Robert Purvis. At least two-thirds of *The Liberator's* early subscribers were Negroes; and when Garrison suffered financial reverses, Forten bailed him out. Addressing the Negro convention of 1831, Garrison, too, flatly opposed colonization.

Two years later when the American Anti-Slavery Society organized at Philadelphia, Negro leaders participated actively—dentist Alexander McCrummell, Robert Purvis, Boston reformer James G. Barbadoes, ministers Samuel E. Cornish, Theodore S. Wright, and Peter S. Williams. Among the Society's fifty-eight vice presidents were Forten and William Watkins. When internal disputes over Garrison's insistence on "moral suasion" as opposed to political action split the antislavery movement in 1839, most Negro leaders joined the Weld-Tappan faction in forming the American and Foreign Anti-Slavery Society.

Many Negro speakers hit the antislavery circuit. Among them, Charles L. Remond of Salem, small in size, elegant in dress, became a polished professional giving talks throughout New England. Another was Samuel R. Ward, a New York Presbyterian minister, whose eloquent speech won him billing as "the black Daniel Webster." The incomparable Sojourner Truth, who after a brief encounter with an eccentric religious sect, emerged as a unique abolitionist voice—all six feet of her, hitting her audience with full-throated conviction.

The most convincing abolitionists were the fugitives, who by their very act of escaping slavery promoted abolition. The remarkable Harriet Tubman, upon escaping, declared her right to "liberty or death" was such that "no man should take me alive." At the risk of both liberty and death, with a $40,000 reward for her capture, she returned to Maryland nineteen times and aided more than 300 slaves to reach freedom. Another former Maryland slave, Henry H. Garnet, who like Ward became a Presbyterian minister, kept up a slashing attack, urging in 1843 a nationwide strike of slaves who should not "toil for the heartless tyrants."

The giant of them all was Frederick Douglass, born in slavery as Frederick Augustus Washington Bailey. Fleeing from his Baltimore owner in a borrowed sailor suit with seaman's papers, he made it to New York and on to New Bedford. Within three years he was on the platform thundering the atrocity of slavery across New England. Tall and powerful, with a flowing mane of hair, throbbing baritone voice, and large forehead over deepset eyes, he was unforgettable, using his skill as a master mimic to make audiences laugh, cry, shout, curse. One hearer recorded: "White men and black men had talked against slavery, but none had ever spoken like Frederick Douglass." His speaking and his *Autobiography* (1845) formed a continuing indictment of slavery. In wide demand as a speaker, Douglass also insisted upon absolute equality. Believing that Garrisonians were confining him to "a stage role as an escaped slave," he struck out on his own and moved to Rochester, where he fought school segregation and lambasted slavery in his own paper, *The North Star*. "Our oppressed brethren are wholly ignored," he complained in 1855, ". . . in the generalship of the movement" for abolition. He demanded "practical recognition of our Equality" in "the Anti-Slavery host." Later, in growing despair, Douglass lashed out: ". . . your Fourth of July . . . reveals . . . the gross injustice and cruelty to which" the slave "is a constant victim."

Harriet Tubman (far left), shown with some of the slaves she helped to escape. (The Sophia Smith Collection, Smith College, Northampton, Massachusetts)

Indeed, some Negroes' despair over the slowness of abolition increased in time to such a point as to bring colonization into favor. Most notable was Dr. Martin R. Delaney (1812–1885) a physician, journalist, and first American Negro nationalist, who gave his children African names and lived up to Douglass' observation, "I thank God for making me a man, but Delaney always thanks Him for making him a black man." Delaney urged Negroes to identify as Africans and look to the old homeland. Later in the Civil War he would recruit Negro soldiers and himself become an army major in the fight against slavery.

3. The Antislavery Tide Swells

In addition to runaway slaves, reformed slaveholders were especially useful in the crusade. Angelina Grimké left her slaveholding family in Charleston and moved to Philadelphia, where she joined the Quakers and published in 1836 a strong attack on slavery. Shortly thereafter, she married Weld and became a frequent antislavery speaker. James G. Birney abandoned his Alabama plantation in order to publish an abolitionist paper in Kentucky and urge political action.

Abolitionists, foreshadowing today's protest movements, pioneered in the use of nonviolent direct action. They held protest rallies, chanted freedom songs, staged confrontations, demonstrated, picketed, and often wound up in jail. Slaveholders were denounced for violating Christian brotherhood and denying democratic liberty and equality. Most speeches and tracts highlighted in gory detail the brutal cruelties of slavery. The slaveowner was the arch-aristocrat, un-American destroyer of the American dream, the flagrant sinner with a consuming lust for women, liquor, and violence. The picture was often overdrawn—but deliberately so, to arouse Americans to eradicate this insidious evil that was an anachronism in the midst of nineteenth-century American democracy.

Among the most vocal and eloquent converts to the abolition crusade were writers Thoreau, Longfellow, Emerson, Melville, Whitman, and Whittier, and ministers Wendell Phillips, Theodore Parker, and William Ellery Channing, all of whom kept up a running fire against slavery. But the most effective literary work was written by Harriet Beecher Stowe, wife of a Lane Seminary professor. Her *Uncle Tom's Cabin* appeared as a book in 1852; within a year it had sold 300,000 copies and over a million by 1860. Made into a play, which was performed by traveling stock companies, it reached more Northerners than any other abolitionist piece and aroused universal indignation over the heartbreaking agonies of slavery as revealed in the unforgettable characters of Uncle Tom, Simon Legree, Topsy, Eliza, and Little Eva. Years later President Lincoln is supposed to have greeted Mrs. Stowe at a White House reception with the remark "So, this is the little lady who brought on the Civil War."

Abolitionists did not convert the North all at once; indeed, they probably never converted a majority before 1861. As self-righteous social reformers, they were often short-sighted and single-minded. In their eyes, slavery was not so much a social ill as a moral sin. Removal of the cancer of slavery became the end; few abolitionists concerned themselves with the means of the Negro's transition from slavery to self-reliant participation in American society. But the abolitionists' conviction and persistent appeals awakened consciences and in time aroused men to put an end to slavery.

In the 1830's, however, abolitionists faced denunciation as wild-eyed madmen bent on destroying American society and the Union. Many Northern communities refused to tolerate them. Heckled, howled down, tormented, and lynched, they were dealt with as troublemakers and outcasts. Birney was driven from Kentucky to free-soil Ohio in 1836. A year later an Alton, Illinois, mob murdered abolitionist editor Elijah Lovejoy and threw his printing press into the Mississippi. In Boston angry men dragged Garrison through the streets. In 1845, near Lexington, Kentucky, a citizens' committee demanded that Cassius M. Clay, a fiery abolitionist editor, stop "publication of . . . *The True American*, as . . . dangerous to the peace of our community." Clay defied them, mounting two brass cannon at his front door and arming a handful of friends with shotguns. To be an abolitionist in a Southern town entailed such perils as Clay faced.

Southern indignation over abolitionists and their works grew as the assault intensified. In earlier years most Southerners had deplored slavery's existence. But new factors—the spread of cotton-raising in the newer South, and agricultural distress and insecurity in the older South—produced a marked change. The turning point in Southern attitude and utterance on slavery came in the early 1830's. *Walker's Appeal*, Garrison's *Liberator*, and Nat Turner's uprising frightened many. Their backlash led the Virginia legislature in 1832 to reject gradual emancipation plans that had been under serious consideration. Professor Thomas Dew provided the classic rationalization, defending slavery on grounds of (1) its historic existence in past civilizations, (2) Biblical sanction, (3) benefits conferred on the Negro, (4) economic benefits to the country's economy, (5) the injustice of thrusting a freed slave into an economic struggle in which he was unprepared to compete.

Other spokesmen would replay the Dew defense with variations and refinements, but the substance of the Southern stance remained constant for the next thirty years. In the face of abolitionists' attacks, slavery was not to be apologized for, but rather acclaimed as a "positive good," as John C. Calhoun phrased it in 1838 resolutions that passed the Senate. Others argued that slavery was necessary to raise cotton, which was so essential to the Southern economy and to the nation's economy. In the South a tight conformity of thought now took over in defense of Southern institutions. Dissenters either moved out or remained quiet.

As abolitionists' attacks grew, misunderstanding and rigidity also grew on both sides of the Mason-Dixon line. Some Americans saw slavery as a great evil curse; others saw it as a benefit. But focusing on slavery, as many Northerners did in ascribing Southern soil exhaustion and economic distress to slavery, made genuine understanding of real Southern problems more difficult. Southerners, too, tended to oversimplify by attributing their social and economic troubles to overgrasping Northern middle men, high tariffs, and abolitionist attacks. If these factors were removed, they argued, Southern problems would be resolved by Southerners in their own way. But despite their initial unpopularity, Northern abolitionists in the 1830's were not about to let national leaders in Washington ignore the slavery question.

4. Slavery Issue Pushes into Politics

By the 1840's slavery, or more precisely the extension of slavery into new territories, burgeoned into a major issue, convulsing politics and turning otherwise reasonable men into irrational demagogues. In part, the convulsions sprang from the ambiguous response made to slavery by the republic's founders. Two fundamental American phenomena were at war with each other from the beginning. The American conscience, as expressed in the Declaration of Independence, asserted the natural rights of man and pronounced slavery an evil. American law, as expressed in the Constitution, proclaimed slaveholding a property right entitled to protection. How could such a conflict between conscience and law be resolved?

In the republic's first fifty years American political practice had been to dodge the issue when possible and, when not possible, to compromise, hoping the question would stay submerged. The Constitution's Framers had evaded the slavery question and even avoided using the word "slave" in the document; such euphemisms as "persons bound to service" grated less harshly on the conscience. Regarding slavery, the Constitution provided (1) that Congress could prohibit importation of slaves but not before 1808; (2) that for purposes of calculating a state's representatives and direct taxes three-fifths of a state's slave population should be counted (Southerners had wanted all counted; Northerners, none if they were not considered citizens); (3) that fugitive slaves escaping to another state "shall be delivered up on the claim" of the owner; (4) that Congress could "make all needful rules and regulations regarding the territory . . . belonging to the United States," including of course the District of Columbia.

At one time or another Congress had exercised each of these powers. An act of 1807 prohibited the importing of additional slaves. American naval units, along with the British, operated a slave patrol off the West African coast, seeking to choke off the illegal slave running, but not with complete success. Estimates suggest that some 200,000 Africans were smuggled into the United States after 1808. A national fugitive slave act of 1793 provided return of runaways as a matter of interstate comity. The Northwest Ordinance of 1787 barred slavery in territory north of the Ohio River. In 1820 Congress approved a series of measures known as the Missouri Compromise, which admitted Maine as a free state, Missouri as a slave state, and prohibited slavery "forever . . . in all territory" of the Louisiana Purchase north of the 36°30′ line of latitude (a westward extension of Missouri's southern border).

The Missouri controversy, as Thomas Jefferson sensed it, struck like "a fire bell in the night" foretelling the dissolution of the Union. Compromise on the immediate issue, many agreed with Jefferson, decreed for the Union "a reprieve only. . . . A geographical line, coinciding with a marked principle, moral and political, once conceived and held up to the angry passions of men, will never be obliterated" and future "irritations" will aggravate it "deeper and deeper." The coming generation of the fifties would learn all too well the acuteness of Jefferson's observation.

Even in the 1830's "irritations" mounted. As the abolition crusade gained momentum, the flow of antislavery literature through Federal mails into the South became a torrent. While abolitionists believed it their moral duty to get slaveholders to abandon their sinful practice, the latter seethed with anger over the inflow of diatribes, which they viewed as unwarranted meddling, "mischievous, inflammatory and incendiary." After Nat Turner's uprising in 1831, Southerners demanded that the mails be closed to such materials because they were threatening Southern peace and security.

Congress exploded in violent argument over free use of the mails. In the end no restrictive bill was passed. Instead, the 1836 Postal Act stated that it was the duty of a local postmaster not to detain nor to prevent delivery of any mail. But in practice the law was ineffective in the face of Southern state legislation that made delivery of abolition literature virtually impossible—a practice that prevailed until the Civil War.

Even more unsettling was the battle waged in Congress over antislavery petitions. In the 1830's local antislavery societies began deluging Congressmen with petitions to abolish slavery in the District of Columbia. As their volume mounted, just reading the titles of antislavery petitions became a time-consuming bore and nuisance that clogged consideration of other petitions. In 1836 the House responded by adopting a rule that "all petitions relating . . . to . . . slavery, shall, without being printed or referred [to committee], be laid upon the table," without further consideration.

Seventy-year-old ex-President John Quincy Adams, then serving his fourth fiery term as a Massachusetts Congressman, raged against the "gag rule" as a "direct violation of the Constitution, . . . the rules of this House, and the rights" of citizens to petition their government. He would not and could not be bound by an "unconstitutional rule." "Old Man Eloquent" made a public announcement that he would present any petition sent him by any person. In consequence, he was swamped with petitions on slavery and other assorted subjects. Doggedly, each House petition day, he labored to present to the House the mass of documents he had received. As soon as he uttered the word "slavery," the Speaker ruled him out of order and directed him to sit down. Displaying unmatched command of parliamentary tactics and refusing to be silenced, he managed to slip in diverse petitions—some calling for an end to slavery, one asking that Congress not abolish slavery (signed ostensibly by a group of slaves), another announcing that Adams should be shot, still another urging that the House expel Adams for violating its rules.

Acting on the last petition, the House began expulsion proceedings against him. In this debate the aroused veteran defended himself and the right of petition so convincingly that the House settled for a mild reprimand. In the course of his defense, Adams pointed out that in case of a war, "civil, servile or foreign," the President as military commander in chief could emancipate slaves as a war measure—a step Lincoln would take as President a quarter century later. For eight years Adams, amply supplied with antislavery ammunition by Theodore Weld, flayed the "gag rule" finally winning its repeal in 1844. In itself the repeal meant little. Of greater consequence was the spotlight focused by Adams on the cause of free speech, now coming to be identified with the antislavery movement.

Meanwhile, in early 1838 Calhoun launched an effort to settle the constitutional status of slavery. He proposed in the Senate a series of six resolutions, which after slight modification and brief debate the Senate adopted by a 3–1 margin. In substance the Calhoun resolutions affirmed that slavery was a "domestic institution" under "the exclusive and sole" power of the states and that the general government as the agent of the states was bound "to resist all attempts by one portion of the Union," meaning the North, to "intermeddle" with slavery in states where it existed or in the District of Columbia. In supporting rationalization Calhoun abandoned early Southern apology for slavery and instead advanced a spirited assertion that slavery was "a positive good," from which many benefits flowed not only to the South and to the Negro but to the country at large.

In the emerging debate over slavery questions, Southern leaders appeared increasingly touchy and short-sighted. Their insistence upon limiting the use of the mails and upon the "gag rule" was a tactical, self-weakening blunder. It produced an adverse countereffect of driving thoughtful Northerners from former indifference to growing concern over slavery. Many Northerners, previously scorning abolitionists as lunatic fringers, came more and more to acknowledge the threat to freedom in the heavy-handed tactics of proslavery men in Congress. As willingness to entertain antislavery appeals grew, the crusade moved to the verge of respectability in the North by the mid-forties.

Such developments, plus the Texas annexation scheme, which some attributed to the machinations of a Southern "slave power," helped to generate an antislavery political party. Already Thomas Morris of Ohio in the Senate and John Quincy Adams of Massachusetts, Joshua Giddings of Ohio, and William Slade of Vermont in the the House were hammering the antislavery tune in Washington. Even though there were abolitionists like Garrison who spurned political action, James G. Birney launched a drive to organize a party soon after he moved his newspaper to New York in 1837. By 1840 he had the Liberty party functioning and himself listed on the ballot as a Presidential candidate. The 7,059 votes he won, while unimpressive alone, served as an omen of things to come.

In the 1840's the energies and attention of Americans were focused largely upon expanding national boundaries to the Pacific. Actually a desire to spread slavery westward had little to do with the push into the Rockies, the Great Salt Lake basin, Oregon, and California, although it did play a part in Texas. Manifest destiny was on the move, aided to be sure by hard economic pressures. In the American stream of life manifest destiny existed side by side with the desire to reform American society and root out its injustices. By the late forties the irresistible force of westward expansion and the immovable object of social reform collided with a thunderous jolt.

5. Polk, Wilmot, and the Rift in the Democracy

Ominous signs were already discernible in 1844. The submerged question of acquiring Texas resurfaced in that year when John Calhoun, serving as Secretary of State, concluded a treaty of annexation. In his appeal to the Senate for ratification, he sought to convince wavering Senators by submitting the diplomatic correspondence between the United States and Great Britain. Therein Calhoun argued that the abolitionist scheming of Britain in Texas required that the United States annex Texas in order to protect slavery within its own borders. In addition, he appended a long, convoluted defense of slavery itself. Calhoun's labored discourse may have delighted his Southern adherents (who needed no convincing on the subject), but it alienated many Senators, who proceeded to defeat the treaty by a 36–16 vote in the Senate.

What appeared to many as a barefaced grab for new slavery territory reechoed in the 1844 Presidential contest, which was just heating up as the Senate debated the Texas treaty. The leading aspirants, former President Martin Van Buren and ever-available Henry Clay, confidently expecting their respective party nominations and hoping to eradicate Texas as a campaign issue, simultaneously published letters stating opposition to the annexation of Texas. As a result, the Democratic convention rejected Van Buren and named instead James K. Polk, a forty-eight-year-old Tennesseean and Jackson favorite, who had served as House Speaker and governor of his state. Clay won the Whig nomination, but his campaign pussyfooting on the Texas issue alienated many disturbed Northerners and lost him further support. Liberty party nominee James G. Birney captured 62,000 votes, and his appeal in New York cost Clay that state and with it the election. Polk squeaked through with a 30,000-vote plurality. As President, Polk proceeded to fulfill every campaign promise—acquiring Texas, Oregon, and California, lowering the tariff, and establishing an Independent Treasury system.

But before Polk's term ended, the Democratic party began unexpectedly to come loose at the seams. How could so successful a President generate a rift in the Democracy. Part of the answer lay in that very success, part in the country's increasing sensitivity to the wrong of slavery.

During the year Polk was elected, that sensitivity split the nation's largest religious denomination. The Methodist Church's general conference called upon a Georgia bishop to refrain from performing his bishop's duties as long as he remained a slaveholder. When he refused, the ensuing controversy produced the break. The Methodist Church South organized itself as a separate body in 1845. In that year also the second largest denomination, the Baptists, snapped into two branches in a dispute over a slaveholding missionary. The Presbyterians, third largest of the churches, engaged in a running internal fight until 1860 when they, too, divided into Northern and Southern units. Clearly the wedge of slavery was dividing Americans into hostile camps when men of the same faith fought each other in disagreement—each faction, North and South, insisting its view of slavery was correct. Unyielding, stubborn rigidity was seizing control of men's minds.

At the same time, dissension was festering within Democratic ranks. Van Buren and Calhoun were both miffed over missing the Presidential nomination in 1844, and their followers grew restive. Old party regular Francis Blair, veteran Jacksonian editor of the official party organ in Washington, was forced out. Senator Thomas Hart Benton, battling against annexation of Texas, edged toward the opposition. The old Jacksonian coalition was cracking.

President Polk pushed determinedly ahead with his party's program. In 1846 Treasury Secretary Robert J. Walker's tariff bill lowering rates passed Congress over howls of protest from New England. Britain's repeal of her Corn Laws the same year swung open the large English market to the delight and profit of Northwest wheat growers. But a river-harbor improvement bill that would have benefited Great Lakes shipping and farmers of that area died under a Polk veto. Outraged Northwesterners, furious over the veto, joined irate Eastern manufacturers, who were fuming over tariff reduction, in a loud clamor against the administration. A protest meeting in Chicago dubbed the sandbar at the harbor's entrance "Mount Polk" in sarcastic tribute to the man who blocked its removal and checked the city's commercial growth.

The Mexican War also roused angry protests. In New England, James Russell Lowell and others wrote scathingly against it, while Henry David Thoreau, who was jailed for not paying taxes that might aid the war, produced his famed "Essay on Civil Disobedience" justifying a citizen's refusal to follow a government's unjust orders to commit acts that violated the dictates of his conscience. Senator Thomas Corwin of Ohio, damning the war as an aggression against a weak neighbor, expressed the hope that Mexicans would welcome American invaders "with bloody hands to hospitable graves." True, the war's critics were Whigs, but Democrats too were already restless. Their turn soon came.

The war was not yet three months old in August, 1846, when Democratic Congressman David Wilmot of Pennsylvania dropped a time bomb whose ominous ticking amplified steadily over the next fifteen years. The Wilmot Proviso, offered as an amendment to a House military appropriations bill, proposed to prohibit slavery in any territory the United States might obtain from Mexico at the war's end. Passed by the House numerous times, it was regularly defeated in the Senate and never became law. But the voting revealed growing political sensitivity to slavery—the House reflecting the North's larger population and stiffening opposition to extending slavery; the Senate, the South's increasing reliance on equal numbers of free-slave states' Senators to defend the "peculiar institution."

Wilmot's proposal presented an impossible dilemma for the South, whose spokesmen fiercely opposed it. Recently Texas and Florida (1845) had entered the Union as slave states, shortly to be matched by Iowa (1846) and Wisconsin (1848), thereby maintaining the free-slave state equilibrium. Both Minnesota and Oregon were about to seek statehood. Their admission within a few years would throw off the balance and shift it in favor of the free states. Now Wilmot's Proviso would, if enacted, ban creating any future slave states from the vast Mexican cession. The South, seeing a half dozen new free states in the offing, faced the gloomy prospect of becoming a permanent minority. Already outvoted in the House, the South thereby would lose its veto arising from equality in the Senate. The outlook was particularly galling to Southerners as they saw new territories being won by Southern fighting men on the battlefield. Understandably, Southern leaders in Washington fought back. On the other side, growing numbers in the North viewed slavery as an unpardonable evil that must be contained within its present limits, if not eradicated.

But could Congress legitimately bar slavery from Western territories? The answers men gave varied according to their views of the Constitution and the nature of the Union, as well as their practical political aims. Many Northerners held that the Constitution authorized Congress to "make needful rules" to bar slavery in all the territories of the United States, as it had already done in the Northwest Ordinance and the Missouri Compromise legislation. Southerners, like Calhoun, contended that since the "sovereign" states were joint owners of the Western territories, Congress as the agent of the states could not enact policy contrary to the interest of its principal (the states). Moreover, since the Constitution sanctioned property in slaves, owners of such property could not legally be barred from taking their property into territories jointly owned by the states.

One answer was advanced by Northern Democrats Lewis Cass (Mich.) and Stephen A. Douglas (Ill.), who contended for "popular sovereignty" ("let the people decide") as a moderate solution. Let the new territories be created leaving the slavery question open, to be decided by the people who settled there. A plausible democratic solution, many thought. But it left many questions unanswered, and ignored the moral issue.

So the issue remained unsolved as the nation prepared for the 1848 Presidential contest. The "poison" (in Emerson's phrase) of the Mexican acquisition was spreading into politics, demanding a decision that politicians had hoped to avoid. Indeed, the appeal of the "squatters' sovereignty" solution was that it would allow Washington leaders to dodge the question, evade taking a stand, and leave the dilemma to the settlers themselves. Northern newspapers were declaring it was time for men to take a stand on the slavery issue. Legislatures in Michigan and Ohio passed resolutions opposing the extension of slavery. Van Buren Democrats in New York broke with the Democratic administration and party, and created their own organization on an antislavery basis. The South responded in kind. Virginia's legislature adopted resolutions declaring that the Federal government had no power to bar slavery from the territories. Mississippi and Alabama endorsed these resolutions.

For both major parties the situation called for caution. The regular Democrats nominated for President the elderly (sixty-six), innocuous Michigan Senator Lewis Cass, expecting that his previous service with Andrew Jackson would carry him to victory. The Whigs, reverting to their 1840 hoopla tactics, picked military hero General Zachary Taylor, Virginia-born owner of a Louisiana sugar plantation, hoping that his military fame would obscure his slaveowning. Neither party platform mentioned slavery; both appealed for "harmony."

Such evasive tactics alienated many Northerners who viewed slavery as the key issue. Many antislavery Democrats in the North, especially New York "Barnburners" (supposedly willing to burn down the barn to get rid of proslavery "rats"), rebelled against party regulars. So, too, did "conscience" Whigs, as opposed to pro-Southern "cotton" Whigs. In August, 1848, antislavery men of both parties, plus Liberty party adherents, met in convention at Buffalo and organized the Free Soil Party. Nominating ex-President Martin Van Buren for President, the party issued a ringing cry: "We inscribe on our banner 'Free Soil, Free Speech, Free Labor and Free Man,' and under it will fight on, and fight ever, until a triumphant victory shall reward our exertions." Here was a broad enough emotional appeal to attract supporters of many stripes—antislavery men, those wanting a Federal homestead law, others who objected to the effort to stifle free petition, and still others who wanted slavery barred from Western territories to keep the land open for free settlers.

The campaign roused little enthusiasm. Taylor, an unknown in politics, remained aloof, while some dismissed the lethargic Cass as a "pot-bellied, mutton-headed cucumber," and Van Buren could not escape his unsavory reputation as the sly "red fox." Taylor captured the election with 1,360,000 votes (47.3 per cent); Cass got 1,220,000 (42.5 per cent); and Van Buren, 291,000 (10.1 per cent). But one voter in ten made clear he wanted slavery checked. Thirteen Free Soilers won election to the House where they held the balance of power, as they did in fact in many Northern legislatures. A strictly sectional party, showing such strength, meant politicians could not dodge the slavery issue much longer. And Southern fanatics had a new basis for urging moderates to join in forming a united Southern party to fight Northern aggression against the South's rights.

Even before the election, John Calhoun in August, 1848, saw danger for the South in the Wilmot Proviso, the antislavery agitation, and the Free Soil movement. In an address at Charleston he called for a Southern convention to consider, in the light of "our honor and our liberty," what course to pursue. In December, 1848, some 69 of the 121 Southern Congressmen caucused and adopted a formal "Address of the Southern Delegates in Congress to their Constituents." Written by Calhoun, it traced at length the train of abolitionist-inspired aggressions against slavery—the Missouri Compromise, the open flouting of the Federal fugitive slave law, the continued demands for emancipation, the recent bill excluding slavery from Oregon Territory, and the proposed abolition of the District of Columbia's slave trade. It was too much to endure. The South would take no more. All Southerners should unite in their own defense and give the North "a pause." Throughout the South the "Address" was cheered.

The response was shrill and belligerent. If the Wilmot Proviso should pass, declared Virginia's Governor, "then indeed the day of compromise will have passed, and the dissolution of our great and glorious Union will become necessary and inevitable." South Carolinians formed committees of safety and elected a state convention that condemned the Proviso. Calhoun was quoted as saying that "the alienation between the sections" had already "gone too far to save the union," while former Governor James Hammond cried, "the sooner [we] get rid of it [the Union] the better." "The only remedy," one editor wrote, was "*the secession of the slaveholding States in a body from the Union and their Formation into a Separate Republic*." Mississippi's legislature issued in October, 1849, a call for a Southern convention to meet in Nashville on June 1, 1850, to determine what action the South should take.

Elsewhere equally ominous sounds echoed. "Rather than see slavery extended one inch beyond its present limits," wrote a Cleveland, Ohio, editor, "we would see this Union rent asunder." In Ohio's legislature, Free Soilers wielding the balance of power engineered the election of Cincinnati attorney Salmon P. Chase as Senator. Chase was an outspoken foe of slavery, an organizer of the Free Soil party, and a frequent lawyer in fugitive slave court cases. At the same time, Free Soil votes in Massachusetts elevated abolitionist Charles Sumner to the Senate. Meanwhile, Missouri's Senator Benton, though a slaveholder himself, rejected his state legislature's instructions regarding slavery, replying sharply that if slavery spreads into the new territory, "we will light up the fires of liberty on every side until they melt your present chains and render all your people free."

4

Sectional Confrontation

During the decade of the 1850's the American people caromed from one sectional confrontation and crisis to another. Threats of secession were voiced with monotonous regularity by Southerners, only to be matched by periodic outbursts of Northern defiance. Politicians strove to produce satisfying accommodations and compromises that would settle once and for all, it was hoped, the outstanding sectional misunderstandings. In the crisis of 1850, which erupted over California's proposed admission to the Union as a free state, political leaders fought off Southern secessionist drives and fashioned what appeared to be a reasonable compromise. Pronounced satisfactory by men on both sides of the Mason-Dixon line, the compromise seemed to promise a period of sectional peace, if not harmony, despite squawks from extremists North and South.

Meanwhile the country forged ahead on the economic front. Production in virtually every quarter, mills and factories of the North, farms and plantations in the South and the Northwest, mines in the North, and forests in many areas, poured out an ever-rising flow of goods, as the nation's prosperity grew. Internal trade over the rapidly expanding railroad network reached annually higher levels. Foreign commerce set new records as American goods flowed out to world markets borne by the swiftly growing American merchant fleet that would soon match England's in size. Economic expansion and prosperity seemed limitless, but as mid-decade approached, the cloud of slavery controversy would dim the bright prospects of the future.

1. The First Crisis of the Union, 1850

In January, 1848, 3,000 miles west of Washington, a lucky gold strike in the Sierra foothills of California sparked a chain reaction that would ultimately help to split the nation in two. "Gold!" gasped carpenter James Marshall as he fingered the gravel near the sawmill he was building at Coloma, California, on January 24, 1848. "Gold!" echoed in men's throats across the land and the world. Tens of thousands joined the rush for quick riches. Few actually struck it rich, but swarming "forty-niners" quickly swelled California's population to over 100,000. A convention at Monterey, anticipating statehood, drafted a state constitution, prohibiting slavery, and fired off a request to Washington for admission as a free state in the Union.

In December, 1849, California's request for admission was waiting as Congressmen gathered in the capital for the new session's opening. Some members were reported to be carrying Colt revolvers and Bowie knives. Tempers ran at fever pitch. Men were on edge about their section's honor and their own. Many Southerners shared Georgian Robert Toombs's feeling: "If it [Wilmot Proviso legislation] should pass, I am for disunion." Immediately the House was embroiled in a nerve-wracking contest over choosing a Speaker. For three weeks the snarl stubbornly blocked transaction of any business. On the House floor a New Yorker and a Virginian traded hot insults that almost flared into a duel. Finally, Georgian Howell Cobb, who had opposed Calhoun's earlier call for a strictly Southern party, was elected Speaker, curiously with the help of Free Soil votes.

Every day Congress heard shrill threats of secession if "Southern rights" were disregarded, while abolitionists shouted insistently that slavery had to be barred from the new territories acquired from Mexico. California spokesmen pressed demands for admission as a free state. Southerns stood stubbornly opposed. In the early weeks of 1850 the crisis appeared insoluble, and collision by extremists looked inescapable. If each faction insisted on having its own way, breakup of the Union seemed certain. President Zachary Taylor, inexperienced in politics, offered little constructive leadership, urging only that California be admitted at once.

In contrast, elder statesman Henry Clay, now seventy-three years old and wise in the ways of political maneuver, again revealed the skill of "the great pacificator" that he had exercised so deftly in the earlier crises of 1820 and 1832–33. In late January he offered in the Senate a set of proposals he hoped would mollify angry men and save the Union by reconciling conflicting interests. His proposals were (1) California to be admitted as a free state—favored by Western and Northern opponents of slavery's extension; (2) territorial governments to be set up in Utah and New Mexico territories, without either authorizing or barring slavery there—a kind of neutrality pact that avoided offense to either side by postponing settlement of the vexing issue, providing nonintervention by Congress, and leaving the decision on slavery to be made by settlers; (3) a tighter fugitive slave act for recovering runaway slaves—pleasing to Southerners who were distressed over Underground railroad operations; (4) a law abolishing the slave trade (i.e., buying and selling, but not slavery itself) in the District of Columbia—pacifying Northerners' horror over slave markets in the shadow of the capitol; (5) the United States to pay Texas' debts in return for that state's surrender to New Mexico of lands claimed west of the Rio Grande —a proposal attractive and profitable to Eastern bondholders of Texas's depreciated securities amounting to $10,000,000 and designed to attract support by Eastern Congressmen and Senators.

In an eloquent, persuasive plea Clay urged adoption of his proposed measures in the interest of "peace, concord and harmony of these States," whose differences over slavery should be "amicably" adjusted "upon a fair, equitable and just basis." If the sections did not agreeably compromise their differences, the result, Clay forecast all too well, would be "civil war" over the "introduction of slavery into the new territories." What "a spectacle we should present to . . . astonished mankind! An effort to propagate a wrong! . . . in which all mankind would be against us!" Such a catastrophe must be avoided at all costs. In a moving appeal to place Union above section, he exclaimed, "I know no South, no North, no East, no West, to which I owe allegiance. . . . This Union is my country." If any men should try to break the Union, he cried, "so long as God . . . [gives] me voice to express my sentiments, or an arm, weak and enfeebled as it may be by age, that voice and arm will be on the side of my country" and raised to maintain "this Union."

Fellow Senators, aroused by the old man's emotional plea, responded in kind. The debate on Clay's Compromise of 1850 evoked the sharpest Congressional battle of the century and some of its most florid oratory. Opposed to the Clay measures stood (1) President Taylor who pressed for California's immediate admission and denounced opponents as traitors; (2) a fiery phalanx of Southerners including John Calhoun, Robert Barnwell Rhett, and Jefferson Davis; (3) Northern antislavery men like Salmon P. Chase, Charles Sumner, and William H. Seward, who proclaimed a "Higher Law" than the Constitution—God's law—decreed that the evil of slavery must end.

On March 4, John Calhoun, emaciated, feeble, and ghostly, wrapped in flannels, tottered into the Senate chamber to hear his written speech read by a Virginia colleague. "I have . . . believed from the first," Calhoun told the Senate, that antislavery agitation "would, if not prevented by some timely and effective measure, end in disunion." For harmony's sake the South had yielded to the North in all previous controversies—Northwest Ordinance, Missouri Compromise, Oregon Territory. And now came a new Northern demand designed to destroy "Southern rights" in California and the Southwest. This was too much. The South could not with "safety and honor" remain in the Union when her rights were repeatedly overridden. Indeed, the bonds of union were rapidly snapping. A genuine Union must rest on a deep, voluntary feeling of attachment, not on an enforced allegiance demanded by a numerical majority. The North must stop its antislavery agitation and aggressions against the South, observe strictly the fugitive slave law, and guarantee the South's rights. If the North refused, the Union was at an end. California itself was the test of good faith. To admit California as a free state would destroy even the pretense of Southern equality. The alternative for the South was clear.

Other Southern orators echoed Calhoun's objections to the proposed Compromise. Davis, for example, argued that California should not be admitted because it had not passed through territorial status and its proceedings in framing a state constitution were wholly irregular and illegal. He reasserted slaveholders' rights to take their slaves into new territories, California included. To bar them was "an odious discrimination" against their right "to a common and equal enjoyment of the Union," as intended by the Constitution. Disregard of the Constitution, he branded as "fatal to the peace and equality of the States"; it will "lead, if persisted in," to destruction of the Union, "in which the slaveholding States have never sought more than equality, and in which they will not be content to remain with less."

On their side, Northerners like Seward and Chase denounced the Compromise's concessions to slavery in the fugitive slave proposal and in its failure to bar slavery from new territories. No compromise with the moral evil of slavery could be tolerated. President Taylor, too, stood firm against the proposal, advising Congress to reject Clay's "omnibus" bill. Chances for its passage appeared slim as spring melted into summer. Talk in the South grew increasingly strident. Some radicals called openly for "separation from the present Union," a sentiment loudly echoed in the press. The Nashville convention met in early June. Amid torrid denunciations of Northern aggression, the convention adopted resolutions affirming Davis's position taken in the Senate and then recessed to await the outcome in Washington.

But in the face of such disunionist threats, support for the accommodation grew. Earlier Daniel Webster, in his famous March 7 speech, pleaded eloquently for conciliation and compromise as the best means to save the Union. Speaking not "as a Massachusetts man, nor as a Northern man, but as an American," he deplored Northern radical agitation and intemperate talk and called for an understanding of the South and slavery. Since slavery was in fact excluded "by the law of nature" from New Mexico territory with its semi-arid climate, Congress need not "re-enact the law of God." When the aged Clay, worn down by his legislative labors, was forced to withdraw for rest at Newport, young, dynamic Senator Stephen A. Douglas, Illinois Democrat, took charge, divided the Compromise into five distinct measures, and whipped them handily through Congress. Obstacles dropped away, as if by the intervention of fate. Calhoun died in March, Taylor in July. Presidential successor, moderate Millard Fillmore of New York, favored the Compromise. By September the five bills had glided through Congress and were signed by the President. How would the country react?

Southern opinion was badly split. Extreme, radical "separationists" demanded immediate secession of their own state regardless of what other states did. A larger faction, known as "cooperationists," favored secession provided it was carried out by joint action of all slaveholding states. Still others in large numbers, Unionists, contended that the Compromise was satisfactory and the South's continued adherence to the Union insured many benefits that withdrawal would surrender.

A special Georgia state convention, dominated by Unionists, resolved in the "Georgia Platform" that the Compromise be accepted so long as the North also abided by it faithfully. Mississippi's response typified the growing shift in Southern feeling. During the 1851 gubernatorial campaign the Democratic candidate proved so extreme a "separationist" that Democratic leaders replaced him with "cooperationist" Jefferson Davis; and in the ensuing election Davis lost to moderate Whig Senator Henry S. Foote, who endorsed the Compromise. Even South Carolina sentiment, which had been running fever-hot for secession, cooled to the point that Francis Lieber was prompted to exclaim, "The match, the powder horn has been wrested from the . . . daring fools and maniac demagogues. . . . I thank thee, O God!"

And so the crisis passed. At least for the moment the bonds of Union held. Whig leaders in the South, having won in the 1848 election, were reluctant to abandon their own administration in Washington. And cotton, at thirteen cents a pound, assured an economic prosperity that many did not want to jeopardize by irresponsible action in 1850–51. But if the Whig party and prosperity were to disintegrate, would Southerners still favor the Union? Ten years ahead lay the answer.

While most Southerners accepted the Compromise and the Union, some extremist "fire-eaters" remained adamant and worked in the years ahead to convince fellow Southerners that only in secession lay sectional salvation. For one, Robert Barnwell Rhett, a South Carolina lawyer-politician and editor of the Charleston *Mercury*, assumed Calhoun's Senate seat in 1850 but resigned in protest when his state failed to take stronger action against the "oppressive" Compromise. During the fifties he constantly argued that the South must leave the Union to secure its "rights," and he labored for Southern unity through local committees of safety, ultimately earning the title of "Father of secession." In Alabama another lawyer-editor-politician, William Lowndes Yancey, openly advocated disunion and organized the Southern Rights Association and the League of United Southerners. The third major "fire-eater," Edmund Ruffin, a Virginia planter who had long urged fellow Southerners to improve their farming methods, had been stirred into action by the Wilmot Proviso. Thereafter as a zealous disunionist, he devoted full time to organizing local secession societies and rousing separationist sentiment. Other Southern nationalists like William Gregg, James DeBow, Roger Pryor, and James Hammond called for Southern economic self-sufficiency through establishing local manufacturing plants and direct Southern trade with Europe and Latin America.

"Southernism," with increasing stridency in the 1850's, also generated drives for home-printed, home-written Southern textbooks, better local schools and colleges, and boycotting Northern vacation spots. Since the Southern way of life was plainly so superior, why should Southerners send sons north to college or for that matter even mingle with Yankees at Newport or Saratoga Springs? "The few labored," historian Avery Craven has observed, "to prepare the way for a Southern nation. In season and out they strove to build self-sufficiency and self-consciousness." The ten years following the Compromise of 1850 would tell how well they succeeded.

2. *Economic Growth and Distractions Abroad*

Above the Mason-Dixon line many Northerners hoped the 1850 Compromise had permanently eased sectional animosities. But almost immediately devout abolitionists denounced concession to evil, focusing their fire on the Fugitive Slave Act. The law not only authorized Federal marshals to deputize local residents to help hunt down runaway slaves but it also prohibited alleged fugitives from testifying before the United States commissioner (hearing officer) who heard the case, in accordance with Southern state law and contrary to that of most Northern jurisdictions. Further, operating under the fee system, the commissioner was paid a ten-dollar fee if he found that the individual in question was a fugitive to be sent south, and only a five-dollar fee if he was a free Negro. Such patent card-stacking in favor of slave-hunting (even encouraging kidnaping) seemed the height of injustice. The South, despite its adherence to the state rights doctrine, was paradoxically insisting on Federal intervention and enforcement within Northern states.

"I will not obey it," cried Emerson in defying the law. Many shared his feeling. Several Northern states enacted "personal liberty laws" which threw such legal safeguards as right to counsel, confrontation of witnesses, and jury trial around alleged fugitives in an effort to prevent illegal kidnaping of free Negroes. Of doubtful constitutionality since the Supreme Court's *Prigg* decision (1842) had placed fugitive slave cases under exclusive Federal jurisdiction, such laws nevertheless remained on the books.

Northern defiance of the law took various forms. Abolitionist lawyers like Salmon P. Chase of Ohio often served without fee as defense attorneys in fugitive cases. In 1855 an Ohio court set free a Negro whom a Federal marshal was holding for trial as a fugitive. When the marshal rearrested the accused, the Ohio court ordered the arrest of the marshal, who won release only on appeal to a Federal court. In Wisconsin, abolitionist editor Sherman Booth, arrested for aiding a fugitive, was freed by the state supreme court, which declared his conviction illegal and the Federal Fugitive Slave Act unconstitutional. Even after the United States Supreme Court

KIDNAPPING AGAIN!!

A MAN WAS STOLEN LAST NIGHT BY THE

Fugitive Slave Bill COMMISSIONER!

HE WILL HAVE HIS

MOCK TRIAL

ON SATURDAY, MAY 27, AT 9 O'CLOCK,

In the Kidnapper's 'Court,' before the Hon. Slave Bill Commissioner,

AT THE COURT HOUSE, IN COURT SQUARE.

SHALL BOSTON STEAL ANOTHER MAN?

Thursday, May 26, 1854.

A Boston poster showing defiance of the Fugitive Slave Act.

overturned the Wisconsin ruling in *Ableman* v. *Booth* (1859), Wisconsin courts continued their defiance.

Northern Negroes joined the defiance, responding to Frederick Douglass's booming call that "nothing short of resistance on the part of the colored man was imperative" and that "every slaveholder who meets a bloody death in this infernal [slave-catching] . . . is an argument in favor of the manhood of our race." Negroes and whites persisted in defying Federal law throughout the fifties as the "Underground Railroad" sought to whisk runaways across Ohio and Pennsylvania to freedom in Canada. Negro "Vigilance Committees" had been functioning in Northern communities since the 1830's. William Wells Brown, who later became an American Antislavery Society agent and the first American Negro novelist with *Clotel: Or the President's Daughter* (1853), was aided by abolitionists in his 1834 escape across Ohio. When he settled at Buffalo he became active in helping other fugitives make their getaways. Vigilance Committee men like David Ruggles, Theodore Wright, Charles Ray, and Frederick Douglass in New York, and Robert Purvis and William Still in Pennsylvania rendered frequent aid. Whether the "Underground Railroad," as historian Larry Gara suggests, was relatively ineffective, it provided a symbol of Northern refusal to acquiesce in slave hunting.

In some Northern communities, where local feeling ran high, it was hard to get a man to accept appointment as Federal marshal since he would then have to capture runaways. If a man did take the job, he found it difficult to get local deputies and often faced social ostracism in his home town. Some deliberate baiting of marshals occurred in extreme abolitionist towns.

To aid a fugitive and to refuse to help Federal marshals recapture runaways were of course violations of Federal law. In parts of the North such violations were frequent and open. In Ohio a band of men boarded a southbound train at Wellington, near Oberlin, and wrested a Negro slave from the marshal escorting him back to the South. When the mob's ringleaders were arrested and brought to trial, a local jury refused to convict them of what was clearly law-breaking. At times abolitionists in Boston and upstate New York towns pried fugitives from jails and speeded them north to Canada. When Anthony Burns, captured in Boston, was shipped back to slavery, stores and offices draped their windows in black. At Christiana, Pennsylvania, after a crowd fought off a slave-seeking posse, its leaders were acquitted in the subsequent trial.

While a small portion of people in the North took such action, the vast majority were absorbed in more mundane, economic pursuits, seeking to improve their individual fortunes. Acquiring land, farming, buying and selling, manufacturing, shipping, speculating, trading, railroading, and organizing varied financial ventures engaged Northern attention. One major advance, the "transportation revolution," in historian George Taylor's phrase, was transforming the face of America's economy. Road and bridge building projects, sponsored by local communities, states, and private firms, were followed by the canal building mania of the 1820's and 1830's. The most useful of the resulting canals was New York's Erie Canal, which lowered freight rates from $100 to $10 per ton, opened the Great Lakes interior, and resulted in half of the nation's foreign trade funneling through New York City in the 1850's.

The coming of steam power further fueled the transportation revolution. Introduced on the Ohio River in 1811, the steamboat soon dominated the vast Mississippi-Ohio waterways. By the 1850's over 700 steam vessels on western waters were carrying peak loads in a colorful trade that was highlighted in the writings of Mark Twain. However, a rash of accidents and explosions brought early Federal regulation in the Steamboat Act of 1851.

Even more telling economically was the swift expansion of railroads. Railroad construction proceeded rapidly, pushing the nation's lines from 3,000 miles in 1840 to over 30,000 by 1860. A network of lines was developed across the Northeast and into the Great Lakes and Mississippi valley. By the early 1850's several lines tied Chicago, hub of western railroads, with the Atlantic seaports. The flow of rail freight tended to redirect trade from the north-to-south pull of Mississippi steamboats to an east-west axis—a commercial shift of decisive importance in 1861.

In communication the electric telegraph, developed by New York artist-inventor Samuel F. B. Morse, transmitted messages in 1844 over a line built with Federal aid between Baltimore and Washington. By the 1850's many small lines had been merged into the dominant Western Union combine. By 1861 telegraph messages could be sent all the way to California, and in 1858 New Yorker Cyrus W. Field ran a transatlantic cable to England.

Good transportation facilities, opening broad domestic markets, gave a boost to manufacturing. Indeed, as the 1850 census showed, manufactures produced $1 billion of goods and had temporarily passed agricultural production. This figure would double in the next decade. While most industry rested on an agricultural base, the two largest in terms of value of manufactures were flour and meal milling and lumber production, which together accounted for one-sixth of the 1860 manufacturing total.

Factors contributing to America's growing industrial strength at mid century included improved technology, mechanization with better machines run by steam and water power, a degree of specialization and concentration, increasingly available supply of labor and capital, plus faster transportation and distribution to an enlarging market. Technological changes included wider application of Whitney's interchangeable, standardized parts principle, introduction of Elias Howe's sewing machine in 1846 to be further improved in a few years by Isaac M. Singer, Charles Goodyear's rubber vulcanizing process, A. L. Dennison's technique for machine-production of watches, and a host of other developments. The increasing flow of immigrants provided a low-paid labor force. Capital in the early years came largely from merchants, and entrepreneurs usually plowed back profits into their businesses. Governments, too, state and local as well as national, often responded to appeals for grants. British investors also supplied funds, more often to transportation than to manufacturing. By 1850 what had begun years before under Wall Street's famed buttonwood tree became regularized in New York's stock exchange where old and new issues of securities attracted private capital. And the corporation, swiftly becoming the most common form of business organization, made possible the raising of the large sums of capital needed by ever-enlarging enterprises.

Most spectacular industrial gains were made in the Northeast. By 1850 this section accounted for three-fourths of the nation's manufacturing. Textiles, boots and shoes, and men's clothing led the way in both numbers of employees and value added by manufacture. Having improved efficiency and quality by 1860, New England cotton factories commanded 70 per cent of their industry and turned out 75 per cent of the nation's cloth, with the average mill operating 7,000 spindles and 163 looms. The pattern in woolens and in boot and shoe making, which grew rapidly in the 1850's, resembled that in cotton with increasing specialization and concentration. Iron making, which had been largely a small, local operation, centered mainly in Pennsylvania, produced 580,000 of the nation's total of 987,000 tons of pig iron in 1860. A shift from wood to anthracite coal and coke (half-burned soft coal) helped improve iron production, and thereafter rolling mills took over from hand forges. But William Kelly's development of blast-furnace techniques in 1847 were not generally adopted till years later. Most pig iron was converted almost immediately into farm implements and machines like seed drills, threshers, cultivators, and into stoves, railroad iron, wire, cable, sheet, and other consumer products. By 1850, manufacturing employed close to a million workers (up from 349,000 in 1820).

At a time when the North was enlarging and diversifying its economic pursuits, the South doggedly devoted its energies to producing staple crops —tobacco, rice, sugar, and most importantly, cotton. In consequence the South's economy became less and less flexible, and more and more dependent on cotton growing, which spread 1,000 miles west from the Carolinas to Texas and 600 miles up the Mississippi valley. As already noted, slavery spread along with cotton raising. Foreign immigrants avoided the region. And since a man's social standing in the South was tied to owning land and slaves, few whites wanted to engage in business or work for wages, since being under another man's direction implied a form of demeaning servitude.

As the price of cotton moved upward from eight cents a pound in 1845 to thirteen cents by the mid-fifties, cotton production rose steadily, as did the demand for new land and slaves. In 1859 output reached its pre-war peak of 5,387,000 bales, and cotton made up more than 60 per cent of the nation's exports. Paradoxically, rising cotton production made the Southerners even more dependent on the North and more resentful of their economic status. Since much of the money paid for cotton was siphoned off for shipping, storing, selling, insurance, and interest charges, planters resented losing half their return in the pockets of Northern businessmen. Making loans to cover these charges left Southern borrowers owing Northern financiers almost $200 million by 1860. Southern indignation against Yankee creditors mounted, especially in years of low cotton prices.

Dixie's cotton, the Northwest's grains, and the Northeast's industrial activity all combined to produce a spectacular rise in the nation's foreign trade, up to a high of $687 million in 1860 from $125 million in depression-plagued 1843. The trade deficit, caused by an excess of imports over exports, was partially offset by the rising export of Western wheat and flour; and of the half-billion dollars of gold mined in California by 1857, 80 per cent went abroad to pay foreign bills. America's ocean-going commerce gloried in its glamorous heyday as the magnificent three-masted sailing Yankee clipper, stretched out by ship designers like David McKay to impressive length and speed, outsailed all ships at sea. American vessels, which carried 75 per cent of the foreign trade, returned with an increasing flow of immigrants. Each year during the early 1850's, more than 300,000 newcomers, largely German and Irish, arrived in America, where they supplied much needed labor in factories, farms, mines, railroads, and construction.

While economic growth burgeoned, the continuing political calm following the 1850 Compromise pleased Northeastern businessmen, Western farmers, and Southern planters. In 1852 both major parties, seeking to avoid discord on the slavery question, nominated inoffensive candidates for President. Democrat Franklin Pierce, a former Senator who had served in the Mexican War and was billed as a Jacksonian "Young Hickory" from New Hampshire, defeated Whig rival, General Winfield Scott, conqueror of Mexico City. Pierce's 250,000-vote margin gave him just over 50 per cent of the total popular vote, making him the only President to win a popular majority between 1840 and 1864. Even the Free Soil vote shrank by half, indicating that Van Buren followers of 1848 were rejoining the Democratic ranks.

For a time overseas distractions drew attention away from domestic cares. Cuba had long been desired by American expansionists. Polk had offered Spain $100 million for the island in the late forties. In the early fifties several private military groups were fitted out in the United States for assaults on Cuba, seeking to topple Spanish authority and ready the island for annexation. Governor John A. Quitman of Mississippi supported one such expedition, and Colonel H. A. Crittenden, nephew of Fillmore's Attorney General, was killed accompanying the abortive Lopez raid of 1851.

Although the new Pierce administration hoped to acquire Cuba, it was not prepared for a public fuss over it. American diplomats in Europe, James Buchanan, Pierre Soulé, and John Y. Mason jointly urged that the United States make a new $120-million offer; if rejected by Spain, then "by every law, human and divine," we "shall be justified" in seizing Cuba. When this "Ostend Manifesto" leaked to the public, the embarrassed administration quickly repudiated it. Northern papers screamed that the "Cuba grab" was a Southern plot for an additional slave state. Talk of acquiring Santo Domingo drew the same condemnation. And when some Southern extremists urged reopening the long-closed African slave trade, Northern abolitionists protested in horror over the barbarous proposal.

Northern charges that Southern expansionists sought to annex Carribean lands to make new slave states were not entirely unfounded. A private military expedition, led by adventurer William Walker, dubbed "the grey-eyed man of destiny," invaded Nicaragua and seized political control. Walker installed himself as president. He served until he got into trouble with New York shipping magnate Cornelius Vanderbilt by cancelling Vanderbilt's lucrative, exclusive concession for carrying California-bound passengers to and across Nicaragua. Again the charge resounded of Southern scheming for a future slave state. In the Panama isthmus, negotiations with New Granada (now Colombia) produced a treaty granting Americans the right to build a railroad, which was completed by 1855, despite incredible obstacles. One route was now assured to California and the Pacific.

American commercial interests had long been intent on expanding trade opportunities in the Pacific. Indeed, Yankee ships had touched the China coast shortly after the American Revolution. When the British forced open additional Chinese ports in 1842, Americans gained similar trading concessions. In 1853, Commodore Mathew C. Perry sailed his four Navy ships into Yedo Bay, Japan, and insisted on delivering a a letter from the President to the Emperor. In March, 1854, a treaty of commerce granted Americans trading rights in two Japanese ports. The strategically located Hawaiian Islands in mid-Pacific, which for years served American whalers and merchant ships as a supply point and drew Yankee missionaries, looked more and more appealing.

The desire to expand America's Pacific trade became linked with the drive to tie California closer to the rest of the country. A transcontinental railroad appeared to be the obvious solution. By the early fifties, proposals for such a line were loudly voiced. Among the voices, none spoke more vigorously than that of Stephen A. Douglas. A Vermont native, Douglas had headed west as a young man, settled for a time in downstate Illinois, then moved to Chicago where he invested in extensive real estate holdings in the booming city's south side. A short man of restless energy and driving ambition, barrel-chested with a booming voice, Douglas moved rapidly up the political ladder from judge to Congressman to United States Senator in 1847. His congeniality and dynamic personality attracted many supporters to him as he swiftly emerged as the most prominent of Northern Democrats. In 1850 the thirty-seven-year-old Senator sponsored and pushed through Congress the law providing Federal subsidies for building the Illinois Central Railroad to run parallel to the Mississippi River from Chicago to New Orleans. Here was a measure that would strengthen Douglas's hold on Illinois voters and broaden his appeal up and down the Mississippi valley as Northwest-South trade could be expected to increase. Railroad politics would soon become entangled with sectional antagonisms growing over the extension of slavery into newly created Western territories.

5

Mounting Sectional Crises

Sectional harmony that had seemed assured just a few years earlier in the wake of the Compromise of 1850 now shattered under the impact of the Kansas-Nebraska Act of 1854. Removing the bar against slavery's spread into Western territories, the act generated a series of unexpected, highly significant results. Its immediate result was to bring on a political revolution as the old Whig party faded and a new vigorous Republican party sprang up. The outbreak of open violence in Kansas pumped adrenalin into renewed sectional clashes. The rising Republican party, the Supreme Court's sanction of slavery's westward spread, and an economic panic coupled with a religious revival set the stage for mounting sectional crises. Finally, an armed abolitionist raid into Virginia fired Southern tempers to the flashing point, as the decade drew to an ominous close.

1. "The Crime Against Kansas"

To build a railroad to the Pacific would require government aid, as all could see. It would also require agreement on the route. If the line were to serve the interests of Chicago and the upper Mississippi valley, the route would have to pass through an as yet unorganized, Indian-occupied region west of Iowa. An ardent expansionist, Stephen Douglas had long advocated opening the vast western plains region to settlement and organizing territorial government there. As 1854 began, Douglas in his eleventh year in Congress was serving as chairman of the Senate Committee on Territories. On January 4, with the above considerations in mind, he reported a bill to organize Nebraska as a Federal territory. Looking toward Federal subsidies for a Pacific railroad with its eastern termini at Chicago and St. Louis, the Senator argued that the railroad must be built to further progress and prosperity in "the spirit of this age" and that territorial government must be established and settlers allowed to take up farms in the region west of Missouri-Iowa. Initially the bill sought simply to facilitate a future railroad and had nothing to do with slavery. It was soon apparent, however, that the 1850 Compromise's "non-intervention"-by-Congress provision, allowing territorial popular sovereignty, would have to be included. Having secured the administration's blessing, Douglas anticipated easy passage of his Nebraska bill.

At this point unforeseen pressure forced three modifications in the bill, largely to satisfy diverse railroad expectations as well as Southern interests.

The first, pushed by Senator David Atchison of Missouri, explicitly denied Congress's power over slavery in the Nebraska Territory and specified that power to be in the hands of "the people residing therein." With that concession, Douglas was also compelled to accept in the bill a statement that the Missouri Compromise (which since 1820 had barred slavery north of the 36°30′ parallel) was "void and inoperative" since it clashed with the Congressional nonintervention principle. Railroad strategy dictated the acceptance by Douglas of the third alteration. A government survey showed that, based on engineering considerations, the southern route near the Mexican border was the most practicable for the Pacific line (and indeed the Gadsden Purchase of 1853 was made to secure that route). Douglas naturally favored a more central route, as did others. To satisfy various factions of central route advocates (some wanting the railroad to run through the area due west of Missouri and others favoring a slightly more northern route due west of Iowa), Douglas reluctantly agreed to split the region into two territories, Kansas and Nebraska. Already aware of an impending political storm, Douglas hoped that these modifications would win over enough legislators to insure the bill's passage.

At the close of January, 1854, he opened the debate arguing for the adoption of the Kansas-Nebraska bill on the grounds that it provided democratic self-determination, that it would banish the disruptive slavery issue from the halls of Congress to the western plains, that "in that climate . . . it is worse than folly to think of its [Nebraska's] being a slaveholding country," and that settlement of the new area would stimulate the nation's growth. After months of wrangling, the Kansas-Nebraska Act passed the Senate 37–14, squeaked through the House 113–100, and became law on May 30, 1854.

The vote, reflecting a sharp sectional division, marked the start of a revolution in party alignment. In the House all Northern Whigs (45 in all) and almost half the Northern Democrats joined in voting against the bill. The remaining Northern Democrats with their Southern cohorts, both Democrat and Whig, engineered the bill's passage. Sectional cleavage was eroding national party unity. The national Whig party would soon dissolve. Cracks in the Democratic ranks would widen. A new sectional party was about to be born.

The response in the North was explosive. Senator Chase of Ohio, with help from Giddings and Sumner, published an "Appeal of the Independent Democrats in Congress to the People of the United States." It denounced the repeal of the Missouri Compromise as a "gross violation of a sacred pledge" that would allow the flow of slavery into all territories. Douglas's bill was "a criminal betrayal of precious rights" and "part and parcel of an atrocious plot to exclude from the vast unoccupied region immigrants from the Old World and free laborers from our own States, and to convert it into a dreary region of despotism, inhabited by masters and slaves." In a direct appeal to Northwest voters, Chase proclaimed that the act by lifting the bar against slavery would destroy freedom, wreck chances for a homestead bill, and block free farmers from new farm lands. Only by resisting the spread of slavery could men save "the Union formed to establish justice and secure the blessings of liberty."

Incensed Northerners reacted so vehemently in castigating Douglas that the "Little Giant" said he could travel from Boston to Chicago by the light of the bonfires burning him in effigy. When he did return to Chicago to explain his position, he found flags flying at half staff and church bells tolling in mourning. A Saturday night crowd of 10,000 shouted steadily to drown out his efforts to address them until Douglas at length pulled out his watch and exclaimed testily, "It is now Sunday morning; I am going to church, and you can go to hell!"

When Kansas Territory was officially opened to settlers in mid-1854, the Federal government had not yet extinguished Indian titles nor surveyed the land into parcels for individual purchases. As migrants began to move in from next-door Missouri and other states, the resulting chaos intensified the usual frontier scramble for the best lands, for sites for future towns, potential county seats, rail junction points, and strategic commercial locations. Often men used violence to grab possession of land long before anything resembling a valid title could be obtained. Normal frontier aggressiveness was further heightened by the struggle for political jobs, lucrative mail,

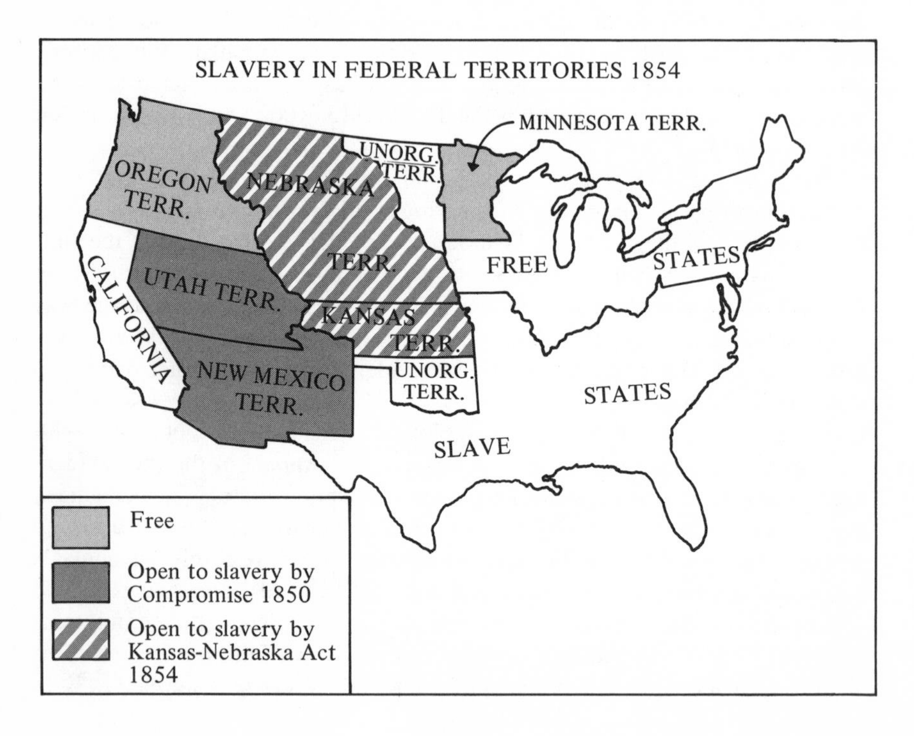

army, and Indian contracts, and concessions for railroad schemes. Some who went to Kansas were there simply to take advantage of opportunities for a quick profit. Other migrants, more numerous, were small farmers moving across from Missouri and other nearby states seeking land for better farms. For most of these the slavery question was of little interest or concern.

But other newcomers, convinced that the slavery issue would be finally settled on the Kansas plains, as Douglas had argued in his popular sovereignty speeches, were determined to make the decision in Kansas on the side of freedom. In distant Worcester, Massachusetts, Eli Thayer organized the New England Emigrant Aid Company to cover the costs of free-soilers moving to Kansas. Funds were raised, and volunteers were recruited. Similar societies were formed in New York, Ohio, Connecticut, and Washington. Within a year over a thousand free-soil emigrants were rolling westward in their wagons carrying cartons of "Beecher's Bibles," the nickname for rifles that antislavery preacher Henry Ward Beecher said would do more than Scriptures to stop slavery in Kansas. Southerners, crying foul, attempted to recruit volunteers in a counter-effort but managed to get only a few hundred from the Lower South to join Jefferson Buford's Kansas-bound expedition.

Nearer at hand, Missourians tended to view the new territory of Kansas just to the west as an extension and even a colony of their own state. Clearly the new territory would be economically dependent for transportation, trade, and services upon Missouri towns like Kansas City and St. Louis. Any effort by Yankee meddlers to dominate Kansas was deemed intolerable. To secure slavery in Kansas, as Senator Atchison saw it, was part of the stakes "we are playing for." "If we win," he told a colleague, "we carry slavery to the Pacific Ocean; if we fail we lose Missouri, Arkansas and Texas; the game must be played boldly." Missourians were urged to do their duty in repelling Yankee efforts to steal Kansas for the free-soil camp. When elections were held on March 30, 1855, Missourians acted "boldly" by crossing the border in large numbers, some armed, dominating the voting and casting ballots themselves before returning to their state. The returns showed 5,427 proslavery votes and 797 antislavery, even though official rolls carried only 2,905 registered voters' names. Territorial Governor Andrew H. Reeder, a Pennsylvania lawyer appointed by Pierce, tried to unseat one-fourth of the legislators on grounds of election frauds, only to be overruled by the President. Despite the governor's protests, the new legislature rammed through the adoption of laws similar to those of Missouri and enacted a slave code, which among other provisions made it illegal even to challenge slavery's legality in Kansas.

Reeder attempted to get the President to reverse these actions, assert Federal authority in the territory, and implement fairly the popular sovereignty provisions. Pierce demonstrated his weakness as a leader, from the viewpoint of Northerners, by complacently dismissing the suggestions. Shortly thereafter, he removed Reeder, charging him with improper land speculations.

As newspapers reported the outrageous developments in Kansas, indignation and a sense of outrage were building in the North. In Kansas free-soil men, rejecting the previous actions as frauds, proceeded to choose a convention and draft a free-soil constitution. Submitted to a referendum in December, without interference by Missouri "border ruffians," this Topeka constitution was approved by a 1,731-to-46 vote. In subsequent elections free-staters chose Reeder as territorial delegate to Congress, and Emigrant Aid Company agent Charles Robinson as Governor. They also chose a legislature of their own.

While the administration in Washington remained immobile, the stage was set for open violence in Kansas. Within a few months Robinson was arrested and jailed for usurpation by proslavery officials. In May, 1856, a Federal marshal organized a posse and called upon other "law-abiding men" to aid him in arresting free-soil officials in Lawrence. His invitation was accepted by bands of armed proslavery men who quickly made their way to Lawrence. That community, which had been founded by Emigrant Aid men and boasted a fortress-like "Free State Hotel," had long been the target of the proslaverite's ire. The arrests were made, the posse was dissolved, and then the marshal himself dined amicably at the hotel. But gangs of armed proslavery men, numbering perhaps 750 and encouraged by an irate proslavery sheriff, prowled about town, attacked two free-state newspaper offices and destroyed their presses, smashed windows and houses, and ultimately set fire to the hotel, before fading back into the countryside and over the Missouri line. Only one man was killed, and he paradoxically was a proslavery man struck by a falling brick. On-the-spot news correspondents hastily telegraphed exaggerated stories of the "sack of Lawrence" that inflamed readers of Eastern antislavery papers.

The Lawrence affair touched off a wave of brutal reprisals that engulfed Kansas in a nasty guerrilla war, as revenge and murder superseded reason and persuasion. Abolitionist John Brown, his eye bright with the zealous fire of an Old Testament prophet ("God's angry man" he was later called), had come to Kansas seeking a new start on a farm at Osawatomie after failures in the East. Taking literally the Biblical injunction of an "eye for an eye," Brown led four of his sons and two friends at midnight to a small proslavery settlement on Pottawatomie Creek, roused five men from their beds, and killed them on the spot. In the wake of Brown's attack, Kansas flared under raids, counter-raids, pillage, plundering, and murder by "jayhawkers," "bushwackers," and "border ruffians," with a toll of more than 200 lives lost. Fearful echoes of this war soon resounded far beyond the borders of Kansas.

Shortly, echoes shook the legislative halls in Washington. With the Pierce administration doing nothing, Congress had for months been wrangling over a policy for Kansas. On May 19, 1856, Charles Sumner launched into a well-rehearsed Senate speech on "The Crime Against Kansas." For two days he ranted against the Kansas "swindle," proslavery men, and the "murderous robbers" from Missouri. In caustic, blistering language he berated the South and particularly the absent South Carolina Senator, elderly Andrew P. Butler, "who has taken a mistress . . . the harlot Slavery." Numerous Senators walked out during the tirade, which one witness characterized as "the most un-American and unpatriotic speech" he ever heard. With Butler's personal honor impugned, his nephew, Preston Brooks of South Carolina, took matters into his own hands. Two days later, Brooks found Sumner seated at his Senate desk and attacked him from behind, pounding his cane repeatedly on Sumner's head so hard that the cane broke and Sumner, trying to rise, wrenched his desk loose before falling unconscious to the floor. Douglas's hope of banishing the slavery dispute from the halls of Congress to be decided on the Kansas plains had backfired with a double vengeance.

Tempers, pride, and honor were so aroused by this point that the sequel to the Sumner-Brooks fracas reads like fiction. "Bully" Brooks resigned from Congress and went home to South Carolina where he was dined, feted, lauded for standing up to insolent Yankee fanatics, and presented with a supply of new canes to replace his broken one. Sumner, whose popularity had earlier sagged so low that his reelection was doubtful, suddenly became a hero, a martyr to Northern freedom. Physically unable to serve for three years, he was nonetheless reelected by the Massachusetts legislature so that his vacant Senate seat would serve as a silent, continuing reminder of Southern brutality bred of slaveholding.

2. *Forging the Republican Party*

"Bleeding Sumner" and "Bleeding Kansas" were byproducts of the emotional turmoil engendered by Douglas's Kansas-Nebraska Act. A more direct result of this bill was the outrage inspired by Senator Chase's "Appeal of the Independent Democrats" of 1854. In the Great Lakes region disaffected men were already enraged over Polk's earlier river-harbor vetoes and the surrender of part of Oregon in the 1846 settlement. Now they rose in resounding protest, first over the "treacherous betrayal" of Congress in removing the Missouri Compromise block against slavery's spread into western territories and then over the sellout of Kansas to the "slave power."

Their moral indignation boiling, men joined rallies and meetings in villages and small towns to vent their anger. At a little white school house in Ripon, Wisconsin, protesters assembled; at the same time, in June, 1854, a mass meeting convened in an oak grove at Jackson, Michigan. Both groups resolved to form a new political party. Both took the name "Republican," out of respect for the ideals of the earlier Republicans' Thomas Jefferson and vowed to fight the extension of slavery into the territories.

Other groups calling themselves such names as "People's Party," "Anti-Nebraska" men, "Fusionists," and "Free Democrats" mushroomed throughout the upper Northwest region. A Pierce veto of new river-harbor appropriations and the blocking of a homestead measure merely intensified the spreading discontent. Rebellion against the old, stand-pat, regular parties raged across the Northwest and fanned out eastward. In the 1854 elections Ohio voters ousted every Congressman who had voted for the Kansas-Nebraska Act. In other Northern states similar results were reported. What had been a Democratic majority of 158 in the previous House would become an anti-Nebraska Republican plurality of perhaps 117 in the new House. After a prolonged deadlock that lasted more than two months, the Republicans were able to determine the new House Speaker, Nathaniel P. Banks of Massachusetts.

Meanwhile the grass roots support of the Republican party was growing. In Illinois former Whig Abraham Lincoln, who earlier had left politics to resume the full-time practice of law, was jolted out of complacency. The repeal of the Missouri Compromise by the Kansas-Nebraska Act aroused him, he said, as he "had never been aroused before." He plunged actively into politics again, stumping for anti-Nebraska candidates. He expressed a common feeling when he declared that removing the old bar on the extension of slavery revealed the South's eagerness to spread slavery. "I hate it [slavery]," he had cried, "because of the monstrous injustice of slavery itself . . . because it deprives our republican example of its just influence in the world—and enables the enemies of our institutions, with plausibility, to taunt us as hypocrites. . . ." To Douglas's view that outsiders should not dictate to Kansans whether they should have slavery or not and that he cared not whether they "voted it up or down," Lincoln rejoined, "inasmuch as you do not object to my taking my hog to Nebraska, therefore, I must not object to your taking your slave. Now I admit this is perfectly logical if there is no difference" between the two, but men cannot shed their "human sympathies" nor deny "their consciousness that, after all there is humanity in the negro."

Conceding Douglas's assertion that "the doctrine of self-government is right," Lincoln countered that its application in Kansas "depends upon whether a negro is *not* or *is* a man. . . . When the white man governs himself, that is self-government; but when he governs himself, and also governs *another* man, . . . that is despotism. If a negro is a man, why then my ancient faith teaches me that 'all men are created equal;' " and that "there can be no moral right in . . . one man's making a slave of another." In Lincoln's view the prospect of slavery entering Kansas and

Nebraska was the concern not only of residents there but of all Americans: "The whole nation is interested that the best use be made of these territories. We want them for the homes of free white people. They cannot be . . . if slavery shall be planted within them. Slave states are places for poor white people to remove FROM, not to remove TO. New free states are places for poor people to go and better their condition." Here he touched a responsive chord in farmers of the Northwest by insisting that "the free territories . . . be kept open for the home of free white people."

In 1854–56 the new Republican party engineered the start of a revolution in American politics. New adherents flocked into its rapidly growing ranks from many different points within the political spectrum. Whigs like William Seward (New York), Thaddeus Stevens (Pennsylvania), and Lincoln banded together with free-soil followers of old Jacksonians Francis P. Blair, Thomas Hart Benton, and Martin Van Buren, with former Democrats like Salmon P. Chase (Ohio) and Lyman Trumbull (Illinois), and with radical abolitionists like Joshua Giddings (Ohio), Ben Wade (Ohio), George W. Julian (Indiana), and Charles Sumner (Massachusetts). At first a makeshift coalition of disparate factions holding differing and often clashing views, the Republicans presented a united stance solely in opposing the extension of slavery into the western territories. On this basis their appeal lay exclusively in the North. In less than two years, their phenomenal upsurge sent Trumbull and Wade to the Senate, Chase to the Ohio governorship, and a sufficient flood of Congressmen to Washington to give them working control of the House, as noted above.

The Republican tide surged ahead as its first national conclave met in Pittsburgh on February 22, 1856. With Francis P. Blair as chairman, Republicans established a national organization, reasserted their unshakeable opposition to the extension of slavery, and at Giddings's insistence affirmed their belief in the principles of the Declaration of Independence. Four months later their nominating convention at Philadelphia named as candidate for President John C. Frémont, the glamorous forty-three-year-old "Pathfinder of the West," who had served briefly as a California Senator. The platform denounced the Kansas-Nebraska legislation and other efforts to push slavery into territories formerly closed to it.

Erosion of the crumbling Whig party continued as many Northern Whigs moved into the Republican ranks. In the middle states and upper South, other Whigs fell under the spell of the four-year-old native American party. This nativist group, alarmed over the growing number of immigrants arriving at an annual rate of over 300,000, played upon fears that the country would soon be dominated by foreigners and particularly by Irish Catholics. Since the party operated with a degree of secrecy and members refused to discuss its inner rituals, outsiders began calling it the "Know-Nothing" party. Its appeal was strongest in Northern cities where new immigrants were taken in tow by and hence supported the growing Democratic political machines. The "Know-Nothing" party also won a broad following among former Whigs in the upper South. In 1856 the American party nominated ex-President Fillmore as Presidential candidate on a platform that was silent on slavery but urged limits on immigration and restrictions on foreigners.

The Democrats, convening at Cincinnati, passed over Pierce as inept and Douglas as too controversial. Instead, in a rare show of party harmony, they agreed on James Buchanan of Pennsylvania. At sixty-five, Buchanan, a veteran Jacksonian with experience as Senator, Secretary of State, and Minister to England, was known as a cautious moderate. He had not been involved in the Kansas ruckus during the preceding years because he had been abroad; consequently, he was acceptable to both Northern and Southern Democrats. On the critical issue of slavery in the territories, the party platform adhered to noninterference by Congress, with any disputed questions to be referred to the Federal courts. Democratic campaigners pictured Republicans as wild-eyed agitators bent on inflaming sectional hatred that would rupture the Union.

The outcome of the fall balloting gave Buchanan 174 electoral votes to Frémont's 114 and Fillmore's 8. "Old Buck's" popular vote of 1.8 million (45 per cent) topped Frémont's 1.3 million (33 per cent) and Fillmore's 872,000 (21 per cent). Democratic spokesmen claimed that the result indicated a nationwide desire for an end to agitation and a renewal of sectional harmony. But a look at the voting raised doubts. While Buchanan did draw votes in all parts of the country, Republican Frémont captured all New England, New York, and most of the Midwest. His high totals in Illinois, Pennsylvania, and Indiana placed him within striking distance of victory. Indeed, if Republicans had taken these states, Frémont would have been President—a circumstance that was not lost on Republican strategists as they looked ahead to 1860 with smiling anticipation.

3. Critical Years, 1857–1859

Buchanan's election quieted fears of Southerners for the moment, although many were apprehensive over Frémont's large vote. With "Republicanism sweeping over the North like a tornado," Buchanan himself had observed privately during the campaign that Frémont's election would mean the "dissolution of the Union." A sturdy Unionist himself, Buchanan (the nation's only bachelor President, whose niece Harriet Lane presided over the White House) appeared dignified if a bit odd with his head tilted permanently to one side and an ever-present puzzled look on his long, narrow face. Looking ahead, he counted on canniness bred of long political experience and innate caution to calm the turbulence of sectional hostility. His inaugural address forecast that the Supreme Court would shortly lay to rest the long agitated territorial slavery question.

True to prediction, on March 7, 1857, Chief Justice Roger B. Taney handed down the fateful decision in the case of Dred Scott. A Missouri Negro slave, Dred Scott, had accompanied his master, an army doctor, who was stationed for several years at Fort Snelling on the upper Mississippi River in Federal territory where slavery was prohibited by the Missouri Compromise law of 1820. Some years after returning to Missouri, Scott sued for his freedom on the grounds that his residence in free territory released him from slavery. His plea was rejected by Missouri's highest court, which held that regardless of his status in Federal territory Scott was a slave by Missouri law upon his return to that state. In 1853, having been acquired by a New York owner, Scott filed suit again, this time in Federal court. The case was appealed to the Supreme Court and was elaborately argued there in December, 1856, with the distinguished Montgomery Blair serving as Scott's counsel. By then the suit had become celebrated as a test case to get a Supreme Court ruling on slavery in the territories.

In preliminary deliberations the justices appeared ready to rule that since Missouri state law barred Negroes from citizenship Scott was therefore not a citizen and hence not entitled to sue in Federal court. But disagreement arose, and it was determined, partly through Buchanan's urging, to render a decision dealing with the larger aspects of the territorial issue. The questions to be decided were (1) was Scott a citizen and therefore entitled to sue in Federal court? and (2) had he become free by virtue of residence in a free, Federal territory? In its reasoning, the Court was badly divided, eight different opinions being offered. On the first question, six judges joined eighty-year-old Taney in holding that, regardless of what Scott's status in free territory might have been, he was a slave upon his return to Missouri. Since he was not a citizen by Missouri law, he had no right to sue in Federal Court. Taney, in his own written opinion, elaborated a highly prejudiced view of the Negro as inferior and not intended for citizenship by the framers of the Constitution.

On the second question, the Court's majority also answered no—Scott was not freed by residence in a free territory. The judges stressed the rights of property, and they held slaves to be property. Then, citing the provision of the Fifth Amendment that "No person shall be deprived of life, liberty or property without due process of law," the majority held that the Missouri Compromise's ban against taking slaves into Federal territories violated this clause, since it deprived an owner of his property (i.e., slaves) when moving to a territory. Therefore, Congress had no power under the Constitution to exclude slavery from Federal territories, and the Missouri Compromise was and always had been unconstitutional and void. By inference, also, a territorial legislature, as a creature of Congress, could have no more authority than its creator; hence, if Congress could not exclude slavery, neither could a territorial legislature. In a vigorous dissent, two Northern justices declared that Congress had the power to prohibit slavery in the territories and had in fact legally done so in the Missouri Compromise and that Scott was therefore a free citizen entitled to sue in Federal court.

At one blow the Court's *Dred Scott* decision, by decreeing that Congress had no power over slavery in the territories, demolished the Republican Party's fundamental objective of getting Congress to bar slavery in the territories. It also seriously undercut Douglas's popular sovereignty doctrine. In impact, it further strengthened the growing Southern insistence on Federal legal protection of slave property in the territories. Around these three positions—the Republican, the Douglas Democratic and the Southern—political battling would rage with mounting fury for the next three years.

Buchanan's administration was off to an ominously bad start. The Court's decision was greeted in the North with derision and condemnation. Many pointed out that the justices holding the majority view came from Southern states; some were slaveholders and, hence, obviously biased on the questions at issue. Republicans lambasted the decision as a "wicked and false judgment," reflecting the will of "the slave power," and "the grossest crime in the judicial annals of the Republic." Lincoln voiced a more moderate Republican assessment in June, 1857: "We think the Dred Scott decision erroneous. We know the court that made it has often overruled its own decisions, and we shall do what we can to have it overrule this."

In addition to the *Scott* ruling, four other developments of 1857 further fanned men's emotions and inflamed sectional animosities. *The Impending Crisis of the South*, a book by North Carolinian Hinton R. Helper, focused on the South's deteriorating economic position. By citing relevant census figures, Helper demonstrated how Southern economic production, even in its boasted domain of agriculture, was falling behind the North's. The South was digging its own economic grave, argued Helper, by clinging to its outmoded, archaic labor system of slavery, "the root of all the shame, poverty, ignorance, tyranny and imbecility of the South." Helper's widely publicized assault on the "peculiar institution's" harmful effects infuriated Southerners. Called a "miserable renegade," he was forced to leave his Carolina home. His book became political dynamite during the next few years; anyone who endorsed it incurred Southern wrath.

In August, 1857, a financial panic, brought on by over-extension of credit, excessive speculation, and shaky railroad and industrial schemes, precipitated an economic crash that threw thousands out of jobs, closed mills, mines, banks, and business offices, depressed prices, and produced general distress. In the North both businessmen and farmers, suffering the pinch of falling prices and dwindling markets, began urging higher tariffs and homestead legislation. Blaming the party in power for the economic slump, many shifted to the Republican ranks. And as so often happens in the wake of depression's threat to economic security, a wave of religious evangelism swept the country with all the super-charged emotionalism of revival meetings, as jobless men "hit the sawdust trail" grasping for a salvation that this world's troubles denied.

In such a state of spiritual and economic turmoil, the prickly Kansas question again riveted the attention of official Washington. In October, 1857, a proslavery convention meeting at Lecompton, Kansas, drafted a constitution guaranteeing slavery in the proposed state. The constitution was submitted to a popular "referendum." Voters were given the choice of approving the constitution "with slavery," which meant slavery was permanently established in Kansas, or approving the constitution "without slavery," which meant slavery would exist undisturbed until 1864 when a new vote would be taken on the question. Either way, Kansas would get slavery. Free-soil Kansans understandably boycotted the voting. Amid countless irregularities and intervention by Missourians again, the election produced a paper majority of 6,000 votes for the Lecompton constitution "with slavery" over 600 against.

In December, President Buchanan recommended to Congress that Kansas be admitted as a slave state under the Lecompton constitution. Rebellion erupted among Northern Democrats. Senator Douglas denounced the whole Lecompton proceedings as a fraud and a travesty on his popular sovereignty. He would unyieldingly oppose the admission of Kansas under Lecompton. Summoned to the White House and warned by Buchanan that President Jackson had broken Democratic Senators who opposed him, Douglas snapped defiantly, "Andrew Jackson is no longer President." Later Illinois' "Little Giant" declared war on the administration, reportedly saying, "By God, I made James Buchanan President, and by God, I'll unmake him!" But the Kansas admission bill passed the Senate, Douglas joining the Republicans in voting against it. In the House, Douglas Democrats, mainly Northwesterners who well recalled the public outcry over the Kansas-Nebraska Act, provided the margin to defeat the admission of Kansas and to insist on a new try for a fair popular sovereignty decision in Kansas. In a new referendum in 1858 Kansas voted to reject the Lecompton constitution by 11,812 to 1,926. Even allowing for a proslaveryite boycott of this election, it appeared that Kansans opposed slavery by 2 to 1. And so things stood, until 1861 when Congress admitted Kansas as a free state.

Douglas's break with the administration brought instant retribution upon him and his supporters. All postmasters, district attorneys, Federal marshals, and other office holders who held patronage jobs as friends of Douglas or his adherents were immediately fired by Buchanan, and their places were filled with loyal, pro-administration Democrats. Douglas returned to Illinois to seek reelection to the Senate in the face of hostility from these new job holders, who labeled him a "renegade" and actively worked for his defeat. However, his adamant stand against a slave state, Kansas, won support from other quarters and put him in the national spotlight. Greeley's

New York *Tribune* advised Illinois Republicans not to oppose Douglas for reelection, since he had furthered Republicans aims for a free Kansas.

But Illinois Republicans were not about to adopt Douglas. Instead, in June, 1858, they nominated for Senator attorney Abraham Lincoln. In a self-description, Lincoln recorded, "I am, in height, six feet four inches, nearly; lean in flesh, weighing on average 180 pounds; dark complexion, with coarse black hair and gray eyes." At age forty-nine Lincoln had come a long way from his Kentucky farm boyhood. Largely self-educated, he had tried his hand at surveying and storekeeping before settling into the law and politics. His intelligence, earthy humor, keen logic, and command of terse English had won him respect as a lawyer and a place in politics, having served in the Illinois legislature and one term in Congress. In accepting the nomination, Lincoln labeled Douglas's popular sovereignty policy a failure because it aggravated rather than resolved the issue. "A house divided against itself cannot stand," he said. "I believe this government cannot endure, permanently half *slave* and half *free*. I do not expect the Union to be *dissolved*—I do not expect the house to *fall*—but I *do* expect it will cease to be divided. It will become *all* one thing, or *all* the other." Slavery, he believed, must be put "in the course of ultimate extinction," as the Founding Fathers intended.

When Lincoln campaign rallies failed to draw large crowds, he challenged Douglas to a series of debates. Held in seven Illinois towns from late August to mid-October, the encounters drew tens of thousands who cheered, howled, and shouted as "Abe" and the "Little Giant" pummeled each other mercilessly. Each candidate had an hour and a half to present his own argument and a half hour to rebut his opponent's. The sharp contrast between the tall, gangling Lincoln speaking in rather high-pitched tones and the short, barrel-round Douglas with a booming voice heightened the interest of the vocal listeners, who often interjected with "Hit him again, Abe," "You got him there, Steve," and more.

Douglas quickly attacked Lincoln as unfit to be Senator because he favored abolition and Negro equality, refused to accept the Supreme Court's *Dred Scott* ruling as the supreme law of the land, and incited sectional hostility that could end only in a "war of extermination." Lincoln sharply refuted these indictments and charged Douglas with conspiring with Pierce, Buchanan, and Taney to spread slavery throughout the land, thereby destroying liberty, equal rights, and popular government. In explaining his own views, Lincoln said, "I have no purpose directly or indirectly to interfere with . . . slavery in the States where it exists . . . nor to introduce political and social equality between the white and black races, . . . but I hold . . . the negro is . . . entitled to all the natural rights enumerated in the Declaration of Independence. . . ." How, asked Douglas, could Republicans defy the Supreme Court's ruling on slavery in Federal territories? Lincoln replied that the Court erred in constitutional interpretation and that Republicans would continue to oppose slavery's extension.

In the Freeport debate Lincoln threw Douglas a barbed question: "Can the people of a United States territory . . . exclude slavery from its limits prior to the formation of a State constitution?" To answer no, Douglas would have to abandon his popular sovereignty doctrine, thereby alienating many loyal Democratic followers; to answer yes, he would defy the *Dred Scott* decision and risk losing his already dwindling pro-Southern support locally and nationally. Douglas clung boldly to his doctrine, asserting that the people of a territory "can . . . exclude slavery from their limits" by refusing to enact "local police regulations" to protect slavery. Douglas's answer, as Lincoln had expected, raised Southern hackles even more and drove deeper the wedge of dissension among Democrats that his earlier stand against Lecompton had initiated. Douglas's "Freeport doctrine," and his later elaboration of it in a *Harper's* article, would further solidify Southern opposition to him and thereby cost him the Presidency in 1860.

The 1858 balloting produced an Illinois legislature that reelected Douglas to the Senate (even though in aggregate Lincoln candidates for legislative seats won more popular votes than Douglas men). Having repelled both administration and Republican efforts to dislodge him, he returned to Washington in full strength. Lincoln, too, emerged from the contest stronger and more visible nationally. Having battled to a virtual draw with the nation's top Democrat, he was a man for Republicans to consider seriously in selecting a nominee two years hence.

In 1859 the ghost of Kansas that perennially haunted the nation's affairs struck again. Old John Brown, obsessed with a divine mission and financed by wealthy abolitionists, gathered together a private "army" of twenty-one men, including two of his sons and five Negroes, on an abandoned Maryland farm and provided them with weapons. His long-planned scheme was aimed at establishing communities of refuge in the Southern mountains, which would be supplied with arms. Then, with runaway slaves joining the communities, he would establish a provisional free state and liberate other slaves.

After dark on October 16, 1859, Brown's band seized the Federal arsenal at Harper's Ferry, Virginia, fifty miles northwest of Washington. The town was thrown into turmoil for a time. A few residents lost their lives, but the expected mass rush of Negroes to join Brown did not materialize. Within forty-eight hours a company of United States marines under Colonel Robert E. Lee's command rushed to the scene, overwhelmed the insurgents, killing ten and taking Brown and others as prisoners. Tried six weeks later for conspiracy to commit murder and treason, Brown was convicted and hanged on December 2. Upon mounting the gallows, Brown made a final appeal for Negro freedom that moved many who deplored his violent act to admire the quiet courage of his last words: "I . . . forfeit my life for the furtherance of the ends of justice, and mingle my blood . . . with the blood of millions in this slave country, whose rights are disregarded by wicked, cruel and unjust enactments. . . . Let it be done."

As an act, taken by itself, Brown's raid meant little. But, in death, Brown swiftly became the symbol of conflict between the sections. Southern "fire-eater" Edmund Ruffin sped to Harper's Ferry and gathered up the raiders' weapons which he displayed on a tour of Southern towns, telling listeners the weapons were intended for use by slaves against them. This visible evidence drove a shudder of fright through Southerners, who visualized the horrors of a mass slave uprising. Many with no direct connection with slavery and formerly indifferent to sectional controversy were now convinced that abolitionists posed a direct threat to the South's security. Abolitionists had mounted an armed invasion of Southern soil; they must be resisted at all costs. Disunionist sentiment rose sharply. Legislatures affirmed a state's right to leave the Union, while Mississippi and South Carolina appropriated funds for military forces. What Seward had called an "irrepressible conflict" a year earlier now moved a notch nearer. In the eyes of many Southerners all Northerners became equated with John Brown the abolitionist who raised "the terrible swift sword."

In reality, most Northerners deplored Brown's resort to armed attack. Lincoln observed that Brown's concern over the "wrong of slavery" did not "excuse violence, bloodshed and treason." But others hailed him as a "new saint" who dared to die for his conviction that slavery must be rooted out—a martyr to the cause of human freedom. "John Brown's Body" would soon become more than a marching song; it would be the symbol of freedom breaking the shackles of black bondage.

Even as John Brown died, hostility was rising in the new Congress then meeting in Washington. Republicans, dominating the House, pushed through bills for a protective tariff, homesteads, and the admission of Kansas as a free state. All of these measures were negated either by the Democratic Senate or by Presidential veto. Sectional wrangling killed hopes for getting the Pacific railroad project moving. But already in 1858 the Butterfield Overland coaches had begun providing mail-passenger service to California. By early 1860 a rival outfit offered ten-day mail delivery through the celebrated "pony express," while plans were rapidly maturing for the completion of a transcontinental telegraph line that would become a reality in 1860. Economic progress would not wait while politicians procrastinated.

Ironically east-west bonds of communication were strengthening as the north-south political ties were unraveling. Northern resentment over Southern blocking of economic policies on tariff, land, and transportation was building higher. Republican leaders would turn this resentment to advantage in the upcoming Presidential contest.

PART II

The Civil War, 1860–1865

When Abraham Lincoln was elected President, seven Southern states withdrew from the Union in the conviction that their vital interests were in danger. In February, 1861, they formed the Confederate States of America. Two months later the showdown over Fort Sumter erupted in a Southern assault on the fort, and the country was at war.

During the four years that followed, Americans engaged in a costly, tragic struggle to determine whether the nation would survive intact. Northern men in field, in factory, and in arms labored and battled to preserve the United States as a single country. With equal dedication Confederates fought to create a Southern nation. In time virtually all resources, human and material, were thrown into what became a total war.

What started as a war to preserve the nation soon developed into a larger struggle for human freedom. Elimination of slavery, the storm center of political controversy that generated the war's coming, now became a Union war aim. With Lincoln's Emancipation Proclamation and the Thirteenth Amendment that followed, human bondage was at last ended in the United States.

The fighting of the war created a vast demand for material goods to fuel the war machine. The North's economy responded with an immense outpouring of production from farm and mine and mill. Under Republican direction, national economic policy was geared to encourage agriculture, stimulate industrial production, extend transportation, expand banking, and step up immigration.

By the fighting's close in 1865, the war had clearly preserved the nation, but its revolutionary effects of winning Negro freedom and pushing men on the path to an urban, industrial society were only beginning to be felt.

6

War Erupts, 1860–1861

During the year and a half following John Brown's execution, events flew by at a dizzying pace, faster than men could comprehend them, more swiftly than politicians could cope with them. In 1860 the last remaining national link shattered when the Democratic national convention found agreement or compromise impossible to achieve. The following Presidential contest pitted four candidates against each other in a crucial battle. Voters cast their ballots in an atmosphere of apprehension and fear over the outcome. In the final tally Lincoln emerged as President-elect. Secession, long threatened by Southern fire-eaters, now burst into open reality.

As lame-duck President James Buchanan looked on helplessly, the lower South quickly voted itself out of the Union and formed its own Confederacy. The new President, assuming office on March 4, 1861, would have to determine the nation's course in dealing with the "erring sisters." What Lincoln would choose to do would submit the fate of the nation to trial by battle in a fiery civil war. Men who had for years sought to avert armed conflict now had to decide which loyalty to follow—to go with their state or to stay with the Union. For many the choice would not be easy. For all Americans the ordeal ahead spelled tragedy.

1. Battle by Ballot: Election of 1860

As the year 1860 opened, an uneasy tension gripped the country. In an atmosphere of nerves stretched taut since the days of the Kansas fracas, the people viewed the coming Presidential campaign with apprehension and alarm. Somehow men sensed instinctively that the nation's survival hinged upon the contest's outcome. Could antagonisms and hostilities, stirred by the contentions of the past decade, survive the fevered rhetoric and angry recriminations of a bitter Presidential campaign without bursting the remaining bonds of Union? All signs were ominous.

In late April the Democrats opened their nominating convention in Charleston, South Carolina, where secession talk was loudest and angriest. Many Southern delegates were determined to secure Southern "rights" to slavery in the territories (and they had been so instructed by the state conventions that chose them). Northern delegates, mostly firm Douglas backers, found themselves brushed aside by convention managers into crowded, makeshift living quarters where the city's stifling humidity aggravated already taut tempers. Hostile local crowds in the convention hall gallery hooted at Northern speeches and wildly applauded Southern efforts.

Immediately a fight broke out over the party platform's plank on slavery in the territories. Southern spokesmen demanded Federal legislative guarantees and protection of slaveholding in all Federal territories. Indignantly, Ohio Senator George E. Pugh, speaking for the Douglas delegates who formed a majority of the convention's total, shouted, "Gentlemen of the South, you mistake us. We will not do it!" When the showdown vote came, the Southern plank for Federal protection of slavery in the territories lost. Fire-eater William L. Yancey, whose delegation was under instructions to secure the proslavery territorial plank, raced to the platform and announced his delegation's immediate withdrawal from the proceedings. Delegates from all lower South states quickly followed, filing out of the hall amid rousing cheers from the galleries. Of the remaining 202 delegates (out of an original total of 303), most favored Douglas's nomination, but the party's rule requiring a two-thirds vote for the nomination made that impossible.

The convention adjourned to reassemble at Baltimore. There, six weeks later, Southern delegates bolted again, but the convention proceeded to nominate Douglas on a nonintervention-by-Congress platform. Southern delegates who had bolted gathered in a rump session and named Vice President John C. Breckinridge of Kentucky for President on a Federal-protection-of-slavery-in-the-territories platform. With this action, the nation's last political bond lay shattered.

Elated over the Democratic rupture, the Republicans met in Chicago on May 16 in an exuberant mood. Among many hopefuls, New York Senator William H. Seward had strength based on long experience in Washington, but his "irrepressible conflict" speech of two years before gave pause to moderates. Handicaps haunted other contenders, too: Salmon Chase of Ohio was identified with extreme abolitionism; Edward Bates of Missouri was tainted with "know-nothing" nativism; Simon Cameron of Pennsylvania, with heavy-handed machine politics. Lincoln, who at the outset had fewer pledged delegates than any of these four, enjoyed the advantages of being almost everyone's second choice and of having a friendly convention gallery that rocked the Wigwam meeting hall with cheers at every mention of Lincoln's name. Realizing that his position had been gaining strength since his Cooper Union speech in February, Lincoln advised his convention managers to make no deals in his name. To another friend he wrote: "I suppose I am not the *first* choice of a very great many [delegates]. Our policy then is to give no offence to others—leave them in a mood to come to us. . . ."

And come they did. After the first ballot gave Seward 173½ votes, Lincoln 102, Cameron 50½, Chase 49 and Bates 48, Lincoln's strategy paid off. Pennsylvania, Ohio, and Indiana delegations switched to "Honest Abe" and gave the "Illinois rail splitter" the nomination. While taking a strong moral position of opposing the extension of slavery into the territories, the Republican platform also made a calculated appeal to economic interest by advocating a protective tariff, free homesteads, Federal aid for a Pacific railroad, and the encouragement of immigration. Party strategy for victory required holding all the states that went Republican in 1856 and picking up at least Pennsylvania and Illinois. The tariff plank was designed to bring in Pennsylvania, while "native son" Lincoln hopefully would swing Illinois into line. It was a masterly combination of moral idealism and hard-headed practical politics. As one historian has observed: "Here was . . . political maturity that blends ideals with materialism, . . . a base broad enough to satisfy the old Whigs, catch its share of the foreign element, attract the eager forces of the new expanding economic order, and yet hold its original members . . . in a great moral crusade" against slavery. The campaign rallying cries were "Lincoln and Liberty," "vote yourself a farm," and "Honest Abe the railsplitter."

A fourth political group, the Constitutional Union party, making its appeal to the remnants of the old Whig and American parties, convened at Baltimore and named John Bell of Tennessee for the Presidency. Hoping to capitalize on Unionist loyalty, it urged voters to stand by the Constitution, the Union, and the enforcement of the law.

The ensuing campaign produced the unique spectacle of two contests for President: Lincoln versus Douglas in the North, Breckinridge versus Bell in Southern states (in most of which Lincoln's name did not even appear on the ballot). The tradition of Presidential dignity required nominees to remain at home, leaving speech-making to their backers. But Douglas, sensing the vital significance of the outcome, broke tradition and threw himself into a man-killing, cross-country drive that carried him through New England, the middle states, and as far south as Mobile, Alabama. He sought voters' support as the only national candidate, contending that the choice of either Lincoln or Breckinridge as sectional nominees would jeopardize the Union. It proved a valiant though futile effort.

The fall balloting gave Lincoln 1,866,000 votes (only 26,000 of them cast south of the Mason-Dixon line). Douglas garnered 1,376,000, Breckinridge 849,000, and Bell 588,000. Clearly no candidate won a majority. Lincoln's total barely topped 39 per cent; Douglas took 30 per cent; Breckinridge, 18 per cent; and Bell, 12 per cent. The electoral vote distribution revealed a sharp sectional slant—Lincoln carried all seventeen free states (except New Jersey whose vote he split with Douglas); Breckinridge took every slaveholding state, except Kentucky, Virginia, Tennessee (won by Bell), and Missouri (Douglas's only state). The electoral college warped the vote to 180 for Lincoln, 72 for Breckinridge, 39 for Bell, 12 for Douglas. The people had spoken, but with many voices, and precisely what it all meant was far from clear.

To say that Lincoln was a "minority President" is accurate. But to say he won because of the division of votes among his opponents is false. Lincoln won because he carried the populous states with large electoral votes, although by slim popular margins. Even if votes for his three opponents had gone to a single candidate, the result would have been the same, except in New Jersey, California, and Oregon, the loss of which would have reduced Lincoln's electoral total from 180 to 169 votes, still a majority of 35 votes.

2. Dark Winter of Secession

Although many Southerners had anticipated Lincoln's election, its actuality in November came as a shock. Convinced that the "animus of the North" was reflected in "the election of an irrepressible conflict" candidate (Lincoln) as President, spokesmen in the Deep South were sure that Southern interests could not be safe in a Union presided over by a "Black Republican." Many Southerners believed that the growth of Northern political power, reflecting the North's increasing population, placed the South, her "peculiar institution," and her way of life in peril.

But was the South really in serious danger? Lincoln had often denied any intention to interfere with slavery where it existed. True, he resisted the extension of slavery into the territories, but he alone could not make policy. His party would control neither the Supreme Court nor the Senate, where Southern interests surely could be safeguarded. Without control of Congress, Republicans could take no action, even if they had wished to undermine the South. What, then, moved the states in the lower South to withdraw from the Union in the wake of Lincoln's election? In the preceding decade three new free states (California, Minnesota, and Oregon) had joined the Union, but no new slave states had been formed during that time. The political power of the North, based on a burgeoning economy and population, gave every sign of continuing to grow. The old Northwest was now tied tightly by rail bonds to the Northeast. New territories would surely soon be voted in as free states. The South would shortly be fully submerged as a permanent political minority. Ultimately, as Southerners saw it, Northern votes could change the Constitution so that protection of slavery would vanish and Southern institutions and civilization would be stifled—if not now, before long. Money-grubbing Yankees would soon take command. Worse still, to unthinking Southerners Lincoln looked like a John Brown who would launch the fury of an assault upon slavery and Southern society. To many he represented a potential, if not an immediate, threat to the South's security. Of what value was the Union in such circumstances? Why wait until it was too late? Why not withdraw now, swiftly, peacefully if possible?

In South Carolina, the fever for secession ran high. The legislature, while in session in November to cast the state's electoral votes, authorized the governor to act. A state convention was called for December 20 to set a course of action. Already a revolutionary atmosphere pervaded the area; mass meetings, parades, fireworks, waving of the "palmetto" state flag, and drilling of minute men left no doubt that the decision would favor secession. "The die is cast," cried one eager secessionist, "the stake is life or death."

At Washington, Congressmen gathering in early December faced an unprecedented crisis for the Union. President Buchanan, as Douglas had said earlier, was no Andrew Jackson. While denying the Southern claim that states have the right to secede, Buchanan conceded at the same time that the Federal government had no power to coerce an unwilling state. To escape the dilemma he sought salvation in efforts at conciliation.

Leaders in Congress, too, searched for a workable compromise. A House committee of thirty-three and a Senate committee of thirteen labored painfully through December to mold an acceptable accommodation in an effort to save the Union. The committee in the House framed a constitutional amendment that would deny Congress any power to touch a state's "domestic institutions," meaning slavery. The Senate committee wrangled endlessly over propositions also designed to reassure the South. Most seriously considered was the Crittenden compromise offered by Kentucky's moderate, respected Senator John J. Crittenden.

The most vital provisions of that proposed compromise called for unamendable amendments that would (1) bar Federal interference with slavery in any state and (2) reestablish and extend the Missouri Compromise line of 36°30′ to the Pacific, with slavery permitted south of the line and prohibited northward. Senate Republicans were inclined to approve this compromise, but when they consulted President-elect Lincoln, he replied firmly on December 11: "Let there be no compromise on the question of extending slavery." Here he would not budge, although he expressed willingness to accept the amendment to protect slavery in states where it already existed. He insisted: "Entertain no proposition for a compromise in regard to the *extension* of slavery. The moment you do, they have us under again; all our labor is lost, and sooner or later must be done over again. Douglas is sure to bring in his 'Popular Sovereignty.' Have none of it. The tug has to come and better now than later." Lincoln's position boiled down to this: let the South be reassured by constitutional amendment, if need be, that slavery would be left untouched where it already was; let a tough fugitive slave law be enforced; beyond that no concession.

Lincoln has been criticised for refusing to compromise on the territorial question. But in his situation as President-elect, having just championed before the voters the blocking of slavery's extension, he could not have yielded. To do so would have exposed him as a hypocritical opportunist, repudiating all he had asserted as morally right for the past six years. More than that, the amalgam of factions in the Republican party would have dissolved at the moment of victory, if its prime spokesman had abandoned the one principle on which all party adherents agreed.

While standing firm against slavery extension, Lincoln sought to make clear his position in a letter of December 20 to his old Whig associate in Congress, Alexander H. Stephens of Georgia: "Do the people of the South really entertain fears that a Republican administration would *directly* or *indirectly* interfere with their slaves, or with them, about their slaves? If they do, I wish to assure you, as once a friend, and still, I hope, not an enemy, that there is no cause for such fears. The South would be in no more danger in this respect than it was in the days of Washington. I suppose, however, that this does not meet the case. You think slavery is *right* and ought to be extended; while we think it is *wrong* and ought to be restricted. That I suppose is the rub. It is certainly the only substantial difference between us." Clearly the difference was *substantial*—between right and wrong.

As the year 1860 came to an end, compromise proposals were hopelessly bogged down. South Carolina's convention met on December 20, revoked the state's ratification of the Constitution, and formally announced the state's withdrawal from the Union. But when state authorities demanded that Federal forts in Charleston harbor be handed over, Buchanan not only refused but also approved Major Robert Anderson's removal of his Federal garrison from land-based Fort Moultrie to the greater security of the island-based Fort Sumter on December 26.

During the next six weeks, Alabama, Mississippi, Florida, Louisiana, Georgia, and Texas also withdrew from the Union, following a process similar to that of South Carolina. In Georgia, where pro-Union feeling ran strong, the vote for secession was razor thin. In Texas, Governor Sam Houston used every means to thwart secession, only to be deposed from office by a secession-bound legislature. On February 4, 1861, delegates from the "Gulf squadron" of seceding states met in Montgomery, Alabama, and formed a provisional government of the Confederate States of America. A constitution, resembling closely that of the United States but guaranteeing slavery and stressing state sovereignty, was drafted and submitted to the states later for ratification. Jefferson Davis of Mississippi was installed as President, and Alexander H. Stephens as Vice President. Both were inaugurated on February 18, later to be chosen for six-year terms in a general election throughout the Confederacy. Appeals to other slave states were rebuffed for the time being by North Carolina, Tennessee, Arkansas, and the border states, which chose to await developments.

Leaders of the border states, all too well aware that their region would be the battleground in any military showdown, anxiously pushed a new compromise effort. A hastily assembled gathering, initiated by Virginians and billed as a "Peace Convention," brought together in Washington men of good will and good intentions serving as delegates from twenty-one states. Beginning on February 4, this "old gentlemen's convention," chaired by ex-President John Tyler of Virginia, deliberated for three weeks and devised a scheme closely resembling the earlier Crittenden compromise. At about the same time Congress adopted a proposed Thirteenth Amendment to the Constitution, which ironically assured noninterference with existing slavery in the states. But when sent to the states for ratification, it died for lack of action.

Meanwhile, Buchanan's stance toward secession had been stiffening. He reshuffled his cabinet, replacing disloyal Southerners with firm Unionists like Edwin M. Stanton of Pennsylvania and John A. Dix of New York. Urging all Americans to observe January 4 as a day of national "humiliation and prayer," Buchanan lent aid to divine appeals by dispatching an unarmed merchant ship, the *Star of the West*, with 200 soldiers, arms, and munitions to bolster Fort Sumter. On January 8, as the ship neared Charleston harbor, South Carolina shore batteries opened fire and forced the vessel to withdraw. In a sense, the Civil War began at this point, although Buchanan took no further forceful action that might commit his successor.

3. Lincoln Braves the Storm over Sumter

On March 4, 1861, when Lincoln emerged on the east portico of the capitol for the inaugural ceremonies, he had just turned fifty-two. Standing six feet four inches tall, he faced the elderly, shrunken Chief Justice Taney and raised his hand to take the oath as President. Senator Stephen Douglas reached forward to hold Lincoln's hat in a symbolic act of unity. But the nation's unity was already shattered. The Confederacy loomed as an accomplished fact—seven seceded states had already seized most Federal installations, such as customs houses and forts, within their borders. The new President would have to meet the situation.

In his inaugural address, emphasizing his view that "the Union of these States is perpetual," Lincoln rejected secession, declaring that "no State can upon its mere notion lawfully get out of the Union" and any secession ordinances and "acts of violence against" Federal authority are not only "illegal" but are "insurrectionary" and "revolutionary." For his own part, he would see that Federal delivery of "the mails will continue to all parts of the Union" and Presidential power "will be used to hold, occupy and possess the property and places belonging to the government." But "there will be no invasion—no using of force," "no attempt to force obnoxious strangers among the people" for these ends. Seeking to invigorate Union feeling in the South, Lincoln addressed himself to "those who really love the Union," saying "I have no purpose . . . to interfere with the institution of slavery where it exists. . . . I have no legal right to do so, and I have no inclination to do so." He had no objection, he repeated, to amending the Constitution to this effect and making the amendment unamendable.

Stressing the practical futility of splitting the Union, the new President asserted, "Physically speaking, we cannot separate. We cannot remove our respective sections. . . . [The sections] cannot but remain face to face; and intercourse, either amicable or hostile, must continue between them. Is it possible, then, to make that intercourse more advantageous or more satisfactory, *after* separation than *before*? Can aliens make treaties better than friends can make laws?" And if war comes, "you cannot fight always; and when after much loss on both sides, and no gain on either, you cease fighting, the identical old questions are upon you." Southerners should pause to think before acting. Cautioning those who defied the government, Lincoln observed, "In your hands, my dissatisfied fellow-countrymen, and not in mine, is the momentous issue of civil war. The government will not assail you. You can have no conflict, without yourselves being the aggressors. You have no oath registered in Heaven to destroy the government, while I shall have the most solemn one to 'preserve, protect and defend' it." Given his benign temperament, Lincoln made a closing plea for harmony: "We are not enemies, but friends. We must not be enemies. Though passion may have strained, it must not break, our bonds of affection. The mystic chords of memory, stretching from every battlefield and patriot grave to every living heart and hearthstone all over this broad land, will yet swell the chorus of the Union when again touched, as surely they will be, by the better angels of our nature."

As his term began, the new President was beset by troubling problems on all sides. Not only was the country split, but his own Republican party, assuming power in Washington for the first time, hungered for the fruits of victory. Hordes of office-seekers swamped the capital and in weary, worrying array pressed their claims upon the harassed Chief. Lincoln had to choose cabinet secretaries, bureau chiefs, and assistants from party adherents, none of whom had had previous national administrative experience. Hundreds of Congressmen and party leaders pushed deserving friends to fill vacancies. Seeking to pay political campaign debts and insure party cohesion, he balanced cabinet appointments neatly—placing Seward (former Whig) in the State Department, Chase (Free Democrat) in the Treasury, Simon Cameron (Pennsylvania boss) in War, Gideon Welles (former Democrat of Connecticut) in Navy, Montgomery Blair (ex-Democrat) in the Post Office, Edward Bates (former Whig of Missouri) as Attorney General, and Caleb Smith (Indianan of Whig background) in Interior. A hybrid cabinet crew, but it satisfied the party's varied factions and paid overdue political bills. Overall, the cabinet added up to better than average in political ability and acumen. Despite the Seward-Chase rivalry as prima donnas, Lincoln managed by tact, good humor, and firmness to manage so effectively that Seward came to acknowledge "he is the best man among us."

In framing a policy toward the South, three courses of action were open to Lincoln: (1) let the seceded states go in peace, as some Northerners suggested, a policy Lincoln firmly rejected in his inaugural address; (2) move immediately with armed force to compel adherence to the Union, a step that would have ignited immediate war and driven away the border states; (3) continue for the time the Buchanan wait-and-drift technique. Lincoln chose to follow the third alternative, partly in the hope that Union sentiment would reassert itself in the South, partly out of a desire not to alienate the upper South, and partly because he wanted to assess the situation deliberately before taking action he could not reverse.

Having announced in his inaugural address that he would "hold and possess" Federal properties, Lincoln could not delay too long in deciding what to do about the two Federal posts remaining in loyal hands—Fort Pickens at Pensacola and Fort Sumter. He could neither risk a credibility gap nor acknowledge Federal weakness by meekly abandoning them. By late March, stiffening Northern feeling and word from Major Anderson that Sumter could be held only by a heavy infusion of assistance compelled the President to act.

All cabinet members, except Blair and Chase, favored quietly evacuating Sumter and making a stand at Fort Pickens, where Federal relief ships already stood offshore and were prepared to land troops. In a private memo Seward even suggested to Lincoln a scheme to make impossible demands on England, Spain, France, and Russia, thereby producing an international crisis that would rally the South in renewed allegiance to the imperiled Union. Lincoln quickly filed away this wild proposal and forgot it. At the same time Seward in an indirect exchange with Confederate commissioners in Washington gave them to understand that Sumter would eventually be evacuated.

Not wishing to drive the border states into Confederate arms, Lincoln determined to make a stand in a way that would be nonagressive and, he hoped, nonoffensive to the South. He dispatched orders to land troops at Pickens. At the same time, he ordered an expedition under naval escort to carry provisions to Fort Sumter, notifying the Governor of South Carolina that "no effort to throw in men, arms, or ammunition will be made" if there was no local attempt to block the landing of provisions.

The dilemma of responding was now thrust upon Confederate leaders. At Montgomery, President Jefferson Davis had put together a cabinet, choosing one member from each Confederate state, including Robert Toombs of Georgia as Secretary of State, Stephen R. Mallory of Florida as Secretary of the Navy, and Judah P. Benjamin of Louisiana as Attorney General. Since Davis himself was a West Point graduate and had served as an officer in the Mexican War and as Secretary of War under President Pierce, he assumed direction of military affairs. He appointed Pierre G. T. Beauregard as brigadier general of the new Confederate army and dispatched him to take command at Charleston. Confederate leaders faced a double risk. If provisions were allowed to reach Sumter, the fort would remain in Charleston harbor as a mocking threat to Confederate authority. If they repulsed peaceful ships carrying food, the onus of firing the first shot and precipitating war would fall on them.

Hoping to avert the dilemma, General Beauregard demanded immediate surrender of Sumter on April 11. Anderson refused but indicated he would have to evacuate in three days unless resupplied. With the Union relief expedition nearing the entrance to the harbor, Beauregard on instructions from the Montgomery government served notice that he would open fire in one hour if Anderson did not yield. At 4:30 A.M., April 12, the first harbor battery guns thundered through the dark. (One report said that old fire-eater Edmund Ruffin insisted on pulling the lanyard of the first gun

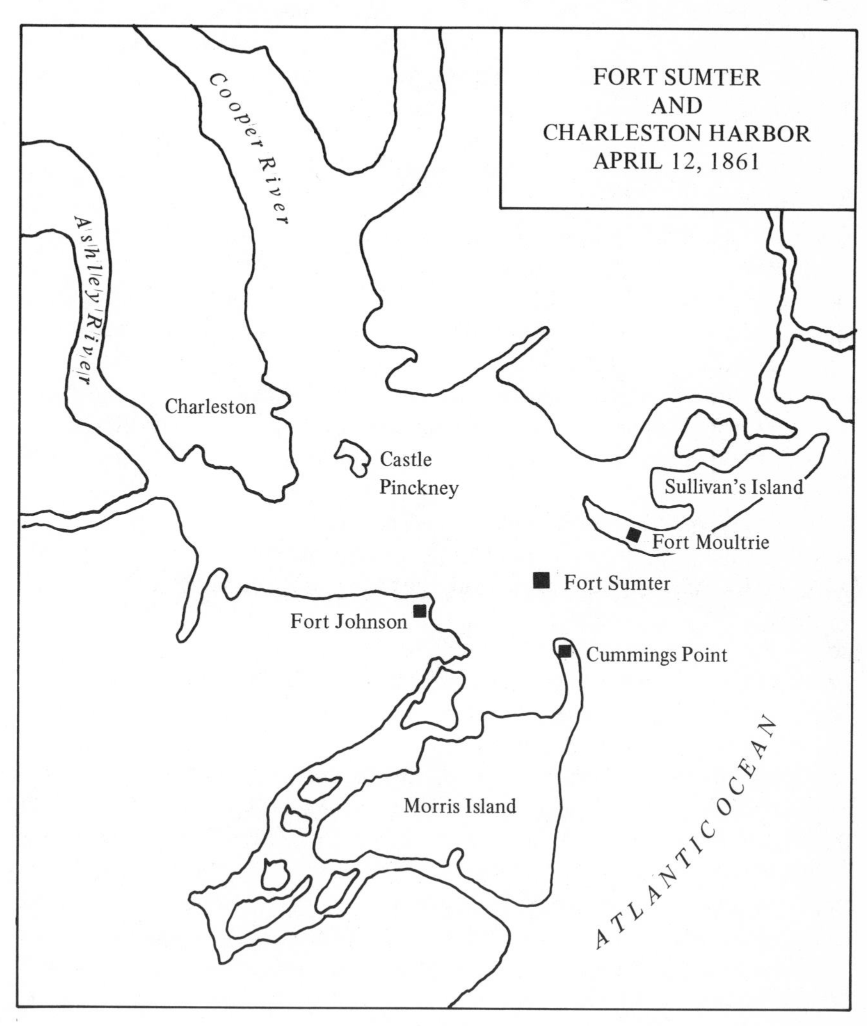

himself.) The fort was soon under a resounding crossfire. Sumter's guns barked back. But after more than thirty hours, his ammunition exhausted, Anderson surrendered. Having saluted the flag before lowering it, Anderson and his men were permitted to row in small boats to the Federal relief ships waiting offshore.

The booming guns over Sumter galvanized Lincoln into swift response. On April 15 his proclamation to the nation called for 75,000 volunteer troops from "the several States of the Union" to put down an unlawful "combination too powerful to be suppressed" by ordinary legal process. The tension of suspense was now broken; a wave of relief swept the land. Now there would be action to replace the endless words and fidgetings of the last four months. Ohio's governor promised to send 200,000 men to Washington in three weeks. Similar replies flooded Lincoln's desk. On April 19 another Presidential proclamation decreed a naval blockade of all Southern ports, designed to cut them off from all foreign trade—a move that touched off international repercussions.

4. Turmoil in the Borderland

Lincoln's April 15 proclamation, while consolidating sentiment in both Confederate and Northern regions, sent a wave of shock and anger through the states of the upper South. Border state men, whom the President had long sought to avoid offending, were now incensed that Northern armies would assail their sister states of the deep South. On April 17 Virginia's state convention, which in three months of intermittent sessions had stood firm against disunion, now reversed its course and voted 88–55 for immediate withdrawal. A week later the "Old Dominion" officially joined the Confederacy. A statewide referendum in late May approved the action. In June the Confederate government, acknowledging Virginia's psychological importance, moved its capital from Montgomery to Richmond, situated scarcely 100 crow-flight miles from Washington. Soon the area between the two capitals would become the most fought over piece of real estate in North America.

In swift succession three other states followed in the wake of Virginia's exit from the Union. North Carolina's convention unanimously approved secession. In Arkansas, Unionist feeling had been running strong until Lincoln's call for troops drove extremists into a fury against "Northern mendacity and usurpation." In short order they rammed a secessionist ordinance through the state convention of May 6 and refused to permit a popular plebiscite. In Tennessee the clash was sharp and bitter. Many shared John Bell's "plague on both your houses" view—indignant over secession but incensed by Washington's resort to force. While the Tennessee legislature was authorizing a referendum, the governor in early May agreed to supply 55,000 soldiers to the Confederacy. On June 8 voters affirmed by a 2–1

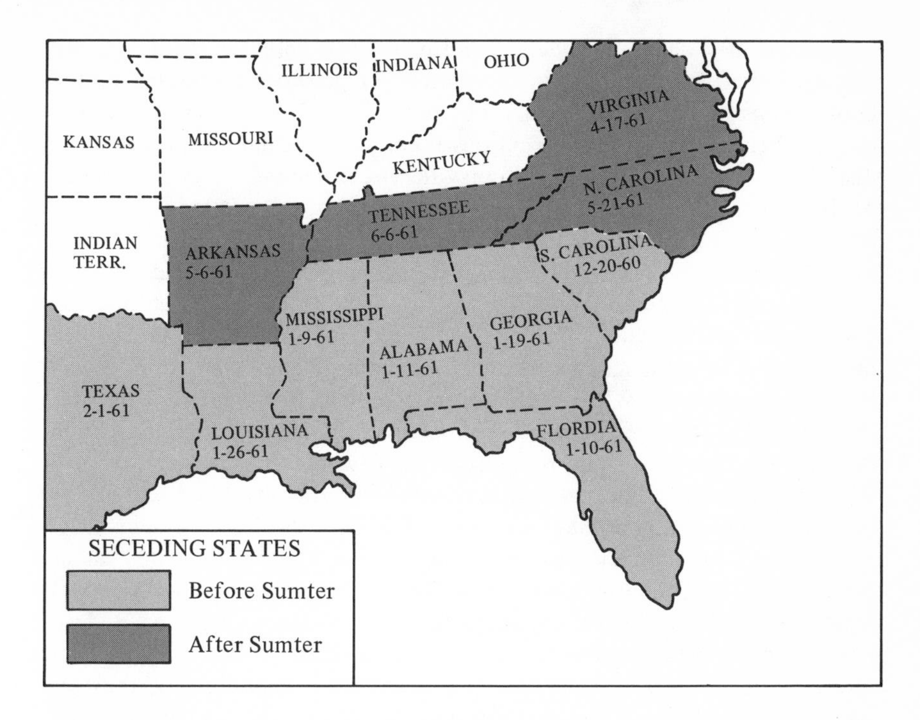

margin the decision already made to join the Confederacy, but in eastern Tennessee, Union loyalty remained so strong that during the war the area supplied more volunteers to the Union than to the South.

In Maryland, Kentucky, and Missouri, the close split between Unionist-secessionist sentiment precipitated an eye-gouging, knee-in-groin brawl for control. From Washington's viewpoint, retaining Maryland was vital to the Federal government's very existence. Disunionists in that state were not only numerous and vehement in pushing to join the South, but they also wielded much political leverage. Baltimore's secessionist mayor for a time blocked all communication through his city from Washington to loyal states to the north. A Massachusetts regiment on its way through Baltimore's streets was attacked by a stone-throwing mob that killed several soldiers. Realizing that Maryland's withdrawal would isolate Washington in an enclave surrounded by Confederate territory, Lincoln made drastic moves to hold the state. Suspending the writ of habeas corpus on his own initiative and stationing Federal agents and troops at key points, he secured the arrest and detention of pro-secession members of the legislature. Thereby that body was prevented from meeting, and possible secession was forestalled. Other Maryland extremists organizing military companies were rounded up and thrown into military prison at Fort McHenry. These actions, high-handed as they were, held the state in the Union until new elections brought to power a legislature and governor devoted to supporting the Federal government.

In Lincoln's native Kentucky, sentiment was split down the middle. Governor Beriah Magoffin, in an attempt to preserve neutrality, refused both Union and Confederate calls for troops. Recruiting by both sides went on nonetheless and led to such curious spectacles as Confederate volunteers marching down one side of a Louisville street waving to Union recruits on the other side. Senator John J. Crittenden's sons followed opposite paths—George becoming a Confederate major general while Thomas held the same rank in the Union army—in pursuing what became truly "a brothers' war." Lincoln reportedly said, "I hope to have God on my side, but I must have Kentucky." His efforts at divine support are not known, but he went to great lengths to avoid offending Kentuckians in any way. His efforts paid off. When a Confederate military force invaded the state in September, 1861, the legislature proclaimed its adherence to the Union, even though later a separate rump convention would declare Kentucky part of the Confederacy. The state settled down to staying loyal and sent 75,000 of its sons into Union armies as against 35,000 for the Confederacy.

Missouri's government expressed strong sympathy for the South at the outset. But pro-Unionists, with Washington's sanction, formed an extra-legal government of their own. Pro-secession Governor Claiborne F. Jackson's military force glowered at gathering units of pro-Union recruits. Rioting in St. Louis streets led to a "massacre" of twenty-eight persons and drove some moderates into secessionist ranks. Within six months after Sumter, the legitimate and extra-legal governments, each with its own forces, clashed in an intrastate civil war. Formal conflict rapidly degenerated into bloody neighbor-versus-neighbor fighting with sniping guerrilla bands of bushwhackers ravaging the countryside in search of plunder and victims. Ruthless, senseless outbreaks of border violence were joined in by Kansas "jayhawkers" seeking revenge for remembered "border ruffian" raids of the 1850's. Roving irregular gangs like W. C. Quantrill's raiders bred those later outlaws Jesse James and the Younger brothers. Brutal attacks, night rides, rape, murder, and robbery punctuated the Missouri struggle. The "show-me" state remained technically in the Union, supplying 100,000 men in blue and only 20,000 grey-clad soldiers. But the hideous horrors of civil war struck home hardest here. On the border, then, the nationalism of Clay and Benton prevailed over the sectionalist pull of Davis and Atchison—but at ferocious cost.

Decision was not easy for many men of the border. The question of loyalty wrenched the inner being of Virginia's Robert E. Lee. Son of "Lighthorse" Harry Lee, a hero in the Revolution to establish the nation, and husband of Mary Ann Custis (daughter of George Washington's adopted son), Lee after graduating at West Point gave thirty years of devoted military service to the nation. Master of beautiful Arlington estate above the Potomac facing the capital, he disliked both slavery and secession, but he loved his home and his state. Called to Washington in April, 1861, he was offered command of the Federal field army by fellow Virginian Winfield Scott, then the nation's top officer. Lee asked twenty-four hours to consider. Back at home he suffered the agony of self-torture in deciding. His wife reported that he paced the floor all night in silent, internal struggle, wrestling with his dilemma—remain loyal to the nation he had served all his life or stand by his state? In the morning he rode into Washington and informed Scott he could not raise his sword against family, neighbors, and friends, he must resign his commission and go with his "country," meaning Virginia. In time his hope to remain uninvolved at Arlington flickered out. When requested to take a Virginia military command, he dutifully accepted in 1862.

While Lee found the tug of loyalty to his state irresistible, other Virginians disagreed. In the state's western counties, the rugged mountainous area between the Shenandoah Valley and the Ohio-Kentucky border, men responded to national allegiance and refused to accept secession. Calling a convention at Wheeling, they organized their own withdrawal from Virginia and with Federal encouragement established the state of West Virginia, which Congress admitted to the Union in 1863.

5. Why War?

So far, this account has chronicled what happened between 1830 and 1861 leading to the outbreak of civil conflict. A pause in the story for a moment is necessary to consider the reasons why the North and South girded for battle. Why the Civil War occurred is a question that has long absorbed the attention of historians. But no consensus has emerged over the causes of the conflict. Historian Carl Becker's comment seems apt: when we ask the Muse of History the question "what," she answers readily; when we ask "why," she remains silent and lets us answer our own question.

Most historical writers concede that the question of causation in human affairs is at best complex and intricate, involving the historian in selecting historical evidence and making judgments. Some suggest that the assigning of causes for historical events simply reflects a particular historian's philosophy, biases, or moral values. Some would even avoid speaking in terms of causes and plainly assert that the Civil War, like other complex human events, resulted from an intricate web of intertwined forces and factors operating within a particular set of economic, social, political, and cultural circumstances upon the generation of Americans living in the mid-nineteenth century. But facing the causation question, most historians subscribe understandably to the view of pluralistic causes, but within a broad context some insist that certain "causes" or "factors" or "forces" deserve more weight than others in explaining why Americans went to war. Hence many explanations have been offered—ranging from slavery to fate, from economic and political to social and psychological to legal and constitutional factors.

Some historians, and many contemporaries of the Civil War era, have seen slavery as the basic cause of the war. Without slavery's existence no such controversy as that which developed in the 1850's could have arisen. Some see an added factor of an aggressive "slavocracy" seeking not only to preserve but to extend slavery beyond its Southern confines. At times Lincoln himself viewed the conflict's cause in this light, holding that the Founding Fathers' intention to place slavery "in the course of ultimate extinction" was being thwarted by those who sought to extend the "peculiar institution." Such extension, in the view of Lincoln and others, had to be prevented because human bondage was morally wrong. As Lincoln observed, "All knew that this interest [slavery] was, somehow, the cause of the war." As Senator Henry Wilson, politician-turned-historian, explained in the 1870's, it was "slavery" and a "dominating and aggressive" "Slave Power," subverting "the natural rights of millions" by reducing "man to property" that brought on the "irrepressible conflict" culminating in civil war. In the late nineteenth and early twentieth centuries this view was shared by many historians in the North. Historian James Ford Rhodes put it most bluntly in 1913: "And of the American Civil War it may safely be asserted there was a single cause, slavery."

In recent years slavery as the main cause has received renewed emphasis. In his monumental, impressive eight-volume *Ordeal of the Union*, historian Allan Nevins declares judiciously: "The main root of the conflict (and there were minor roots) was the problem of slavery *with its complimentary problem of race-adjustment*; the main source of the tragedy was the refusal of either section to face these conjoined problems squarely and pay the heavy costs of a peaceful settlement" (italics in original). Others, too, have focused on the moral issue of slavery, as does Arthur M. Schlesinger, Jr., in insisting that "moral differences" over slavery became uncompromiseable and lay at the heart of the controversy and conflict.

Sometimes joined to the slavery explanation was another view, which implied that power over man's affairs lay outside man's own hands and beyond his control. Something larger—God or Providence or Fate—directed human destinies regardless of man's wishes, desires, or efforts. Lincoln, who was not an especially religious man in the conventional sense, declared in his Second Inaugural Address of March 4, 1865: "If we shall suppose that American Slavery is one of those offences which, in the providence of God, must needs come, but which, having continued through His appointed time, He now wills to remove, and that He gives to both North and South, this terrible war, as the woe due to those by whom the offence came, shall we discern therein any departure from those divine attributes which the believers in a Living God always ascribe to Him?" And earlier, in the midst of the war, Lincoln had observed, "I am almost ready to say that this is probably true—that God wills this contest." To those who subscribe to the notion of divine direction of human affairs, this view explains everything and makes seeking other causes superfluous. To others it explains nothing.

The Fate or Providence theory is too mystical for skeptical twentieth century minds. Instead, some writers offer explanations placing greatest stress upon economic factors. Rejecting the slavery thesis, historian Charles A. Beard, for example, contends that clashing, fundamental economic interests and drives formed the basis of the conflict between "the planting aristocracy of the South" and the "capitalists, laborers and farmers of the North." The former, who, according to Beard, had for years determined Federal policies on tariffs, land, money and banking, public subsidies for transportation, resisted the efforts of the latter to gain national dominance that would spell changed economic policies to the advantage of Northern capitalists or "expectant capitalists," as later writers added. Defeat in the 1860 election sent Southerners out of the Union. They would take the risks of separation from the Union rather than endure the threatened change of economic policies within it. Northern success in the war, as Beard saw it, produced a "Second American Revolution" whereby industrial capitalism triumphed over agrarianism and drastically altered the course of America's history. American Marxist writer Algie M. Simons explained the Civil War as essentially "a contest to secure" control of the national government between "Northern capitalists" and Southern "slave chattel" and land owning capitalists, each aiming at securing its own interests. More recently some historians, refining the economic thesis, have focused on the clash between two highly developed class structures as providing the key to understanding why the war came.

Some earlier writers developed the explanation that Southerners, convinced of the superiority of their own way of life in the struggle of "incompatible civilizations" and pursuing "Southern nationalism" to its logical extension, entered upon or were prodded into a "war for Southern Independence." Others have argued that the growing mid-nineteenth century threat of increasingly centralized, consolidated power in Washington produced in reaction a "war between the states." Those who cast human affairs largely in legal terms offer a variation of this theme in ascribing the conflict to the clash of loose constructionist consolidationists and strict constructionist states' righters.

Another explanation that won broad endorsement in the 1930's and 1940's was the "revisionist" view laying great stress on the psychological, irrational, emotional factors in the genesis of the war. "Extreme fanaticism" of radical Southern "fire eaters" and wild-eyed Northern abolitionists distorted reality, exaggerated supposed differences between North and South, whipped up an atmosphere of mutual suspicion and hatred, and generated artificial crises over fancied issues, in which a "blundering generation" of inept politicians stumbled needlessly into "a repressible conflict." By injecting the moral issue of slavery into politics, fanatics brought on the "breakdown of the democratic process" of free discussion and compromise—a process, it was argued, incapable of handling emotionally charged issues clothed in moral righteousness. Critics object that this explanation misses the point by neglecting to analyze and explain the substance—be it economic, political, or whatever—from which the emotionalism arose. Such critics contend that abolitionists should be praised rather than damned for prodding nineteenth century Americans to face up to the evil of slavery and eradicate that cancerous anachronism from America's democratic society.

But enough of hindsight. What did the participants themselves think the war was all about? On this point the leaders were clear. In his April 15 call for troops, Lincoln appealed to citizens to aid the government "to maintain the honor, the integrity, and the existence of our National Union." The first Congress in Washington during the war also declared emphatically in the Crittenden-Johnson resolutions of July, 1861, that "this war is . . . waged . . . to defend the *supremacy* of the Constitution and to preserve the Union." Many times during the first year and a half of the war Lincoln reiterated that the war's aim was to restore the Union and demonstrate to a skeptical world that America's "experiment" in popular self-government based on "free institutions" which seek to "elevate the condition of men" could sustain itself.

When pressed in mid-1862 to declare war on slavery, Lincoln responded to Horace Greeley's "Prayer of Twenty Millions" by saying, "My paramount object in this struggle is to save the Union, and is *not* either to save or to destroy slavery. . . . What I do about slavery, and the colored race, I do because I believe it helps save the Union; and what I forebear, I forebear because I do not believe it would save the Union." This did not mean Lincoln opposed ending slavery. Far from it. But he studiously avoided giving offense to the border slave states that remained in the Union, regularly urging them to adopt a plan of gradual, compensated emancipation.

In September, 1862, the war acquired an additional purpose for the North with Lincoln's issuance of the Emancipation Proclamation. From that point on, it became not only a war to save the Union but also a war to wipe out slavery within the restored Union. In his Gettysburg Address dedicating the national cemetery on November 18, 1863, Lincoln tied together the two war aims to save the "nation conceived in liberty, and dedicated to the proposition that all men are created equal," adding with firm eloquence "that we here highly resolve that these dead shall not have died in vain—that this nation, under God, shall have a new birth of freedom—and that government of the people, by the people, for the people, shall not perish from the earth."

On the Confederate side the purpose of the war, as President Davis put it in his inaugural address, was to win independence from "the tyranny of an unbridled majority, the most odious and least responsible form of despotism." Time and again during the conflict, Davis reemphasized that Southerners sought only independence and liberty. "We are in arms," he said, "to renew such sacrifices as our fathers made to the holy cause of constitutional liberty," in a reference to the American Revolution of 1776. In Southern eyes the struggle was the Revolution all over again—Southern patriots determined to shake off the shackles of Northern oppression as their fathers had battled to rid themselves of British tyranny. Indeed Davis's father, like Lee's, had fought in the American Revolution.

It was, then, a defensive war for Southern independence, for the right to be left alone without offensive Yankee interference and officious meddling in the domestic concerns of Southern states. Obviously the defense of slavery, though seldom referred to explicitly by Confederate leaders, was implied in the drive for independence, and it tarnished the Southern appeals for assistance from abroad. Toward the end of the war, the desire for independence overcame the desire to preserve slavery. Davis dispatched agent Duncan F. Kenner to Europe to seek diplomatic recognition in return for a Southern pledge of gradual emancipation, while the Confederate Congress was voting to free those slaves who volunteered to serve in Southern armies. But Europe was no longer listening. The Southern fight had become truly a "Lost Cause."

6. Combatants Gird for War: Manpower and Resources

The shock of Sumter in April, 1861, united sentiment in the North and also in the South. Each side glowered at the other across the Potomac. Each side knew it enjoyed advantages and suffered from limitations. The loyal states numbering twenty-three counted a population of 22 million giving the Union a gross population margin of 2½ to 1 over the 9 million people of the eleven seceded states. Of the Confederacy's total population, some 3.5 million were Negroes, who while serving as farm workers and cooks, teamsters and laborers in army camps would not be called on as soldiers. The margin in military manpower appeared to be 3–1 in the North's favor, rising to 5–1 by the war's last year. But it took many months to mobilize this strength, while a good many Northerners "crossed over" to join the Southern cause, and others in large numbers opposing the war as wrong engaged in obstruction tactics or refused support. The effective Northern margin was thereby reduced.

The North's military manpower edge was partially offset by certain factors on the Southern side. At the war's start the advantage of superior, experienced officers lay clearly with the South. In Southern society, in contrast to the North, a lifetime military career carried much social prestige. Military academies flourished, some like Virginia Military Institute rising to first-rate college level. For a quarter century preceding Sumter the Federal army had been largely dominated by Southerners, headed by General Scott. This situation insured advancement for Southern officers and so discouraged Northern West Pointers like William T. Sherman, George B. McClellan, and Ulysses S. Grant that they resigned to pursue more promising civilian careers. Further, most Southern young men having grown up on farms were accustomed to outdoor life, riding, hunting, handling horses and firearms; for them the transition to life in the field was less difficult and trying than it was for Yankee boys from "the sidewalks of New York" or the mill towns of the Merrimac, who were unfamiliar with the physical rigors of outdoor life. This difference was perhaps less true than Southerners believed, especially in regard to Union soldiers from the Northwest.

Southern armies, as the war developed, would be fighting on interior lines of an arc-like front. The Federal forces would have to move men and supplies over long lines of transportation that stretched even farther as Union forces pushed deeper southward. This meant, too, leaving occupation garrisons en route, thereby cutting the North's manpower edge. Southern forces, on their side, could and did use Negro slaves for fatigue duty, handling supplies and other logistical support operations. Besides, since the nature of the war made Northern armies an invading force, the psychological edge lay with Southern soldiers who were bolstered by the visceral feeling that they were literally defending their homes and families against Yankee intruders. And in terms of tactics, military experts calculated that an army attacking fortified, entrenched positions needed at least a 6–1 margin in men to overrun such points. Clearly the advantage, strategically, psychologically, and tactically, lay with the defenders—an advantage the South hoped to exploit to the full.

On its side, the North had the capability of fielding much larger armies than its foe, but it did not come close to exploiting its manpower advantage fully until late in the war. With roughly 4 million military-age men available, the North engaged about half that number in service; to these were added, beginning in 1863, nearly 180,000 Negro soldiers, who despite initial skeptical predictions and discriminatory treatment in pay contributed hearteningly to ultimate victory. On its side, the South with a manpower pool of 1½ million men increased its enlistments steadily to a total of 900,000 reaching its greatest effective strength of about 480,000 by late 1863. In the first two years of war as the size of battling armies was nearly even, the South might have won the war by decisive military success. But as the war dragged into its third year Yankee forces, despite heavy losses, kept driving on in growing numbers while large rebel casualties were irreplaceable and drained the South's manpower barrel to the bottom.

More decisive Northern advantages lay in the areas of industrial production, finance, and trade, which would prove crucial as the conflict blos-

Union army camp. (National Archives)

somed into total war. The North's 110,000 manufacturing plants, representing in 1860 an $850-million capital investment and employing 1.1 million workers, produced $1.5 million worth of goods annually, including the bulk of the nation's shoes, textiles, iron and steel products, 97 per cent of America's firearms, and 96 per cent of its railroad equipment. By comparison, the South was a pigmy—18,000 plants, $95 million in capital, 110,000 workers, $155,000 in value of products. Most of the commercial shipping and mercantile firms were quartered in the North, whose banks and financial firms not only dominated the domestic credit–monetary field but maintained close ties with British counterparts. In a long war, such access to financial resources and foreign trade would prove critically decisive. Even in agriculture Northern production managed to expand, despite loss of workers to the army, by increased use of labor-saving machines like the thresher, reaper, planter, and cultivator. In contrast, Southern farm production declined under the strains of war, loss of slaves, and military devastation.

In transportation facilities, too, the North's edge was impressive. As the conflict became a war of movement, the side that could move men and supplies more speedily to strategic points wielded a large lever of success. The North had more wagons, draft animals, steamboats, and barges than its foe. And in critical rail facilities, the North's 20,000 miles of railroad lines were more than double the South's. Besides, Southern lines were often short, had big gaps between rail heads, and used many different gauges, making long-distance transportation impossible. As locomotives and rolling stock broke down or were destroyed, Northerners could replace theirs; the South could not. As the war lengthened, Confederate rail lines deteriorated seriously and by the war's last year were near collapse.

When the guns roared over Sumter, the regular United States army troops numbered only 17,000 men, scattered mainly in distant frontier posts. The loss of a major portion of the officer corps to the South was a severe blow. But it was offset by the navy, whose officers for the most part remained loyal. Although navy ships at the outset numbered only ninety of which only forty-two were in active service and mostly on distant stations, and only twenty-nine were steam-powered, Union sea power would ultimately provide a decisive margin. Under the supervision of Navy Secretary Gideon Welles and his able assistant, Gustavus V. Fox, ships were built, purchased, leased, and adapted until the navy in the war's last year boasted over 650 vessels of all types including ocean packets, ferry boats, sailing ships, and fishing trawlers as well as those designed for war purposes. The navy's mission of sealing off thousands of miles of Confederate coast line in the blockade was a taxing and impossible task. Rebel blockade runners managed to operate in and out of Mobile, Charleston, Wilmington, and lesser ports until the navy's strength grew and imposed a strangling economic warfare that ultimately isolated the South from outside help and undermined morale. In addition, on the rivers, notably the Mississippi, Cumberland, and Tennessee, navy units transported men and supplies and supported the army in assaults upon Southern strongpoints. At many points naval power gave the margin of victory to the North.

With such overwhelming superiority ranged on the Union side, how could the Confederacy manage to stretch the war out for four long, bloody years? Part of the answer lies in the North's lack of preparation at the start and the delays and inefficiency in mobilizing Yankee manpower and materiel. In part, the South's defensive position and high morale in the early years account for the length of the conflict. The need of Northern armies to leave garrisons to occupy captured points and the fact that winter cold and spring mud made fighting impossible for four or five months each year also contributed to lengthening the war.

The South placed great hope in its control of the world's main cotton supply. Since England's textile industry imported over 80 per cent of its raw cotton from America, employed one-fourth of Britain's workers, and accounted for 50 per cent of her export trade, Confederate leaders expected that cutting off the cotton supply would impel British intervention on the Confederate side. In the first year of war the South sent diplomatic commissioners to England in the hope of winning sympathy and material and financial support. For a while it appeared that they might succeed. But as time

Confederates in army camp. (Library of Congress)

passed, the possibility of Britain's intervention was offset by other factors —a large heldover cotton surplus from the preceding two years, the slavery issue, and England's desire for cheap Northern wheat. The Confederacy's announced intention of resorting to privateering, which had been outlawed by European nations adhering to the Declaration of Paris of 1856, also cooled some British fervor for the South. In the end, Southern hopes for British intervention would be dashed.

7

The Fighting Rages, 1861–1863

After all the talk and boasts and the initial rush of men to arms in April 1861, little action took place in the field for some months. Preparations went forward in taking in new volunteers, drilling, training, equipping, and supplying them. But the training was skimpy, equipment sometimes defective. On such a basis leaders on both sides appeared reluctant to launch a major military drive. At length after considerable skirmishing, Federal forces advanced southward from Washington only to be hurled back in disarray in the First Bull Run fiasco. In consequence, both sides became aware that what they had originally seen as a short, swift war was bound to stretch into a prolonged, increasingly bitter conflict.

New recruits were called to the colors, existing armies enlarged, new armies formed, equipped, and readied for battle. In the second year of the fighting a major Federal thrust was repulsed on the outskirts of the Confederate capital at Richmond. Further Federal efforts to gain ground in northern Virginia were stopped cold. Similarly a Confederate thrust into Maryland was turned back at Antietam. Only in the western theater did Union forces gain ground, taking firm possession of western Tennessee and New Orleans.

In the war's third year a tenacious Federal campaign won full control of the Mississippi River area in a stunning drive culminating in the fall of Vicksburg. At the same time a second Confederate northward drive penetrated into southern Pennsylvania only to be sent reeling back by Union guns at Gettysburg. The turning point had been passed, but the war was far from over. The North took heart as Union armies secured east Tennessee by the year's end and stood poised in northern Virginia for a major thrust to the south.

1. Struggle on Sea and Land, 1861–1862

After the fury and histrionics over Sumter subsided, each side had to settle down to determining basic strategy to achieve the objective it was fighting for. Since Washington's aim was to subdue rebellion and restore the Union, it must take the offensive against the Southern insurrection. General Winfield Scott, the seventy-five-year-old commander of the Federal army, at the outset originated the main lines of Union overall strategy: throw a large noose around the Confederacy with the navy patrolling the coasts on the east and south and with land armies driving down from the border states,

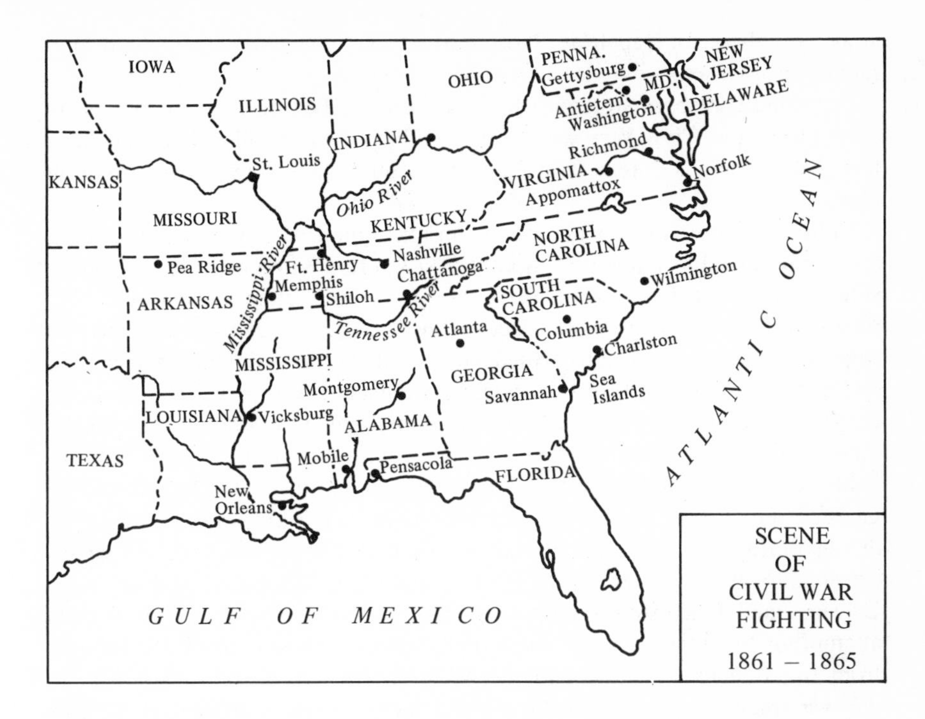

split the enemy's holdings along the Mississippi, and then draw the noose tighter and tighter to the point of strangulation. This "Anaconda" strategy, as the newspapers called it, remained to the end basic Federal policy and in the end produced ultimate success.

On the South's side, since its aim was to win independence, President Jefferson Davis believed the proper strategy was a defensive one, based on a chain of forts to be constructed from Virginia westward to beyond the Mississippi. From this defense line Northern attacks would be readily repelled. Once established, the government should seek recognition and material aid from England and Europe, holding out unlimited cotton as the bait to win commercial treaties, accumulate needed supplies, and bind foreign nations to the Confederacy. With this accomplished, overthrow by the North would be impossible. With some justification, critics harped on the Confederacy's failure to capitalize on the ten peaceful weeks between the Montgomery convention and Sumter by obtaining large supplies of arms, equipment, and supplies from abroad. General Beauregard was calling for an immediate, large-scale offensive against the Yankees. But if her objective was independence and defense of Southern rights, the South could ill afford to appear as an aggressive military power in the eyes of the world. Seeking to win foreign sympathy for a people pictured as an oppressed minority, Davis stressed defense, not attack; he insisted the South wanted separation not war, only to be left alone, not to be embroiled. Hence overall defensive strategy called for repelling Northern attacks wherever they came, not mounting invasions of Federal territory.

From the start both strategies had their critics. But throughout four years of fighting, the Civil War was to be fought out essentially along the lines laid out in Davis's defensive policy and Scott's "Anaconda" strangulation plan.

In implementing Scott's plan, Lincoln made the first move by announcing a Federal naval blockade of all Southern sea ports. With only a few effective ships available at the moment, the Union navy lay scattered and weak. Secretary Welles moved in short order to buy, lease, and commandeer private ships and convert them into armed vessels in the government's service. In addition, with the aid of his talented assistant, Gustavus V. Fox, he launched a massive naval building program, gathered supplies and equipment, trained new men, and got the navy moving in ship-shape fashion. With over 3,500 miles of Southern coast to patrol, extending from the Chesapeake Bay to Texas's Rio Grande border, the blockade was a paper dream during the first year of the conflict. Ships stationed in squadrons off major Southern ports like Norfolk, Charleston, Savannah, Mobile, New Orleans, and Galveston sought to intercept Southern and foreign vessels attempting to enter or leave these harbors. But elusive blockade runners from the Bahamas, Cuba, and the West Indies, eager for rich profits in the war trade, resorted to shallow-draft, swift, small boats that could dart into obscure, shallow harbors along the Carolina-Georgia-Florida coast. These proved almost impossible to detect and capture. Not until mid-1862 did the Union navy mount sufficient size and strength to apply an effective squeeze on this funnel of goods flowing into Dixie.

At length Union supremacy at sea would prove decisive. In the first year naval units pecked away at Confederate coastal defenses. Amphibious forces made raids and even landings at scattered points along the coast. By the second year they would become even more effective.

The Union navy suffered a severe scare in March, 1862, when the *Merrimac*, a Federal warship scuttled when Union forces left Norfolk Navy Yard, was raised by the Confederates, refitted as an ironclad with heavy armor plate and an iron ram at her prow, and rechristened the *Virginia*. With four inches of solid iron protecting her sides and mounting ten guns, she steamed out of Norfolk and proceeded to attack the Union naval squadron in Hampton Roads, ramming and sinking one thirty-gun warship and setting fire to another. As the news flashed northward, panic gripped government officials in Washington in fear that Union shipping was doomed.

The following day an odd-shaped Union craft, the *Monitor*, appeared on the scene. Ordered by the navy five months earlier and designed and built by Swedish engineer John Ericsson, the *Monitor* looked like a "tin can on a raft" with its flat iron hull topped by a revolving turret that mounted two heavy guns. In a classic encounter the *Monitor* traded an all-day barrage with the Confederate ironclad. Neither ship could pierce the iron plating of the other. The resulting draw forced the rebel vessel back into harbor from which she never emerged again. But the lesson was clear. The engagement, foreshadowing the obsolescence of wooden ships, introduced a new factor in naval warfare. Ironclads would become increasingly important in Federal flotillas as the Mississippi River campaign gained momentum.

In the next few years Confederate ingenuity produced some remarkable innovations in naval warfare. On the Mississippi an ironclad was pieced together from wood, wire, rails, and scrap metal and given the name the *Arkansas*. With her deadly, sharp-pointed prow, she spread havoc on the Mississippi for a time in 1862 as she rammed and sank Federal ships. After a heavy Union bombardment her engines failed, and the helpless craft was scuttled by her crew. "One of the happiest moments of my life," Federal Captain David Farragut sighed in relief. In 1863 Southerners built at Mobile the first submarine, christened the *H. L. Hunley* for its designer-builder. Though it sank four times during test runs with the loss of its seven-man crew each time, it was raised and finally hauled overland to Charleston, where in February, 1864, it sank the U. S. S. *Housatonic* with an exploding torpedo that also sent the *Hunley* and its fifth crew to the bottom.

If the fighting at sea and on water formed one stage of war, on the land geographic features decreed that the war would be fought in three additional theaters. West of the Mississippi, considerable fighting took place in Missouri, as noted above. Ultimately Union forces drove southward and occupied the upper part of Arkansas. Although later in the war Federal troops attempted an up-the-Red-River expedition, the trans-Mississippi theater remained relatively inactive, especially after the fall of Vicksburg in July, 1863.

In the middle area lying between the Appalachians and the Mississippi, usually called the western theater, Federal strategy aimed first at gaining control of the Mississippi River from Kentucky to its mouth and then seizing eastern Tennessee preparatory to a drive through Georgia that would cut the eastern part of the Confederacy in two. In the eastern theater, situated between the Appalachians and the Atlantic, Federals attempted to drive south from Washington to the rebel capital at Richmond.

In 1861, military operations on land cranked up slowly in the wake of Fort Sumter. Since neither side was then adequately prepared for large-scale movements, only small skirmishes engaged contending forces in the mountainous western Virginia country during the early summer, the Federals gaining the upper hand there. Shortly voluble spokesmen on both sides were clamoring for a swift and deadly thrust that would end the war quickly. "On to Richmond! Forward!" shouted action-hungry Northern newspapers and Congressmen. Even Lincoln was persuaded that the war could be finished off in short order.

When in June, 1861, General Beauregard's main Confederate army moved to Manassas Junction, a critical railroad point within thirty miles of Washington, political demands for action grew irresistible. With "three-month volunteers" nearing the end of their term of service, General Irwin McDowell ordered his 30,000-man army forward, their ultimate target Richmond. His raw, inexperienced men marched gaily southward out of Washington, singing and chanting in carefree optimism. Beauregard, with 24,000 equally green recruits, dug in on the south bank of a small stream called Bull Run.

In the morning of July 21 charging Federals crashed through the rebel center on their way to seeming victory. Only one block stood in their way. On the Confederate right General Thomas J. Jackson, commanding troops composed mostly of his students from Virginia Military Institute where he had been a professor of mathematics only a few months earlier, held like a "stonewall" against the Yankee onslaughts. His excited men, loosing a wild, fierce shriek (soon to be famous as the frightening "rebel yell") stopped the Federals cold. (Their commander would thereafter be known as "Stonewall" Jackson.) By afternoon some 9,000 Confederate reinforcements, brought up speedily by General Joseph E. Johnston from the Shenandoah Valley, rushed into action and drove the Federals from the field. What started as a Yankee success, turning into an orderly withdrawal, soon degenerated into a wild stampede as frightened youngsters, shucking packs and guns, sped toward Washington and homeward, their three months service done. Newsmen, Congressmen, government clerks, and wives, who in a Sunday picnic mood had followed Union troops out from the capital to witness the expected easy victory, now found themselves ensnared in narrow roads choked with tangled masses of men, horses, wagons, abandoned baggage, and artillery pieces. Not all made it home safely—at least one Congressman suffered the indignity of capture and wound up in Libby Prison, Richmond.

Bull Run drove home the savage clout of war. Of more than 63,000 men engaged, the Federals lost 2,896 killed, missing, and wounded; the rebels, 1,982. Obviously the war was going to be neither easy nor short. New calls for troops flashed across the wires from Washington and Richmond.

One incidental effect of Bull Run appeared quickly in Washington. Responding to the President's earlier call, Congress had gathered in special session beginning on July 4. To the Congress, Lincoln reported and asked approval of all emergency, extra-legal measures he had taken on his own since Sumter—increasing the size of the regular army, calling out volunteers, borrowing money, contracting for supplies and equipment, appointing officers, and among other things, suspending the writ of habeas corpus in certain areas. Jealous of its own powers, Congress had at first refused to validate the President's prior actions and had even turned down his request for additional men and money. Then came Bull Run's disaster. Within days both houses shouted through approval of the Lincoln measures, the habeas corpus suspension excepted. The lawmakers went even a step further and on August 6, at the instigation of abolitionist Radical Republicans, adopted the first Confiscation Act authorizing the President to seize all property, including slaves, used in furthering the rebellion. After some hesitation, Lincoln signed the measure.

In June an earlier Federal push had started toward Richmond, led by one of Lincoln's many ''political generals,'' Benjamin F. Butler, who had been a Massachusetts Congressman before the war. At Big Bethel Church near Yorktown, a Confederate counter thrust drove Butler's troops back to their Fortress Monroe base on the peninsula's tip. In this command Butler took the unusual step of refusing to return runaway slaves who came within his defense lines, declaring them to be ''contraband'' of war. He refused Confederate demands for their return, contending that Confederates had used the slaves for military support tasks, and he now put them to work on Union fortifications. Other Federal reversals ensued, notably a disaster at Ball's Bluff on the Potomac River, where prominent Senator Edward D. Baker was killed and Oliver Wendell Holmes, Jr., (later to be a Supreme Court justice) was wounded. Arising from this, a Congressional furore led to the creation of Congress's Joint Committee on the Conduct of the War, which for the war's duration would continue under Senator Ben Wade's lead its probing, second guessing, and often partisan meddling with military management both in Washington and in the field.

From the west came discouraging news in August. A Federal force in Missouri, hoping to drive rebel troops from that state, attacked a Confederate army twice its size at Wilson's Creek near the Arkansas border. The men in blue suffered not only defeat but also loss of their General, Nathaniel Lyon, who died in a burst of rebel bullets. Blame for the defeat and for Lyon's death fell on General John C. Frémont, commander of the Department of the West with headquarters in St. Louis. Frémont was soon in trouble on another score. To deal with local disorders and violence plaguing Missouri, he had issued a proclamation establishing martial law and declaring free all slaves held by persons resisting the authority of the United States. Apprehensive over repercussions in Kentucky and other loyal border states, Lincoln overruled the proclamation and replaced Frémont in November. In as new commander for the West was General Henry W. Halleck, a professional soldier with a vast book knowledge of war, who was dubbed ''Old Brains'' by his cohorts.

Following the Bull Run reversal in the east, Lincoln replaced McDowell, designated a new Army of the Potomac, and installed General George B. McClellan, fresh from limited successes in western Virginia, as the new commander. A talented West Pointer who had earlier seen service in the war with Mexico and as an observer in the Crimean war, McClellan had designed an improved cavalry saddle, had gone into civilian business, and become a railroad president. From that post he resigned to offer his services at the outbreak of war. A short, dark man, with supreme self-assurance, the commander at age thirty-five felt the weight of his new eminence with Napoleonic majesty. "All tell me," he wrote his wife, "that I am held responsible for the fate of the nation. I shall carry this thing *en grande* and crush the rebels in one campaign." Shortly McClellan took over as overall commander, replacing aged Winfield Scott, who retired. Hope ran high at first for the young new leader, who cut a dashing figure riding through Washington's streets, organizing and disciplining the new recruits who were streaming into the city in the fall of 1861. Surely here was a man with the technical skill, youthful vigor, verve, and confidence to inspire the army and drive on to Richmond and victory. Months passed. More drilling, more marching, more building of forts on the city's outskirts. No action. More months gone. Still no action. Men began to wonder.

McClellan, a man endowed with a larger share of vanity and caution than most mortals, conceived his duty to build the capital's defenses and mold an army that would respond to orders with disciplined precision. As an organizer and trainer he succeeded remarkably well. When Congress convened in December some leaders marveled at his work. But others wondered. Soon callers beseiged the White House demanding to know when the grand offensive would start. But continued drilling, marching, and fortifying closed out the year 1861 with still no sign of what "Little Mac" intended to do.

While McClellan's Army of the Potomac swelled to a magnificent force of over 100,000 well-trained, well-armed men, the largest army ever assembled in the Western Hemisphere, Union prospects did not brighten noticeably. In the western theater desultory fighting continued. Again in Missouri a Federal army was beaten, this time at Belmont as the year dragged to its weary end. The losing general was an unknown officer from Illinois—thirty-nine-year-old Ulysses S. Grant.

2. *Union Gains in the West, 1862*

As the year 1862 opened, some regularity of form was beginning to clothe military operation in certain respects. For one, terminology was now worked out—the North naming its armies for large rivers, the South for land areas. For example, the Federal Army of the Potomac fought against the Army of Northern Virginia; the Confederate Army of Tennessee against the Army of the Tennessee. In naming battles, the North usually used the name of the nearest river or stream, like Bull Run, the South the nearest town, like Manassas.

By 1862 also the two separate theaters of military action were now clearly discernible. The Appalachians, knifing through the South from Maryland to Alabama, thrust a rough barrier that blocked easy passage between eastern and western fronts and impeded free movement of troops between the two. In consequence, for much of the war the eastern armies fought an almost totally distinct war from those of the west. Not until 1864 did effective coordination of the two develop. In contrast to twentieth century military strategy, Federal armies aimed more for enemy cities than for opposing armies. Thus Richmond in the east and New Orleans and Vicksburg in the west served as the main Union targets; later it would be Chattanooga and Atlanta, strategic Southern rail centers.

At the start of 1862, Confederate defensive strategy in the west rested mainly upon Kentucky. There one of the South's ablest generals, Albert Sidney Johnston, had seized control of Bowling Green as his headquarters to direct operations in southern Kentucky aimed at thwarting any Federal thrust toward Tennessee. At Kentucky's western end, Southern General Leonidas Polk, a West Pointer who had become an Episcopal bishop, gained possession of the bluffs above Columbus from which point his artillery controlled the Mississippi River. From there the Confederate defense line, thinly manned as it was, stretched all the way east to Cumberland Gap. Union forces in Kentucky were under the command of General Don Carlos Buell, a cautious leader reluctant to move until every detail was in place. To the west of the Mississippi River some 20,000 rebel troops patrolled along the Missouri-Arkansas border ready to check any Federal attempts to penetrate southward.

Clearly, since Confederates attempted to guard a 600-mile defense line from the Appalachians to the Mississippi and beyond, they could effectively protect only selected, critical points along the line. One such point (since most of Kentucky was Union-occupied) lay at the Kentucky-Tennessee border where the two large rivers, the Tennessee and the Cumberland, flowing parallel and within a dozen miles of each other rolled northward toward the Ohio River. Here Johnston stationed defensive units to block any Union drive toward Tennessee.

In early February, 1862, General Grant swung south out of Cairo, Illinois, leading a 15,000-man attack force supported by a flotilla of Federal gunboats commanded by Commodore Andrew H. Foote. Their targets, Forts Henry and Donelson, guarded the rivers' joint gateway opening into central Tennessee and the lower South itself (the Tennessee River's southward loop touching Mississippi and Alabama in their northernmost reaches). After a fierce naval bombardment pulverized the defenses, Grant moved in and seized Fort Henry on February 6. At Fort Donelson, twelve miles to the east, the 12,000 Confederate defenders, after fending off Foote's gunboats, found themselves surrounded by Grant's army. Fort commander Simon B. Buckner asked Grant's terms. "No terms except unconditional surrender,'' shot back the laconic reply. On February 16, Grant possessed the fort, forty artillery pieces, and 12,000 prisoners of war. For the first time Union men had a major victory and a military hero to cheer. Thereafter U. S. Grant would be hailed as ''Unconditional Surrender'' Grant.

Upon the loss of Forts Henry and Donelson, Johnston, who had already pulled his forces back from endangered central Kentucky to Nashville, Tennessee, now retreated even farther southward. The eastern anchor of the Confederate defense line had buckled when Union General George H. Thomas routed an advance rebel force at Mill Springs in eastern Kentucky. At its far western end, too, the rebel line failed to hold. General Samuel R. Curtis' 12,000-man army defeated some 16,000 Confederate troops, including 3,500 Choctaw, Cherokee, and Creek warriors, at Pea Ridge, Arkansas. In southeast Missouri, General John Pope drove Confederate defenders out of New Madrid and seized heavily fortified ''Island No. 10,'' thereby opening the Mississippi River to Union shipping as far south as Memphis. As a result, Johnston was compelled to pull back Confederate forces from western Tennessee and form a new base at Corinth, a rail junction in northeast Mississippi.

Since mid-February the way was open for a Federal thrust through west Tennessee that might well have driven far toward the Gulf. But a month of inept fumbling by ''Old Brains'' Halleck in overall command at St. Louis delayed the kickoff and let the magnificent opportunity pass. By early April, Grant, after being temporarily relieved of command, rejoined his army near Shiloh close to Pittsburg Landing on the Tennessee River just north of Mississippi's border. There he awaited arrival of reinforcements under General Don Carlos Buell. On April 6, Albert Sidney Johnston's regrouped force of 40,000 Confederates suddenly smashed into Grant's encamped and unprepared army, which was driven back to the river's edge in dismay and disarray. Only nightfall and perhaps the death of Johnston, who fell mortally wounded in the first day's fighting, saved Grant from being crushed.

During the night Buell's reinforcements arrived, raising Federal strength to 60,000 soldiers. After bitter fighting the following day, Grant succeeded in dislodging the rebels now led by a less aggressive Beauregard. At this point, Halleck reached the scene, took personal command and again managed to stall a full-scale followup of the retreating Confederates near Corinth. The army was perhaps in no shape to push forward because of the 100,000 men engaged in the Shiloh battle almost one-fourth became casualties (13,047 Federals, 10,694 Confederates) in what was the bloodiest fight to that date on the North American continent. As a result, a healthy mutual respect developed for the military capability on each side. But viewed overall, Shiloh was decisive. There the Confederacy made a supreme effort to recover western Tennessee. Failing there, the Confederates' course ran downhill from then on, as Mississippi—both state and river—lay open to Federal assaults. For the present, however, Halleck failed to capitalize on the opening, and Braxton Bragg succeeded in regrouping the forces he now took over from the defeated Beauregard.

During the lull on land, naval units made a dramatic move. In late April, Federal Navy Captain David G. Farragut (a Southerner of Spanish-American descent and still spry at age sixty) led a Union flotilla in blasting its way past the river forts guarding the Mississippi's mouth and seized possession of New Orleans. Shortly afterwards, Union ships captured Baton Rouge and Natchez and secured control of the lower reaches of the great river. Only Vicksburg, Mississippi, and Port Hudson, Louisiana, remained in Confederate hands.

In New Orleans a Federal occupation force of 18,000 men under the command of General Butler faced the scorn and spite of many local residents. Butler moved swiftly to suppress unrest. One man who tore down the Union flag was executed after sentence was imposed by a military commission. To deal with feminine hostility, Butler issued his notorious order that "any female who should by gesture, words, and looks insult a Union soldier is to be regarded and held liable to be treated as a woman of the town plying her vocation." When the order was condemned as disgracefully barbaric, Butler explained in a letter to a New York editor: "The women . . . were everywhere insulting my soldiers, deliberately spitting in their faces and upon their uniforms, making insulting gestures and remarks. . . . Is the She-adder to be preferred to the He-adder, when they void their venom in your face?" To lock up such insulting women "in the Guard House," as was proposed, "my men must have broken open private dwellings and chased their fair, feeble, fretful and ferocious rebels to their bedrooms to seize them. How many riots do you think I should have had to drag screaming women through the streets to the guard house?" Instead, "my order . . . at once executed itself. . . . How do you regard and treat a lewd woman and her remarks as she passes you on the street? Pass her by, do you not? You are not bound to notice either her acts or her remarks. Some of your New York editors seem to think they must hold dalliance with such a person." Not at all. "After that order every man . . . was bound in Honor not to notice any of the acts of these women. They were no longer insults; they were the blandishments of which Solomon speaks in the Proverbs." The result has been that "since that order, no man or woman has insulted a soldier of mine in New Orleans. . . nor has there been a single cause for complaint. . . . A woman can walk alone . . . through New Orleans at any hour, day or night, free of molestation or insult from citizen or soldier. Can you say as much, O most virtuous Editor, for New York?"

Whatever the merit or menace of Butler's "woman" order, Farragut's seizure of the lower Mississippi deprived the South of its most vital port at New Orleans and sealed off up-river areas from an outlet to the sea—an irreparable loss for the Confederacy. On the Atlantic coast, too, the Federal navy had been busy. Accompanied by amphibious army troops, naval units had attacked and seized many points along the Carolina coast—Hatteras Inlet, Roanoke Island, Port Royal and adjacent islands, Fort Macon, Elizabeth City, New Bern. Nearly all the North Carolina coast, with the exception of Wilmington, had been neutralized by April, 1862, and the capture of Fort Pulaski, in that same month, rendered Savannah, Georgia, useless as a Confederate port. The "Anaconda's" squeeze was beginning to tighten. But it would be a long time before strangulation came.

Several secondary developments diverted attention from the main strategic stage for a time. Federal spy James J. Andrews and twenty-one soldiers slipped into Georgia and near Atlanta stole a railroad locomotive, "The General." Racing north toward Chattanooga they intended to rip up tracks and bridges in their wake. The scheme backfired when Southerners hastily mounted a fast chase by handcar and then by engine. When the raiders ran out of fuel, they were rounded up, and Andrews and seven cohorts met death on the gallows at Atlanta.

Action on the quiescent Kentucky front flared anew in July when Colonel John H. Morgan led a slashing cavalry raid that bagged 1,200 Federal prisoners. In late August, Bragg charged north into Kentucky and came within a whisker of capturing Louisville before joining forces with General Edmund Kirby-Smith. Together they engaged Buell in a messy battle at Perryville that produced heavy casualties, a Union hero in Philip H. Sheridan, and no clear decision.

Withdrawing to Tennessee, the Confederates were at length followed by General William S. Rosecrans, Buell's successor, now in command of the Army of the Cumberland. On the final day of 1862 Rosecrans's 42,000 effectives struck Bragg's 34,000 troops at Murfreesboro, Tennessee. Here on the banks of Stone's River the armies slugged it out in three days of bitter assaults, counter assaults, and heavy firing that ended with 9,000 casualties on each side but no decisive result. While the Confederates drew back toward central Tennessee, the Federals did not strike again for six months. The year that began so hearteningly for the Union armies in the west ended in indecision and stalemate, as Grant and William T. Sherman's forces lay bogged down at Chickasaw Bayou near Vicksburg.

3. Confederate Success, Union Despair in the East, 1862

The Union story in the east for 1862 was even more discouraging. McClellan, still drilling and reviewing troops in Washington as the year began, drew heavy fire from critical Congressmen and prominent editors. With 150,000 men in arms at the capital, he had not yet reached his goal of a 250,000-man military machine, fashioned on European models and supported with the proper proportions of artillery, cavalry, and other units. He became involved in endless conferences, inspections, joint calculations with adjutants, engineers, quartermasters, and commissaries. McClellan seemed furiously busy. Some cynics said it was all busywork and it brought the army no nearer to Richmond and the war no nearer an end.

Doubts about McClellan grew in January, 1862. Some Congressmen, called Radicals because they wanted slavery eliminated at once, viewed McClellan as "soft" on slavery. Others openly questioned whether he secretly harbored pro-Southern feelings (a cousin served in the Confederate army) that restrained him from moving vigorously against the enemy. Lincoln, showing superhuman restraint, bore with his general, who more than once bruskly snubbed the President whose "perfectly sickening" advice struck McClellan as motivated by the "hypocrisy, knavery and folly" of civilian chiefs who knew nothing of war. One such, War Secretary Simon Cameron, had authorized supply contracts that not only defrauded the government of immense sums but also failed to secure materiel and equipment needed by the army. For example, Colt revolvers worth $15 were sold to the government for $35; a Missouri fort built by a contractor for $80,000 cost the government $191,000.

In January, 1862, the President sent Cameron as minister to Russia. In his place he put Edwin M. Stanton, lawyer and former democrat, who for all his cantankerous manner and overbearing arrogance unsnarled the War Department's administrative mess and honestly secured supplies and equipment for the army. Realizing his own limitations, Lincoln had taken to studying military books, pouring over maps, talking and corresponding widely with military men to increase his grasp of war problems and management. He made no claim to expertise, but his native intelligence and diligent study enabled him to enlarge his capability as "a great natural strategist, better than any of his generals," (in the opinion of two modern critics) whose grasp of "larger strategy" did "more than any general to win the war."

At length, exasperated by McClellan's dilatoriness, Lincoln issued General Order No. 1 commanding McClellan to move by February 22. His own view was that a direct drive on Richmond was the best approach since it kept the main Union army between Washington and rebel forces. But he deferred to McClellan's judgment. McClellan's plan, finally revealed to Lincoln in February, called for an elaborate amphibious operation. The navy would transport troops to the eastern tip of the peninsula between the York and James Rivers. The army would then push seventy miles inland for an assault on Richmond. Not enthusiastic about the plan, Lincoln insisted on detaching McDowell's corps of 37,000 troops to defend Washington from possible attack by Johnston's force still at Manassas. McClellan complained that the loss of McDowell's corps materially weakened the offensive before it began.

By April, McClellan was on the peninsula, with close to 100,000 men. Johnston shifted his 60,000-man army to a position east of Richmond. Yorktown, a relatively weak Confederate point on the road to Richmond, might have been quickly captured. But McClellan, with Bull Run's nightmare still fresh in mind, took a month to reduce it. Heavy spring rains on the peninsula turned roads into quagmires. McClellan inched forward at snail's speed—delayed partly by soggy roads, partly by Johnston's harassments, but mainly because he kept hoping for reinforcements from Washington. These, he contended, were urgently needed because he was persuaded by his faulty Pinkerton intelligence agents that he was greatly outnumbered by the foe.

Reinforcements were not sent because of "Stonewall" Jackson's incredibly swift maneuvers in Virginia's Shenandoah Valley just west of the Blue Ridge mountains. Jackson's lightning strikes at many different points giving the impression that he commanded a large body of troops reinforced Washington's fear of a rebel attack through the mountain passes on the capital. Actually Jackson had only 16,000 men. He shifted them speedily to Winchester, Kernstown, Cross Keys, and other points, thereby tying down some 45,000 Federals. About three-fourths of the latter who were intended to cooperate in McClellan's drive on Richmond were prevented from joining that campaign. By early June, Jackson slipped out of the valley and marched rapidly to add his force to Johnston's, now numbering 80,000 in the coming defense of Richmond against McClellan.

By the time Jackson arrived, McClellan had reached Seven Pines whence Richmond's church spires were visible barely nine miles to the west. It was as close as McClellan would get to the Confederate capital. Noting that Federals were divided into two segments by the flooded Chickahominy River, the rebels attacked McClellan's left wing on May 31–June 1 at Seven Pines and Fair Oaks. With Johnston severely wounded in the first encounter, McClellan might have profited by rebel misfortune and confusion and pressed forward with fair prospects of success. Instead, leaving 25,000 troops on the Chickahominy, he withdrew to his base twenty miles to the east, settling down to wait once more for hoped-for reinforcements.

With Johnston out of action, General Robert E. Lee, West Pointer and life-long career soldier now aged fifty-four, took command of what now came to be called the Army of Northern Virginia and assumed the task of defending the threatened Confederate capital. For the next three years, in the face of a 3–2 and often a 3–1 manpower deficit, Lee proved a skilled defensive strategist and a resourceful, inspiring, and inspired leader for his under-manned, ill-equipped army. His chivalric bearing, his gentlemanly manner, his memory for names and his concern for his men kindled a high morale in the army that would "carry the South on its bayonets" in the rigorous campaigns ahead. Focusing on the defense of Virginia and relying heavily on such able lieutenants as "Stonewall" Jackson who responded as though by instinct and without direct command, Lee outgeneraled a succession of baffled Union commanders in a brilliant set of campaigns displaying such high-level professional skill as to make opponents appear almost amateurish by comparison.

From near Richmond, Lee's cavalry chief, colorful, full-bearded General J. E. B. Stuart, flew off on a dazzling but foolhardy three-day ride around the entire Federal army that produced valuable information for Lee but also alerted McClellan, who now readied his forces to meet the advertised Confederate advance. On June 25 Lee's jab at the Federal right wing at Mechanicsville was repulsed. But it touched off the "Seven Days" battles of June 25 to July 1, in which Union troops inflicted heavy damage on rebel attackers, while sustaining large losses themselves. No decisive victory resulted. Both armies, battered, bruised and bloodied, drew back—Lee closer to Richmond, McClellan to a new base established at Harrison's Landing on the James River under cover of Federal navy gunboats.

Here President Lincoln, perturbed and disappointed, came on July 9 to confer with his General. Bluntly McClellan complained that the administration had failed to support his peninsula campaign adequately and handed Lincoln a lengthy document, the "Harrison's Landing Letter," giving extensive and officious advice on political matters, warning against making war on civilians and against confiscation and "forcible abolition of slavery" that would undermine army morale, and opposing arbitrary military arrests of civilians in the North. Sounding much like a Democratic campaign tract, it was a presumptuous, insolent letter that would have stirred most Presidents (as in the Truman-MacArthur affair ninety years later) to fire the writer on the spot. Lincoln pondered, then rejected McClellan's proposal to renew the attack on Richmond, and sadly ordered the army's return to Washington. The President now brought from St. Louis General Henry W. Halleck to take over the overall command, while he retained McClellan in a subordinate command under General John Pope, now in charge of the main Federal army in northern Virginia.

In late August, Pope, as rash as McClellan was cautious, launched a new drive toward Richmond by way of Bull Run. That was as far as he got. His army was caught and chewed between two jaws of Lee's army and suffered disastrous defeat on August 29–30, 1862, losing 16,000 of its 75,000 troops. At home Northerners were engulfed in a sense of futility—a mood Democratic opponents of the Lincoln administration would exploit fully in the coming fall elections. After two campaigns toward Richmond in sixteen months, as historian Douglas S. Freeman has observed, "the only Federals closer than 100 miles to Richmond were prisoners."

The time was now ripe, Lee calculated, for an invasion northward that could win Maryland for the Confederacy and hopefully secure formal recognition by England. In desperation, Lincoln again tapped McClellan to take command of the demoralized army. Upon doing so, ''Little Mac'' was greeted with wild cheers by the dispirited men in blue.

On September 5, Lee's regiments, aglow over their recent Bull Run victory, waded across the Potomac and moved into Frederick, Maryland, where housewife Barbara Fritchie, stars and stripes flying from her window in defiance of rebel occupation, reportedly shouted from her window, ''Shoot if you must this old grey head, but spare your country's flag.'' Here Lee split his forces, sending Jackson west to seize the Federal arsenal and arms at Harper's Ferry, Stuart's cavalry east to report enemy movements, while Lee led his main army northward. Fear gripped Washington, Baltimore, and Philadelphia. At the very least, many thought, the invasion would surely isolate the nation's capital.

For once McClellan moved, slicing through the passes over South Mountain to get at Lee in the valley to the west. By incredible chance, Lee's orders for disposing his troops were picked up by a Union private, who found them wrapped around three cigars on the ground and delivered them to McClellan. Even more incredibly, McClellan now paused, still harboring delusions of enemy strength. He thereby lost the chance of a swift strike to catch Lee off guard and crush his army. The delay allowed Jackson, coming on from Harper's Ferry, to rejoin Lee near Sharpsburg as McClellan's army was closing in. The resulting battle of Antietam on September

Lincoln visits McClellan after Antietam. (Library of Congress)

17 generated a massive, mutual mauling as Federals pummeled rebel positions throughout the day. The grim men in grey fought back stubbornly. McClellan's reluctance to throw in General Ambrose E. Burnside's corps until late in the day has been tagged as the cause for failing to win a full-scale Union success. But the hand-to-hand fighting in the "Cornfield," on the creek's banks, and at the bridge was sheer butchery as blue and grey warriors slaughtered each other with demonic fury. As dusk fell, 25,000 corpses—half Union, half Confederate—blanketed the ground.

Who won at Antietam is still debated. McClellan throttled Lee's invasion, but considering the disparity of manpower (78,000 to 45,000) it should have been a rout. Besides, Lee's army was allowed to slip away unmolested, back across the Potomac to regroup in Virginia and to fight another day. True, Washington had been saved and the Union cause strengthened. Five days later Lincoln announced the Preliminary Emancipation Proclamation. From now on the Federal forces were committed to a war to advance human freedom as well as to save the Union.

The struggle was far from over. Six weeks later Lincoln reassigned McClellan to recruiting duty in Trenton, New Jersey, and placed Burnside in command of the Army of the Potomac. When notified, Burnside recoiled in disbelief, saying, "I am not competent to command such a large army." He then proceeded to demonstrate his statement's accuracy. On December 13, a freezing cold day, he hurled his troops across the Rappahannock River at Fredericksburg to attack Lee's 70,000-man force entrenched in impregnable works on Marye's Heights. Six massive, suicidal assaults by the men in blue failed to budge the defenders whose murderous fire chopped gaping holes in the charging Federal columns. Over 12,000 Union casualties resulted, as compared with fewer than 6,000 for the South.

The year 1862 drew to a close with Federal troops no nearer Richmond than they had been eighteen months earlier. Northern morale sagged sharply. Public credit declined to the point where it took 134 greenback dollars to buy 100 dollars in gold. Looking to the fall mid-term elections, Democrats called for an end of the senseless killing, an end to the administration's suppression of civil liberties, and for a negotiated peace. The voters responded, registering their frustration over long casualty lists, arbitrary arrests, military trials of civilians, Federal centralizing tendencies, and the shift toward Radical policies like emancipation. Republicans suffered serious losses. In fact, so many incumbents lost that Republican control of the next Congress was jeopardized. Questioning Lincoln's competence, some Radicals pushed for a remaking of the cabinet that would force Seward out. Seward offered his resignation in December, 1862. In a showdown Lincoln refused to accept it but maneuvered the more Radical Chase into tendering his resignation. This, too, he refused to accept, but held both resignations in hand for potential future use.

It had been a difficult year, but the President had demonstrated his political mastery. Moreover, in issuing the Emancipation Proclamation, he had given moral substance to the Union's cause. As he reported to Congress, "In giving freedom to the slave, we assure freedom to the free. . . . We shall nobly save or meanly lose the last best hope of earth. . . . The way is plain, peaceful, generous, just—a way which if followed, the world will forever applaud, and God must forever bless." The next year, 1863, would go far in determining whether the hope would be fulfilled.

4. Union Crescendo at Vicksburg and Gettysburg, 1863

The first months of the third year of war featured cavalry raids that smacked more of show-off grandstanding than of solid military advance. Confederate horsemen under General Nathan B. Forrest made a series of quick jabs into Tennessee. In April, Colonel Benjamin H. Grierson led a large Federal cavalry force from Tennessee in a sweep through Mississippi to Baton Rouge wrecking railroads and burning supply depots and softening up the area for Grant's coming Mississippi campaign. Morgan's rebel raiders pushed a summer foray into Indiana and southern Ohio.

Major operations had already begun in Grant's drive to open the full length of the Mississippi River. Frustrated a year earlier at Shiloh in his thrust into the lower valley, Grant carefully planned a coordinated river-land operation to reduce the rebel stronghold at Vicksburg. By this time, that fortified city, standing high on the unassailable east bluffs of the river, assumed a strategic and psychological importance for the Confederate cause as the key point through which contact with rebel forces on the west of the river was maintained and through which western supplies channeled by rail eastward.

After efforts to build a river-diverting canal proved futile, the Union Commander switched plans. Bringing his army south from Memphis to Milliken's Bend, Grant had naval transports ferry the troops to the Louisiana (west) side, where they marched southward at a safe distance from Vicksburg's guns to a point on the river south of that strongpoint. Here he awaited the fleet. At night navy gunboats and transports under Commodore David Porter dashed past the booming Vicksburg batteries, rendezvoused with Grant, and transported his 20,000 troops to the east bank well below Vicksburg. From Port Hudson, Grant's army cut away from its own supply lines. Dashing eastward and living off the land, Grant's men won a series of small, quick victories, liquidated a rebel force at Jackson, Mississippi, and in mid-May wheeled westward to lay seige to Vicksburg, the Confederates' "Gibraltar of the Mississippi." In alarm, Richmond dispatched Joseph E. Johnston (now recovered from earlier wounds) to take command in the west, but how to unite Bragg's army to the east with Pemberton's force now barricaded in Vicksburg remained an impossible puzzle for the Southern command. For six weeks General John C. Pemberton's 30,000 entrenched Confederates remained trapped in that surrounded city, pummeled mercilessly by Grant's artillery from land and Porter's gunboats from the river. Supplies exhausted, they were forced to resort to eating dogs, mules, rats. Inevitably, on July 4 Pemberton surrendered to Grant his entire army, whose members were paroled as prisoners of war. The stunning Federal success sliced the Confederacy in two, gave the Union full control of the Mississippi, raised the nation's morale at home and its prestige abroad. The dogged, cigar-chomping, stocky, forty-one-year-old Grant was hailed again as a true hero throughout the land. When Lincoln was told that Grant hit the bottle heavily, Lincoln reportedly quipped, "Find out what brand of whiskey he drinks; I want to order a case for my other generals."

Not content to rest on his laurels, Grant ordered 40,000 Federal troops under Rosecrans to push forward from Murfreesboro to Tennessee's southeast corner, where they drove Bragg back into Georgia and took possession of the strategic rail center of Chattanooga. Bostered by the arrival of General James Longstreet's 11,000-man force, Bragg rallied, wheeled about, and launched a heavy, sustained assault that tore a hole in the surprised Union lines, smashed the right flank, and sent Rosecrans and two corps reeling back into Chattanooga. The Union left wing commanded by General George H. Thomas, unaware of the breakthrough, stood rock-hard against repeated rebel onslaughts and saved the day from total disaster. As it was, Confederate casualties numbered 18,000 to 17,000 for the Federals. As Bragg closed in on Chattanooga, where Rosecrans remained seemingly paralyzed by the recent shock, "Rock of Chickamauga" Thomas was given command of the Army of the Cumberland. Joining him in east Tennessee was General William T. Sherman, leading the Army of the Tennessee, along with Grant, who had just been elevated to supreme command of all western operations. Two army corps under Hooker were now hustled westward from Virginia to give further reinforcement. Bragg, occupying a ring of hills southeast of the city, found his manpower reduced as Longstreet with 15,000 troops set out for Knoxville, while Grant's remaining force grew to 60,000.

On November 23 just southeast of Chattanooga a three-day battle began when Sherman punched at the Confederate right on the north end of Missionary Ridge. Shortly afterward Hooker hit the rebels' far left wing and in "the battle above the clouds" seized control of Lookout Mountain. On November 25, two of Thomas's divisions under Sheridan and T. J. Wood charged forward (in what was intended as a "demonstration" to relieve pressure on Sherman) under orders to capture the rebel rifle pits at the foot of the ridge. The 18,000 attacking Federals not only took the rifle pits but surged forward, without orders and under spectacular momentum, to the top of Missionary Ridge. There they drove the stunned Confederates from their earthworks, smashed the rebel center and sent Bragg's shattered army fleeing in disarray into Georgia. All eastern Tennessee had been liberated, a large wedge driven into the Confederacy, and Georgia was now ripe for the invasion that Sherman would lead in 1864.

Meanwhile in the eastern theater, the 130,000-man Army of the Potomac under ''Fighting Joe'' Hooker's command drew Lee's army of 60,000 into battle near Chancellorsville in broken, forested, confusing terrain a dozen miles west of Fredericksburg. In the ensuing battle, May 1–5, while Lee's main force feinted at the Union center, ''Stonewall'' Jackson struck and rolled up the vulnerable Federal right flank with such startling violence that Hooker, suffering 17,000 casualties, retired shaken from the field and limped northward toward Washington. Lee's ''masterpiece'' at Chancellorsville cost him heavily—12,000 killed, wounded, and missing. But worse, Jackson, having ridden out from his camp at night, upon returning was shot by his own sentries, who mistook him for an enemy. Shortly before, Lee had extended congratulations to Jackson for the ''victory due to your skill and energy.'' Now on May 10 Jackson lay dead. The Confederacy suffered a grievous blow. At ''high noon'' Lee had lost his ablest ''lieutenant,'' his irreplaceable ''right arm.'' Two months later at Gettysburg Jackson, with his instinct for implementing Lee's battle plans, would be sorely missed.

Army hospital at Fredericksburg. (Library of Congress)

Nonetheless, convinced that the Confederates' hour was now or never, Lee determined to drive northward, spread destruction and shatter already shaky civilian morale in the hope that Washington would be forced to concede Confederate independence. His request for every available man of the 250,000 Confederates under arms was rejected by Davis who justifiably refused to strip defenses in the west just as fighting was stepping up there. Lee with his 75,0000-man Army of Northern Virginia took the grand gamble.

On June 3 Lee's army moved—his Second Corps under General Richard S. Ewell in the lead, followed by the First Corps under Longstreet and the Third under General A. P. Hill. Crossing over into the valley, they marched north passing over the Potomac near Harper's Ferry. Stuart's cavalry, instructed to cover the march, fought off Union cavalry in the war's biggest horse battle at Brandy Station, Virginia, on June 9. Hooker believed the time ripe for a strike toward Richmond. But Lincoln told him firmly: "Lee's army, not Richmond, is your true objective. . . . Follow on his flank and on his inside track," keeping Washington always covered, "shortening your lines, while lengthening his." By June 23, Ewell had pushed his grey troops to within ten miles of Harrisburg, Pennsylvania. At the same time Stuart's cavalry swung completely around Hooker's army, as it moved northward parallel to Lee's and thirty miles to the east. Again a spectacular feat, but it seriously handicapped Lee who was deprived of his "eyes" at a critical moment. By June 25 Lee brought his main army into Chambersburg, Pennsylvania, but he had lost track of Hooker's whereabouts. On June 28 General George G. Meade, known familiarly as "the old snapping turtle," took over command from Hooker and hastened his troops northward to parry Lee's invasion.

On June 30 a detachment of Hill's men, seeking shoes and supplies at Gettysburg, encountered by chance an advance Federal cavalry force. Swiftly word flashed back to the main armies, and both Meade and Lee hurried their troops forward to a fateful three-day showdown. On July 1, Hill's and Ewell's men swept through town, scattering advance Federal troops, who then regrouped on Cemetery Ridge's high ground southeast of town. By nightfall they were joined by other bluecoats in throwing up earthworks and installing artillery pieces on the Ridge. Had the rebels seized this Ridge (which they could easily have done on the first day) with its elevated points at Culp's Hill on the northeast and Little and Big Round Tops three miles to the south, the battle's outcome might well have been different. Instead, Lee's men took up a parallel position on Seminary Ridge a mile to the west across rolling wheatfields. From there, as July 2 dawned, Lee's 75,000 embattled veterans faced the rising sun as it glistened on Federal artillery guns and bayonets across the fields that divided the two armies.

The first day had been given over the feinting, jabbing, probing, and skirmishing. Now, viewing the entrenched Federal position on the eastern

Dead soldiers at Gettysburg. (Library of Congress)

Ridge, Longstreet counseled Lee to avoid a frontal assault and to march instead around the Federals' southern flank and seize a strong position between Meade's army and Washington, which would require Meade to attack. Lee listened but decided to fight it out where he was. On July 2, Lee ordered the attack. After some delay Longstreet and Hill hurled their troops against the Union left and after furious fighting in the Peach Orchard and Devil's Den succeeded in reaching the base of the Round Tops, only to discover the Federals in full possession of these key hills. (Later critics would fault Longstreet's delay in launching the attack for failure to gain the Round Tops and with them the key to the battle.) On July 3, Ewell's efforts came close but failed to crack the Union right wing in the morning. Lee then played his final card. At 1 P.M. Confederate guns laid down a deadly barrage on Union lines. Infantry units formed into assault columns. General George E. Pickett's division, with supporting troops to a total of 15,000 men, moved out smartly from Seminary Ridge, doublequicking in formation across the open fields, heading for the Union center, where General Winfield Scott Hancock's entrenched defenders blinked in disbelief. Grey-clad veterans sped forward in a suicidal rush, as artillery and rifle fire threw a sheet of lead into their faces. The lines sagged, reeled, crumbled as men dropped by the hundreds, but they reformed and kept coming on. A handful pierced the Union center across a low stone wall—"the high water mark of the Confederacy"—but hand-to-hand combat subdued them. Slowly the bleeding fragments of Pickett's force shuddered, staggered, then receded stumbling blindly back to Seminary Ridge. The guns soon fell silent as the sun dropped to the horizon. The war's biggest battle ended as Confederates counted 28,000 casualties, the Union 23,000. Night fell as the blood flowed from "the flower of Southern manhood" strewn over the "yellow fields of wheat."

On July 4 Lee's battered army began its sullen retreat through a driving rain storm. By July 13 Lee was back in Virginia, the remnants of his army still intact. In anguish Lincoln cried out, "Our army held the war in the hollow of its hand and would not close it." Meade, with his giant but bruised army, had failed to pursue the retreating Confederates.

Months later still unburied at Gettysburg lay the corpses of the thousands "who gave their lives that this nation might live." A national cemetery was built in their honor. On November 19, 1863, Lincoln came and in his brief Gettysburg Address dedicated not only the cemetery but solemnly vowed, "it is for us the living to be dedicated here to the unfinished work that they who fought here have so nobly advanced. It is right for us to be here dedicated to the great task remaining . . . that this nation, under God, shall have a new birth of freedom. . . ."

8

War Becomes Revolution, 1863-1865

Gettysburg and Vicksburg drove home to Americans the full import of the war. None could any longer doubt that total war had come and that America would not again be the America of prewar years. From the beginning it grew increasingly clear that war, once begun, was becoming all consuming, demanding the full energies of all. No one could remain neutral or aloof. The entire society—its farms, mines, mills, railroads, ships, shops, and counting houses—were mobilizing and becoming geared speedily to making war. Former institutions, practices, old ideas, former ways of doing things had to give way under the angry impact of war. Total war demanded the citizen's total allegiance. All must serve, cooperate, contribute, endure the pressures to conform.

What started as a limited war for limited purposes soon shed the wraps of accepted conventions and burst into a broad-fronted revolution. Under unprecedented pressures of an internal rebellion, the old Constitution was reshaped as the national government expanded its authority at the expense of the states and the President broadened executive powers at the expense of Congress. The age-old struggle to balance freedom and authority in the area of individual liberty underwent new tests as dissent and protest were largely stifled and shackled. The war, begun in an effort to preserve the nation, shortly became a struggle to smother slavery in "a new birth of freedom." In its most spectacular aspect, the new revolution, through military action, executive proclamation, and constitutional amendment, finally outlawed slavery. After initial delays, blacks soon became soldiers in the crusade to save the Union and wipe out slavery. As the war raged, new doors would begin to swing open to them. And on the economic front sweeping legislation would add other dimensions to the revolution.

1. The Home Front: Mobilizing for War

When in April, 1861, Lincoln acted to mobilize armed men for war, he called upon state governors to place voluntarily recruited state militia units into national service. These units were much larger in number than the regular army forces, which included less than 17,000 at the start and would be substantially increased to over 42,000 during the war. Later Federal calls would go out for volunteers, quotas being assigned to states and Congressional districts. The recruiting of troops was managed by state officials, as were their organization, management, pay, and to some degree their support until they were mustered into Federal service. Energetic governors like John Andrew of Massachusetts, Andrew Curtin of Pennsylvania, and Oliver P. Morton of Indiana worked well with Federal officials but attempted to retain much authority in their own hands. When in the summer of 1861 recruiting proved sluggish, especially after the First Battle of Bull Run, Congress voted the creation of a volunteer army of 500,000, who were known as "United States Volunteers" and came to form the major part of Union troops. In contrast to regular army men, these volunteers took up arms during the emergency, expecting to return to civilian life at war's end. This volunteer force was commanded during the early years of the war by many political generals, appointed by governors or the President, and by regimental officers elected by enlisted men. The lack of a definite system of organization resulted in sloppy discipline, haphazard lines of command, and competition between state governments and the War Department for men, uniforms, munitions, equipment, food, and supplies. All this was accompanied by scandalous graft on contracts, outrageous prices, and shoddy materials.

By mid-1862 the army was so badly cut by battle losses, disease, expired enlistments, and desertions that on July 2 a new call for 300,000 volunteers went to the states. In the face of a slow response Congress then authorized a draft of 300,000 nine-month militia men, with quotas assigned to the states. When this move yielded only 65,000 soldiers, Federal, state, and local bounties (money bonuses for enlisting) were introduced. At first the Federal bounty was $100 (increased by 1864 to $300), but states, cities, counties, and even privately organized outfits offered additional rewards to the recruit, plus fringe benefits to his family at home. By the war's end New York had spent $86 million for bounties; all states over $286 million; the national government $300 million. A volunteer might reap as much as $800 in bounties (an amount not be sneezed at when a private's pay stood at $11 a month). The arrangement led to much confusion, dishonesty, and cheating. A man with no intention of ever serving, could enlist in one place, collect the cash bounties there, move on, enlist under another name in another place, collect again, and repeat the process as long as he could escape detection. Some "bounty jumpers" amassed as much as $8,000, one man boasting of having jumped bounty thirty-two times.

For the army to hold men, once they had been recruited, was not easy. The monotony of tedious garrison duty, rigors of campaigning in the open field, hazards of actual fighting, lack of decent food, fear, disease, the pull of home and family led many to desert. The rate of Union desertions ran at about one out of ten for a total of 200,000 (New York alone figured about 44,000). Under Presidential calls, much confusion resulted over state quotas and enlistment terms of three, six, or nine months or one year or longer. Finally Congress adopted a national conscription act on March 3, 1863, requiring the registration of all able-bodied men between twenty and forty-five years to be subject to call by lottery for national service up to three years. State quotas were retained and could be filled by volunteers. Any deficiency of numbers of volunteers below the quota had to be met by drafting conscripts. A draftee could secure exemption by hiring a substitute or by paying a $300 commutation fee to be used for securing a substitute—a provision denounced as favoritism for upper-income groups.

With all these defects, the conscription system roused evasion and hostility. Altogether, only 46,000 draftees and 118,000 substitutes were raised by the draft. Defiance, evasion, and obstruction were common: enrollment officers were frequently manhandled and lottery drawings violently disrupted. ''Insurrection'' against operation of the draft broke out in certain counties in Ohio, Kentucky, Pennsylvania, and Wisconsin, necessitating intervention by Federal or state troops. In New York, Governor Horatio Seymour protested directly to Lincoln against the impending draft. In New York City where many residents resented the war, abolition, and the Negro, announcement of the draft lottery results on July 11, 1863, sparked an attack by a mob that destroyed the Federal provost marshal's office and mushroomed into a week-long riot. Rioters fought the police, beat up the Police Superintendent, and robbed jewelry stores. After raiding mansions with shouts of ''Down with the rich,'' the mob turned its fury on Negroes, lynching those caught on the streets and burning down a Negro orphanage. Homes and stores lay gutted, and seventy-four persons were dead by the time Federal troops rushed from Gettysburg and restored order to the shocked city.

In order to supply the armies in the field, a vast system of letting government contracts to secure everything from heavy artillery pieces, warships, wagons, and locomotives to bullets, buttons, braid, and brandy had to be developed. The sloppy, costly procurement system originated by Secretary of War Cameron gave way to more orderly, efficient procurement arrangements after Stanton took over, although even then shoddy blankets, uniforms, shoes, defective muskets, and junk were foisted off on the government by crooked suppliers.

To satisfy war demands, the American economy underwent a booming expansion. While not all segments of industry enlarged (some actually were retarded by the war), manufacturing output and profits rose in boots and shoes, woolens, iron and steel, arms and munitions, coal and lumber. Some industries multiplied their prewar production many times over. Old factories were remodeled, new ones were built, and improved technology and machines were introduced. The Howe-Singer sewing machine, for example, revolutionized production of clothing and shoes and boots. The widespread use of Eli Whitney's principle of standardized, interchangeable parts boosted arms-making phenomenally. The government arsenal at Springfield, Massachusetts, which before the war made less than 15,000 rifles a year was soon turning out more than 200,000. Farm output zoomed upward, too, as Northern farmers employed more machines and better methods to expand plantings. Since farm prices also climbed with demand, agriculture enjoyed an era of prosperity. Indeed wheat exports soon tripled the prewar volume.

To pay for the flood of goods, the government resorted to the three traditional fiscal devices—taxes, borrowing, and paper money. In the first two years of the war, duties on imports were hiked twice, internal excise taxes were imposed on most goods including a manufacturer's tax, and personal income taxes were levied. By the last tax, which ranged from 5 per cent on incomes of $600 up to 10 per cent on those over $5,000, the actions of the Federal government came to affect individuals throughout the country directly. In fact the Internal Revenue Act of 1862 imposed, in addition to income and manufacturer's taxes, selected sales taxes, stamp duties, and even occupational license fees.

As gold and silver bullion and coin became scarce in the market because they were being hoarded by private individuals and used to pay international debts, Congress in the 1862 and 1863 Legal Tender Acts authorized the Treasury to run the printing presses and issue $450 million in paper notes, whose green ink caused the soldiers who first received them to call them "greenbacks." Their value in gold equivalent fluctuated widely, reflecting varying degrees of confidence in the government according to the fortunes of Union armies. As late as mid-1864 a greenback dollar was worth only 39 cents in gold and by the war's end had risen to only 67 cents. Continued use of greenbacks, with their inflationary effects on prices, adversely affected laborers and fixed-income groups and generated a political fight that outlasted the war.

Secretary Chase, who distrusted paper money and disliked high taxes, resorted to borrowing as the chief means of financing the war. After trying at first to sell government bonds directly to the people with little success, he turned for help to the bankers. Favoring, as he did, low-interest-rate, short-term bonds, redeemable after five years but before twenty years and known popularly as "five-twenties," Chase had to make concessions to bankers, allowing interest rates of 6 and 7 per cent on terms as long as forty years. In 1862 Jay Cooke's Philadelphia banking firm, engaged to float bond issues at fat commissions, mounted a high-pressure sales campaign that sold over $400 million worth of bonds. Under the National Bank Acts of 1863 and 1864 local banking associations, established under Federal charters, were required to purchase government bonds to the extent of one-third of their capital. Upon depositing the bonds with the Treasury, the local association could issue bank notes up to 90 per cent of the value of the bonds. These could then be lent at interest to local borrowers, thereby doubling the interest-drawing power of the bank. By the war's end over 1,600 nationally-chartered banks helped bolster the market for government bonds and had $200 million worth of bank notes outstanding in circulation. Altogether, Federal war financing rested upon $667 million collected in taxes throughout the war, $2.6 billion from loans, and $450 million in greenbacks.

Besides guns and money, the government offered soldiers and their dependent families assistance through the United States Sanitary Commission. A kind of nineteenth century forerunner of a combined Red Cross and USO, the Commission provided for wounded and sick soldiers ambulance, medical, and hospital services, supplementing the regular military hospitals. It maintained as well snack bars, feeding stations, soldiers' lounges at or behind the front and gave financial aid to dependent families at home. Funds were raised by churches, popular appeals, voluntary donations, and periodic Sanitary Commission fairs in Northern cities. The Commission's mercy missions were extended, where possible, to Confederate as well as Union soldiers.

The Confederacy faced essentially the same kinds of problems that the North did, only more so, since it had to work from scratch to build both a government and a fighting machine. Its constitution established a government similar to that of the United States. The chief differences were limitation on the tariff power, the President's term (six years, no reelection), explicit recognition of "the right of property in slaves," no mention of a power to promote "the general welfare," and a new device allowing cabinet members to sit in Congress. The government proved of necessity to be nonpartisan. A new flag, the "Stars and Bars," was adopted.

The Confederate Congress initially authorized a 100,000-man volunteer army to serve for six to twelve months. After hostilities began, this was

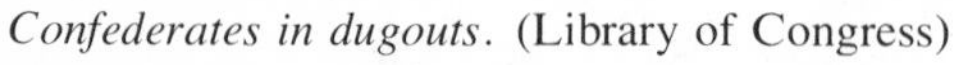

Confederates in dugouts. (Library of Congress)

increased to 400,000 to serve for three years or for the war's duration. Early volunteering, as in the North, produced more men than the government could equip, often raised and outfitted by a wealthy, prominent citizen who recruited friends and neighbors in his local community. But as volunteering dwindled in 1862, a conscription law required registration of all men between eighteen and thirty-five (later increased to forty-five and, in February, 1864, modified to include all between seventeen and fifty). The law allowed the hiring of substitutes and exempted persons in a long list of occupational groups, including anyone who owned twenty slaves, a provision that caused a great outcry against "a rich man's war and a poor man's fight." As with the Federal law, the Confederate draft worked more as a stimulus to volunteering, producing some 300,000 volunteers who wished to avoid the stigma of "conscript."

Obtaining military equipment, munitons, and supplies posed a major hurdle for the Confederacy. At the outset the Tredgar Iron Works in Richmond was the only Southern factory capable of turning out heavy artillery guns, and its capacity was limited. Slowly the South developed other munitions plants, but the output was never large. At the beginning, privately owned arms—muskets, rifles, pistols, revolvers—came from private closets and down from walls (estimates indicate that the number of pieces was substantial). Added to these during the war's first two years were imports from Europe which brought the total to perhaps 330,000 small arms. The states contributed another 270,000, and captures from the enemy are estimated as high as 100,000.

As the war lengthened, supplies of everything in the South—clothing, shoes, blankets, matches, salt, horses, and even food—became scarce. Government-operated factories, newly built, attempted in vain to keep pace with the enormous military demands. Much confusion in management, inadequate transportation facilities, and poor coordination brought on desperate shortages by mid-1863. For the rest of the war, Confederate armies labored under serious handicaps of short rations, supplies, and equipment. That they were able to hang on for so long with so little was no small achievement.

How to finance their operations was a continuous aggravation to Confederate leaders. Export-import duties, in the face of an ever-tightening Federal blockade, produced little revenue at best. A direct tax—on real estate, slaves, and other property—was reluctantly resorted to in August, 1861, but it yielded a disappointingly small $17.5 million. Not until April, 1863, was a general internal revenue measure enacted, levying taxes on sales of virtually every consumer item, on personal incomes, and on every person engaged in a business, profession, or trade. To this was added a tax-in-kind that required all farmers to contribute to the government one-tenth of all the crops they produced. Relatively ineffective, these tax measures taken together yielded only about one per cent of the Confederacy's entire income for the war. Nor did borrowing prove much more

Three Confederate prisoners. (National Archives)

successful. Bond issues at home plus the Erlanger loan in France backed by cotton yielded $712 million, making about 39 per cent of the Southern government's total income. Consequently, the Treasury under Secretaries Christopher G. Memminger and George A. Trenholm was forced to resort to running the printing presses on a massive scale. By war's end, over $1.5 billion of paper notes had been issued. In the face of this deluge, other currency and coins were hoarded, forcing people to resort to the use of postage stamps, privately issued ''shin-plasters'' (small paper notes) and tokens honored by the businessmen who issued them. A Confederate paper dollar, measured in gold, stood at 90 cents in 1861, declined to 29 cents in 1863, skidded to 4.6 cents in 1864 and to 1.7 cents in early 1865. The resulting inflation worked hardships on all sides, as Richmond prices in 1864 clearly showed: ''coats $350, pants $100, shoes $125, . . . bacon $9 per pound, . . . butter $15 per pound, chickens $30 per pair. . . .'' Since wages and salries rose only slightly, the financial pinch was universal and severe.

Such suffering as inflation produced substantially weakened Southern morale. In some areas support for the Confederacy had been scant even at the beginning. Unionist sentiment predominated throughout the counties of the Appalachian chain from Virginia to northern Alabama. In the latter, many agreed with one small farmer's complaint that the war was a slave-holder's plot—''All they want is to git you . . . [to] go fight for there infurnal negroes. . . ." In northwest Arkansas and in German-populated counties of Texas, perhaps one-third of the residents remained neutral while another third supported the Federal cause.

The Southern principle of state rights was many times invoked in resisting Richmond's efforts to concentrate authority and coordinate war efforts. Some governors like Joseph E. Brown of Georgia and Zebulon Vance of North Carolina not only dragged their feet at times but also engaged in outright defiance of Davis's government. Presidential suspension of the writ of habeas corpus, resulting in arbitrary arrests, evoked bitter denunciation and refusal to cooperate at all in some Southern areas. Georgia's legislature went so far as to proclaim the habeas corpus suspension unconstitutional and invalid.

2. *War Reshapes Law and Constitution*

What kind of conflict? In legal terms, what was the Civil War—a mass riot, an insurrection, a rebellion, or an international war? Regardless of what it was called, taking up arms against the United States was treason within the Constitution's definition of "levying war against" the nation, for which severe penalties could be imposed. On its side, the South contended that secession was legitimate, that the Confederacy was a *de jure* and *de facto* government and therefore entitled to international recognition. In the official Federal view, however, secession was illegal and Confederates were engaged in treasonous rebellion. The administration, the Congress, and the Supreme Court all supported this view, Federal documents labeling it officially as the War of the Rebellion, but implementing the theory in practice encountered complex difficulties. In actuality, the United States, while avoiding any act suggesting official recognition of the Confederacy as an independent, sovereign nation, did in fact concede belligerent rights. Lincoln's proclamation of blockade of April, 1861, was in international law an acknowledgement of belligerent status, even though not so intended by the President. When sailors from Confederate raiding ships were captured early in the war, Lincoln had to abandon his initial inclination to execute them as pirates, under threat of Confederate reprisals. Captured Southern soldiers were also treated as prisoners of war (a status accorded only to officially recognized belligerents in international practice), and although prisoner exchanges were few and infrequent, they were spasmodically negotiated throughout the struggle.

When Federal blockaders captured British ships moving into Southern harbors under Union blockade, the seizures were protested by British owners on the grounds that if no international war existed, blockade and captures were not legitimate. In the *Prize Cases* decision of 1863 the Supreme Court ruled that (1) the conflict, whatever its nature internally, was an international war so far as foreigners were concerned, (2) the war began, not by declaration by Congress, but by the President's blockade proclamation, which was

Andersonville with Union POWs. (Brown Brothers)

an exercise of his duty to repel invasion and enforce the laws. Hence from an international standpoint, the war began on April 19, 1861, and seizures of foreign ships violating the blockade after that date were legal.

Clearly participation in armed rebellion against the United States was treason, as the Constitution defined it. But what could be done with the millions of persons engaging in treasonable activities? Congress attempted to supply the answers in a series of wartime statutes. One, the Conspiracies Act of July 31, 1861, provided heavy fines and prison terms for any person guilty of conspiring to overthrow the government or to obstruct its laws. The first Confiscation Act of August 6, 1861, authorized executive seizure of all property actually used "in aid of the rebellion" or for "insurrectionary purposes." A second Confiscation Act of July 17, 1862 (also called the Treason Act) set the death penalty or heavy fine or imprisonment for conviction on treason charges but also distinguished engaging in or aiding rebellion as a separate crime from treason, with lesser penalties of fine and imprisonment. This law also imposed upon Confederate officials and others aiding the rebellion (who after sixty days failed to resume allegiance to the Union) forfeiture of all property, including slaves. Its wording unfortunately was fuzzy, and since it required the sale of confiscated property, how it would be applied to confiscated slaves remained uncertain. The second Confiscation Act, in fact, mixed a curious blend of constitutional and international law. Although the aim of the act was to punish rebellious persons by seizing their property, no provision was made for the trial and conviction of those accused of rebellion. Rather, confiscation was to be a separate action against the property of enemies (as in international law) not against the property of traitors (as in domestic, constitutional law). Lincoln's concern that confiscation of property imposed a penalty beyond the lifetime of the guilty person, in violation of the Constitution, was only partially allayed by an explanatory joint Congressional resolution.

In enforcing these statutes, the Lincoln administration followed a slow, cautious, lenient policy. Where Federal district attorneys obtained indictments on treason or lesser charges, they often acted on the advice of Attorney General Bates and allowed accused persons to remain at large on their own recognizance. Often the indictment was continued from one court term to another, and in many instances the case was eventually dismissed. Lincoln did not wish to antagonize further the border states where Federal power could enforce these laws, and farther south enforcement was impossible since no Federal courts operated at the time the laws were adopted. Significantly, the government did not execute a single person for treason, even in the face of widespread participation in rebellion. The confiscation policy was only selectively applied, the most dramatic instance being Federal seizure of Lee's estate on the Potomac at Arlington, which was later turned into a national cemetery.

National Centralization and Presidential Power. As in all of America's wars, the trend to Federal centralization of power accelerated. As noted previously, military recruiting and procurement, early handled by the states, moved into Federal hands by the war's third year. The railroads were nationalized in May, 1862 for the duration of the war. New paper currency in the form of Federal greenbacks and national bank notes, as described above, became the dominant form of currency when a Federal 10 per cent tax drove state bank notes from the marketplace. Closing both eyes to the Constitution, Congress approved West Virginia's admission as a state in 1863, thereby dividing the state of Virginia without its legitimate consent.

Along with the centralizing of power in the Federal government went an increasing domination at the center by the President. Perhaps executive domination is required by the very nature of war itself, which necessitates swift decision and quick action (for which Congress is institutionally and temperamentally unfitted). Lincoln did not hesitate to use Presidential power to the full. In the spring of 1861 his actions—calling forth the militia, proclaiming a naval blockade, spending $2 million from the Treasury, borrowing $250 million more, and suspending habeas corpus—were all done without prior authorization by Congress, which was out of session and which gave a reluctant consent months afterward.

Lincoln continued to exercise asserted presidential prerogatives and sweeping powers. In September, 1862, disregarding the slave-seizure section of the second Confiscation Act, he based his Emancipation Proclamation on his military powers as commander in chief. In December, 1863, he announced his own policy of reconstruction for the South, and later in 1864 when Congress passed a conflicting policy, he killed it with a pocket veto. And in military affairs the President provided strong executive direction as well.

Individual Liberties and National Security. At the outset Lincoln suspended the writ of habeas corpus in certain areas on his own authority, despite Congressional protests. The Constitution provided that "the privilege of the writ of habeas corpus shall not be suspended, unless when in cases of rebellion or invasion the public safety may require it." Congressional leaders insisted that this provision as part of Article I (the Article on Congress) meant that only Congress could suspend it. In September, 1862, Lincoln went further still with a proclamation subjecting "disloyal" persons to martial law and suspending the writ of habeas corpus in cases involving such persons. He did not alter his policy of arbitrary arrests of suspected security risks, even after Congress adopted the Habeas Corpus Act (March 3, 1863), authorizing the President to suspend the writ, a power which Lincoln believed the President already possessed by virtue of his military authority in wartime. The 1863 act required arresting officers to report the names of all arrested persons to the nearest Federal district court, a provision often disregarded in practice. Under Lincoln's direction the President's office and powers were much enlarged during the Civil War as powerful instruments for decisive action. The precedents set then in expanding and using executive power would later be resorted to by strong Presidents in the twentieth century.

But Lincoln's exercise of power did not go unchallenged. His actions were most questionable in the field of civil liberty—an ironic twist when after 1862 the war became a contest for the liberty of slaves. Anglo-American tradition, reinforced by the Constitution and statute law, has long maintained that every person is entitled to his day in court, to "due process of law," as the lawyers say. A few Congressmen and many citizens challenged the policy of military subjugation of the South and urged peace by negotiation. To win support they often held mass protest rallies, called for an end to fighting, denounced the administration ("Lincoln and his minions," they scoffed) for arbitrary, military arrests and detention of dissenting citizens. With habeas corpus suspended, military commanders often seized such persons on suspicion of disloyalty, without any hard evidence, and held them in military detention for periods of time running from overnight to a few days to many months. During four years of war, estimates suggest that more than 30,000 persons were so arrested and held.

Because the policy of arbitrary arrests raised serious questions for a democratic society, a closer look at its execution, effects, and rationalization is needed. In May, 1861, a Marylander named Merryman, organizer of a secessionist military company, was arrested and jailed by military authorities at Fort McHenry in Baltimore harbor. Upon application to Chief Justice Taney, a writ of habeas corpus, which requires the arresting officer either to release the suspect or bring him to court to hear charges against him and answer them, was issued and served on General George Cadwalader, who was holding Merryman prisoner. Upon direction from Washington, the general refused to produce Merryman in court, stating that he was acting under authority from the President. Outraged by this refusal, Chief Justice Taney issued an opinion declaring that (1) the President had no constitutional power to suspend the writ of habeas corpus, (2) only Congress could do so, (3) the President acted illegally, and (4) the President should insure that the "civil process of the United States . . . be . . . enforced." Lincoln took no official notice of this sharp rebuke. Defenders of the President have observed that it was remarkable that a man like Merryman taking up arms against the nation had even been able to get a lawyer and a hearing in court.

An even more sensational case involving freedom of speech and dissent arose in 1863. General Burnside, commanding the Department of the Ohio, issued General Order No. 38 that persons in "the habit of declaring sympathies for the enemy" would be arrested. In early May at a mass protest rally in Mount Vernon, Ohio, attended by 15,000 people, Democratic ex-Congressman Clement L. Vallandigham eloquently attacked Lincoln's policy of arbitrary arrest and suppression of free speech and shouted that he hereby defied "General Order No. 38, General Burnside commanding." For dramtic emphasis he threw a copy of the order on the platform, stamped on it, and asserted he would contend for individual liberty, as guaranteed in "General Order No. 1, the Constitution of the United States, General Washington commanding." In the front row of the audience two military officers in civilian clothes were busily taking notes on Vallandigham's words. Three nights later Vallandigham was routed out of his bed in his Dayton home, seized by Federal soldiers, and hustled off to military prison in Cincinnati.

Brought before a military commission, he refused to answer questions on the grounds that the military had no authority to try a civilian. His conviction and sentencing to prison for the war's duration embarrassed President Lincoln, who wishing to avoid charges of muzzling political opponents, commuted Vallandigham's sentence to banishment to the Confederacy. This, Lincoln explained in answer to Democrats' protests, was necessary because Vallandigham "was laboring . . . to prevent the raising of troops, to encourage desertions from the army" and thereby "damaging the army, upon the existence and vigor of which the life of the nation depends. . . . Must I shoot the simple-minded soldier boy who deserts [in response to such appeals as Vallandigham's], while I must not touch a hair of the wily agitator who induces him to desert?" Military necessity, dictated by self-preservation of the nation, Lincoln argued, required drastic action against Vallandigham and others like him who sought to hamstring the war effort.

Shipped off to the Confederacy, while still protesting, Vallandigham was allowed to escape by Confederate officials, who wanted no part of him, and made his way to Canada. While in Ontario, he was nominated by Ohio's Democrats as candidate for governor in 1863, ran *in absentia*, and lost by a large margin, which implied popular approval of Lincoln's action. In 1864 in a female disguise he slipped back into the country, was allowed on Lincoln's orders to remain unmolested, and took an active part in the subsequent Democratic national convention.

The question of how to balance order and freedom, authority and liberty, continued to vex Lincoln, as it has other generations of Americans. As he put it, "Must a government, of necessity, be too *strong* for the liberties of its own people, or too *weak* to maintain its own existence." The Supreme Court, although it refused to review Vallandigham's case on appeal, did speak in a later, similar case involving the conviction and sentencing to hanging of an Indiana civilian editor by a military commission. In the case of *ex parte Milligan* (1866), the Court decreed that a civilian could not be subjected to trial by a military court where there was no war or actual fighting in his immediate vicinity and where civil courts were open and functioning. A civilian's right to "due process" in wartime, even in civil war, was thereby reaffirmed.

3. Death Blow to Slavery

In acting to eliminate slavery, the United States lagged well behind other countries. Britain had ended slavery in her colonies in 1833. Latin American nations, except for Brazil, had done the same by the 1850's. In 1861 the Russian Czar decreed a plan for emancipating more than 20 million serfs. President Lincoln was fully aware of these actions taken elsewhere as he was also aware of the contention advanced by Congressman John Quincy Adams in 1837 that in time of war the President as commander in chief could strike down slavery under his military powers.

During the first year of the war Lincoln "struggled," as he said, against pressure, largely from Radical Republicans, to act against slavery. Recognizing the tenuous threads that held four border states (where slavery still existed) in the Union and the fragile unity of the North, where many still clung to the state rights' view that slavery was a domestic matter for state decision alone, Lincoln steered a cautious course. When Generals Butler and Frémont moved to emancipate slaves in their command areas, Lincoln overruled them at once, noting that Kentucky's legislature threatened extreme action and soldiers in some areas refused to fight if Frémont's order stood. In the spring of 1862 when General David Hunter declared slaves free in South Carolina, Lincoln countermanded his order. As war spread in the South, many Negroes left their homes and fled into Union army encampments, where officers often exercised their discretion in keeping them and putting them to work at military support tasks. In March, 1862, Congress prohibited officers from returning runaway slaves to their owners. Six months later War Department approval was given to the accepting of fugitives as army volunteers, an idea that was suggested in Secretary Cameron's report of December, 1861, to the President.

To these measures Lincoln gave his consent, as he did to an act of Congress (April, 1862) abolishing slavery in the District of Columbia with compensation of $300 per slave paid to owners, and to another act (June, 1862) ending slavery in Federal territories without compensation. In March of that year Lincoln offered his own proposal that "any state which may adopt gradual abolishment of slavery" be given Federal funds "to compensate" for its "change of system." His object, he said, was to lure border states, and any others, away from attachment to the "institution." In explanation, Lincoln argued that "the initiation of emancipation" with compensation would bolster border states' attachment to the Union and end the Confederacy's hope of winning them over. When the proposal lost in Congress (border state men voting against it), Lincoln called a White House conference of border state Congressmen. He told them, "If you had voted for the resolution, the war would now be substantially ended" and urged them to "reconsider" the proposal by the coming December, 1862, session of Congress.

By summer of 1862 Lincoln determined to call upon the seceded slave states to return to the Union or face loss of their slaves. Over a period of weeks he labored over preparing a proclamation of emancipation, which he submitted to his cabinet on July 22, soliciting members' suggestions as to wording and timing. Seward persuaded him to delay its issuance, in view of the recent Union army withdrawal from the Peninsula campaign, until a Federal victory provided a more opportune moment. The president agreed.

At about the same time Congress adopted the second Confiscation Act of July 17 imposing as a penalty for treason that all slaves of persons convicted of treason "shall be forever free of their servitude." As noted earlier, Lincoln gave his hesitant consent to the measure. Then in August Horace Greeley pressed for emancipation in his "Prayer of Twenty Millions" letter. Although Lincoln's mind was already made up, he gave no indication of it in his reply stating that what he did or did not do about slavery would be determined by whether he thought it would help save the Union.

At length Union success at Antietam supplied the occasion. On September 22, 1862, Lincoln issued the preliminary Emancipation Proclamation. The heart of the Proclamation declared that in those states still in rebellion on January 1, 1863, "All persons held as slaves . . . shall be then, thenceforward and forever free." For slave states, then in rebellion, that resumed their allegiance within the next 100 days (by January 1, 1863), the Proclamation promised that the President would urge the next Congress to provide "pecuniary aid" so that the states might "voluntarily adopt immediate or gradual abolishment of slavery" with compensation to owners.

True to his promise, on December 1, 1862, Lincoln's message called on Congress to adopt a constitutional amendment providing that any state providing for abolishing slavery "any time before the first day of January, 1900, shall receive compensation from the United States," from funds raised by the sale of government bonds. Here was gradual emancipation coupled with compensation for owners. States still in rebellion on January 1, 1863, would be barred from the offer. Lincoln viewed this as a just solution to a highly complex problem. He stuck to his course, although shoved and buffeted from opposing sides. Conservative Democrats, arguing that tampering with slavery would prolong the war, picked up strength in the 1862 fall elections and now urged going even slower on slavery. But Radical Republicans demanded even speedier action, as Senator Charles Sumner and others led delegations to the White House to press the President.

On January 1, 1863, the "full period of one hundred days" having passed, Lincoln signed the final Proclamation, saying, "I never, in my whole life, felt more certain that I was doing right than I do in signing this paper." Except for Tennessee and limited parts of Louisiana and Virginia, the Proclamation as issued declared that in the Confederate states, still in rebellion, "all persons held as slaves . . . are, and henceforward shall be free." The emancipation move, as Lincoln saw it, satisfied many objectives—as a matter of justice to the Negroes, as a military move to weaken the enemy, as a political necessity to blunt Radical pressures, and as a diplomatic step to forestall foreign governments' recognition of the Confederacy. It did serve all these ends. But above all, "in giving *freedom* to the *slave*, we *assure* freedom to the *free*," Lincoln announced, to make clear to all—in the South and in the world abroad—the "ultimate extinction" of slavery.

During the next few days massive celebrations and public gatherings in Washington, Philadelphia, New York, Boston, and other Northern communities greeted the news of freedom with wild enthusiasm. In Norfolk and New Orleans thousands of Negroes marched in processions of celebration. In Port Royal, South Carolina, young Negro school teacher Charlotte Forten recorded it as "the most glorious day this nation has yet seen." As Union armies pushed into the South in the coming months, thousands of Negroes hailed the "day of jubilee" by abandoning their former masters to greet their Yankee deliverers.

Lincoln's hopes for gradual, compensated emancipation as a reasonable solution to a vexing social dilemma were to be disappointed. But he was still concerned over what would happen to the freed slave in the future.

For many years Lincoln had favored some form of Negro colonization, on a voluntary basis. "I strongly favor colonization," he told Congress in December, 1863; "And yet I wish to say there is an objection urged against free colored persons remaining in the country, which is largely imaginary, if not sometimes malicious." Yet, the Negro's future in America troubled him greatly. In a statement, foreshadowing views of twentieth century black and white militants, Lincoln told a deputation of free Negroes in August, 1862: "You and we are different races. . . . Your race suffers very greatly . . . by living among us, while ours suffers from your presence. . . . [O]n this broad continent, not a single man of your race is made [by law] the equal of a single man of ours. . . . It is better for us both, therefore, to be separated." As President, his interest in voluntary colonization schemes remained strong. He not only followed closely but gave encouragement to the unsuccessful project of a free Negro colony at Chiriqui in Central America and to the disastrous attempt to settle 400 Negroes on Îsle à Vache off the coast of Haiti.

4. The Negro and the War

Lincoln's announcement of the Emancipation Proclamation in September, 1862, giving a new turn to the war, focused the nation's attention on the 4 million Negro Americans. In a war now for Negro emancipation, should not blacks also fight for their own freedom? Indeed, many Negroes had from the start been rendering large assistance in the war effort, unrecognized and unrewarded as they had been. At the outset some blacks in Northern communities had tried to volunteer for military service, only to be turned away. It took dogged persistence for a black man to join, as Nicholas Biddle did when he volunteered for the company recruited in his home town of Pottsville, Pennsylvania, donned the uniform, and accompanied his unit to Washington. In July, 1861, newspapers reported the astonishing exploit of William Tillman, a Negro steward aboard a Northern merchant ship high-jacked by Confederates at sea. Before reaching a Southern port, Tillman engineered an uprising, seized the ship, and sailed it into New York harbor. Farther south at Charleston in May, 1862, Negro sailor Robert Smalls took over a converted Confederate gunboat at dockside, brazenly sailed it past harbor defenses, and delivered it to the Union blockading squadron just offshore.

As Yankee forces launched invasions at various points scattered from Virginia to western Tennessee to the Gulf coast, they found Negroes elated and enthusiastic over the bluecoats' appearance. As one observer recorded, "the first Federal troops were almost smothered by welcoming blacks." At Pensacola, Admiral David Porter noted "Negroes grinning from ear to ear and turning somersaults to show their delight . . . [and] true affection for the old flag." But in addition to providing a welcome, Southern blacks rendered practical help. Not only did they labor at fortifications, wagon loading, toting supplies, and the like when set to work by Butler and other field commanders, but they often provided the best "eyes and ears" Yankee invaders could command. Where Northern troops were new to the areas they moved into, local Negroes were familiar with the terrain, roads, paths, streams, bridges and towns. Coming into Yankee camps, they gave invaluable aid as guides and as intelligence gatherers in the surrounding countryside. General Abner Doubleday (inventor of the game of baseball earlier) ordered all Negroes admitted to his lines because "they bring much valuable information which cannot be obtained from other sources." Another officer noted that "they also know, and have frequently exposed, the haunts of Secession spies . . . and the existence of rebel organizations."

At sea as well as on land contrabands helped the Union cause. In the waters of Chesapeake Bay, off the Carolina coast, off Georgia, and elsewhere, small fishing craft bearing blacks frequently approached Union blockading vessels and offered their services. Again since they knew well the local waterways, the shoals, sandbars, inlets, and anchorages, they served often as guides, even in some instances as pilots steering Federal ships safely through treacherous waters. The navy welcomed their help and began enlisting them as early as August, 1861, as cooks, coal heavers, firemen, and gunners aboard ship.

The first effort to recruit Negro soldiers was made in the spring of 1862 by Union General David Hunter in the Sea Islands of South Carolina. Hunter organized the First South Carolina Volunteer Regiment, grew discouraged over lack of support from Washington, but was happy to see them mustered in officially in November, 1862. Meanwhile General Butler, in command of the Department of the Gulf at New Orleans, having repeatedly pleaded with Washington for reinforcements in vain, turned to enlisting local free blacks. Reviving the tradition of free Negroes defending New Orleans as they had done in 1815 under Andrew Jackson, Butler organized the First Regiment of Louisiana Native Guards, had them mustered into Federal service in September, and assigned them to defensive stations at the forts guarding the entrance to the mouth of the Mississippi.

Reports reaching the North of substantial numbers of Negroes within areas held by Union forces in the South inspired efforts to provide for their transition out of slavery. Voluntary aid societies sprang up in black communities in Northern cities gathering funds to send supplies to their brethren southward. Teachers were recruited, and in March, 1862, a first contingent of fifty-three teachers headed for the Sea Islands. In Washington the Contraband Relief Association was organized under the lead of Mrs. Elizabeth Keckley, who had served as dressmaker for Mrs. Lincoln since the start of the President's term.

Meanwhile Lincoln's proposals for the colonization of freed Negroes abroad encountered general negative reaction and protests for Negro spokesmen. Public meetings in the North, petitions to the President, and even delegations to the White House spoke sharply against it. Only a handful of blacks responded positively to Martin R. Delany's and James Redpath's proposals for emigration to Haiti, while Liberia's agent in America, Edward W. Blyden, found that his plea to "come help us build up a Nationality in Africa" went largely unheeded. But President Joseph J. Roberts of Liberia was received at the White House in August, 1862, as the United States formally gave diplomatic recognition after a quarter century's delay. At the same time Robert Purvis best summed up the general Negro feeling on colonization: "The children of the black man have enriched the soil by their tears, and sweat, and blood. Sir, we were born here, and here we choose to remain."

Lincoln's Emancipation Proclamation, greeted with rejoicing by Negroes when first announced in September, 1862, contained in its final form on January 1, 1863, the promise that freed slaves would be "received into the armed service of the United States." As early as 1861 Secretary of War Cameron had noted that Negroes constituted a potential military resource, but fears and prejudice against employing Negro troops remained strong. In 1862 a beginning was made, as noted above, by Hunter and Butler. But not until early 1863 did the War Department move on a broad front to develop Negro recruiting. Secretary Stanton issued authorization to Northern Governors, and Governor John A. Andrew swiftly organized the Massachusetts Fifty-Fourth Regiment as the first Northern all-Negro unit, which shortly set sail for Charleston harbor. There on July 18 it bore the brunt of the assault on Fort Wagner. Other Northern states, led by Rhode Island, rapidly followed suit during the summer. As Negro enlistments mounted, Frederick Douglass commented: "Once let the black man get upon his person the brass letters U.S., . . . an eagle on his button, and a musket on his shoulder . . . , and there is no power on earth which can deny that he has earned the right to citizenship in the United States."

Meanwhile Adjutant General Lorenzo Thomas had been sent to the Mississippi Valley to recruit Negroes, who, he reported, "eagerly seek to enter military organization." In fact, Thomas's efforts, bolstered by the War Department's new Bureau of Colored Troops employed field officers and special agents George L. Stearns and Augustus L. Chetlain as recruiters in Tennessee, Kentucky, and elsewhere. They produced 20,830 black volunteers by the end of 1863. These were in addition to some 15,000 recruited in the lower Mississippi Valley area by Generals Butler and Banks.

All told, during the war 178,975 Negro soldiers served in Federal armies. About 40 per cent came from the lower Mississippi region, with a total of 90,000 drawn from all seceded states, close to 40,000 from the border, and 50,000 from the North. Blacks constituted close to one-eighth of the entire Federal forces by the last year of the war.

At first prejudice and discrimination assigned black troops lower pay (Negro privates got $7 per month as compared to $11 for whites), poorer quarters, inferior weapons, and less medical-hospital care. Not until June,

A black gun crew that took part in the battle of Nashville. (Chicago Historical Society)

1864, did Congress eradicate the differential in pay, making the raise retroactive to January 1. Negro soldiers also resented their initial deployment almost exclusively on labor details and guard and garrison duty. But in time Negro fighting units were fully engaged at Milliken's Bend and Port Hudson in the Vicksburg campaign, later in the east Tennessee Union drive and in Sherman's capture of Atlanta. General Thomas noted prejudice in the army diminishing "since blacks have fully shown their fighting qualities and manliness," dispelling white doubts. The New York *Times*, commenting on black troops in the Port Hudson battle, observed: "No body of troops—Western, Eastern or rebel—have fought better in the war." In August, 1863, noting the Negro participation at Port Hudson and Milliken's Bend, Lincoln reported that "some of our commanders in the field . . . believe that . . . the use of colored troops constitute the heaviest blow yet dealt to the rebels, and that at least one of these important successes could not have been achieved . . . but for the aid of black soldiers."

Although at first Negro officers were not employed, in time almost 100 Negroes held commissions. When Grant mounted the 1864 Petersburg campaign, twenty-two black regiments marched with him, while Butler's cooperating Army of the James counted fifteen Negro regiments. By December, impressed by Negro fighting skill, Grant organized the all-black

XXV Corps. Among Negro troops, casualties ran extremely high; out of 178,000 soldiers who served, some 38,000 lost their lives. Their record was an impressive one—battling in almost every part of the South, where capture by the enemy meant abuse, torture, or as at Fort Pillow even execution. Black women, too, served with distinction, notably Harriet Tubman and Susie King Taylor who worked as nurses alongside Clara Barton in providing medical attention in the Sea Islands. In the Union navy also 29,511 Negroes formed about one-fourth of the total enlistments, with their battle casualties and related deaths running to over 2,800.

As to the Negro's wartime service, Ben Butler later summed it up best, though perhaps over-optimisitcally, declaring that the Negro soldier "with the bayonet . . . unlocked the iron-barred gates of prejudice, and opened new fields of freedom." But opening "new fields of freedom" required action by Congress and the voters. As black soldiers charged forward with Grant and Sherman, Congress and the nation, too, moved forward toward Negro freedom.

In January, 1865, a number of doors swung open for Negroes. Both Missouri and Tennessee proclaimed that "all persons held to service of labor" were now free, and Illinois repealed her discriminatory legislation against Negroes. At the national level Senator Lyman Trumbull introduced a constitutional amendment to eliminate "involuntary servitude." Adopted quickly by the Senate in April, 1864, it at first fell short of the required two-thirds support in the House until January, 1865, when enough Democrats shifted their votes. Sent to the states for ratification, the Thirteenth Amendment, in diametrical contrast to the abortive one of 1861, became an official part of the Constitution on December 18, 1865.

9

The Fighting Ends

Because the Civil War in America had repercussions abroad, each belligerent sought to gain advantage by a shrewdly directed foreign policy. As Confederates tried to win diplomatic recognition and foreign aid, United States policy aimed to ward off foreign intervention of any sort (recognition, aid, or mediation) in what Washington held to be strictly a domestic affair. After early difficulties Union efforts, reinforced by military victories and other favorable factors, succeeded in neutralizing the threat of Europe's influencing the war's outcome.

At home old political combinations, facing new challenges, had to adapt or lose their followings. Republican dominance prevailed throughout the war, as Democrats fell into partial eclipse. Partly war-inspired, partly reflecting interest group demands, government policies produced major, revolutionary changes in tariffs, subsidies, land policy, banking, currency, education, immigration, financing, and taxes. The resulting changes would reshape the American economy for generations after the guns fell silent at Appomattox.

1. Politics Abroad: Keeping Europe Neutral

The war in America was reflected in a diplomatic struggle abroad. In 1861 the Confederate government, belatedly awakening to the necessity of foreign aid in a long war, sought recognition and material support from European powers. In response, Washington labored to block European aid and diplomatic recognition. European rulers, particularly in Britain, while holding no brief for slavery, were apprehensive over possible infection from the success of American democracy. Consequently, they watched happily as American unity cracked in 1861. Many English leaders, who had long resented America's growing commercial-industrial strength, wished for success of the South, which was after all England's best supplier of raw cotton and a major customer for British manufactured goods. In less than a month after Sumter, Britain and France boosted Southern hopes by recognizing the Confederacy's status as a belligerent, though not as a sovereign independent government.

Seeking more tangible aid, the Southern government sent emissaries William L. Yancey, Pierre A. Rost, and A. Dudley Mann to England, France, Belgium, Russia, and Spain on a mission aiming to win treaties of friendship and commerce. In November, 1861, Confederate diplomatic commissioners James M. Mason and John Slidell en route to London and Paris were seized at sea when the Federal warship, Captain Charles Wilkes's *San Jacinto*, intercepted the British mail packet, the *Trent*, on which they were traveling, and removed them. Hailed at home as heroic, Wilkes's action roused a storm of British protest. A contingent of 8,000 British troops was rushed to Canada, and an ultimatum was delivered to Washington. Having interfered with a neutral ship on the high seas, in contradiction of long-standing American-espoused principles, the Lincoln administration faced a potentially explosive crisis. After some deliberation, Seward dispatched a soothing reply to England's protest and released Mason and Slidell, who were allowed to go on to Europe. England expressed satisfaction, and the two-month *Trent* affair happily blew over without a showdown.

Confederate commissioners vigorously pushed their "King Cotton" diplomacy offering large supplies of cotton at bargain rates well below war-inflated prices in return for delivery of arms, war materials, guns, ships, and supplies. Although English warehouses bulged with cotton left over from huge harvests of 1859 and 1860, Confederates achieved some success in obtaining supplies. In France they even succeeded in securing the help of the Erlanger banking firm in floating a loan, secured by pledging future delivery of cotton, but the ultimate proceeds were disappointingly small.

Their best coup came in placing contracts with English shipyards for building vessels for Confederate use. Since British neutrality laws prohibited the sale of warships to belligerents, the yards turned out the basic ship hulls, which upon taking trial runs were allowed to "escape" to ports in the Azores or the Bahamas, where guns were obtained and fitted into the already prepared gun emplacements on board. Eighteen such raiding ships, known as cruisers, made their way into Confederate service and operated in the Atlantic, Pacific, and as far away as the Indian Ocean. During the course of the war they sank hundreds of Yankee wooden vessels to the tune of over $19 million in losses. The most flamboyant of the Confederate raiders, the 1,040-ton *Alabama* commanded by Captain Rafael Semmes, after accounting for sixty-two Yankee captures, was at length brought to bay by the U.S.S. *Kearsarge*, and in a spectacular gun duel off Cherbourg, France, was finally sent to the bottom on June 19, 1864. An even more serious threat to the North's control of the sea developed when Confederate naval agent, Captain James D. Bulloch, contracted with the Laird shipyard to design and construct speedy ironclad ships carrying a sharp, steel-tipped prow. Dubbed the "Laird rams," such ships, if they got into action, could have swiftly destroyed Union navy wooden vessels, broken the ever-tightening economic blockade, and opened the South's ports to a flow of European supplies that could have spelled Southern victory.

Several factors operated to blunt the thrust of the Confederate diplomatic offensive. For one, British dependence on Southern cotton lessened greatly with the development of alternative sources in Egypt and India. As crop failures hit English grain farmers, the North's "King Wheat" began to displace "King Cotton." The effects of Confederate appeals to the British public were counteracted by the labors of Lincoln's counter propagandists dispatched to Britain—journalist Thurlow Weed, abolitionist clergyman Henry Ward Beecher (brother of Harriet Beecher Stowe), and ex-governor of Kansas Robert J. Walker. In consequence, pro-Southern sentiment began to decline.

Recognition of the Confederacy and intervention by mediation remained a possibility well into the war's second year. In the summer of 1862 (following Lee's second Bull Run victory) British cabinet leaders informally agreed that the time was ripe to move jointly with French Emperor Napoleon III in his standing offer to pursue joint Franco-British mediation of the American conflict. Napoleon, with French troops committed in Mexico in support of Prince Maximilian, his puppet ruler there, eagerly sought the disruption of the United States. Then came the success of the Federal forces at Antietam and Lincoln's Emancipation Proclamation. Henry Adams, secretary of the United States legation, wrote home from London: "The Emancipation Proclamation has done more for us here than all our former victories and all our diplomacy . . . creating an almost convulsive reaction in our favor." The next month England rejected outright Napoleon's proposal for making a joint offer of a six-month armistice in America. In December, 1862, after the Fredericksburg disaster, Napoleon, proceeding alone, made his offer, which Lincoln coolly declined.

The Union's most effective instrument in the diplomatic struggle was Charles Francis Adams, minister to London. Son and grandson of a President with an English boarding school and Harvard education, former Congressman Adams proved to be a man of cultured gentility, intellectual prowess, and stubborn grit, a superb diplomat whose worth matched that of a Union army division. Backed by a Union threat to loose a "flood of privateers" on Britain's nominally neutral shipping, Adams painstakingly gathered evidence in the form of affadavits from Laird shipyard workers on the nature of the ships under construction, gun emplacements and all, intended for delivery to the Confederates. This evidence he presented to the foreign office. In April, 1863, he persuaded Her Majesty's government to detain the newly constructed cruiser, the *Alexandra*. Three months later the news of Vicksburg and Gettysburg bolstered Adams's position to the point where he demanded that the British foreign secretary seize the "Laird rams" that were about to be launched. He warned that if the "rams" were allowed to sail, "it would be superfluous in me to point out to your lordship that this is war." Adams's warning probably simply reinforced a decision already made by the British government. The order went out to hold the "Laird rams" in port. The Union blockade, and with it, ultimate military victory, was now assured. The British showed no further inclination either to intervene or strengthen the Confederacy. In 1864 Richmond played one last, desperate card—offering to abolish slavery in return for recognition and aid—but London and Paris were no longer listening.

During the war years a curious confluence of events—civil conflict in America and in central Europe—drew autocratic Russia and democratic United States closer together. Resembling each other in certain ways—each having pushed its frontiers across a continent, each having retained human servitude long beyond its time, each moving to emancipation at about the same time—the two nations had experienced little contact with each other. In late 1863 squadrons of Russia's naval fleet put in at New York and San Francisco, where expressions of good will were exchanged and Russians were entertained gaily and hailed as friends. Even though an uprising in Russian Poland and a threatened Anglo-French intervention there motivated Russia's sending her fleets out of European waters, most Americans hailed the naval visits as gestures of good will at a time when all Europe appeared unsympathetic if not hostile to the United States.

2. Politics at Home: Reshaping the Economy

While the foreign front was being secured, battling on the political front at home went on. The Republican Party, controlling both the executive and legislative branches, was a coalition of diverse political factions and economic interest groups linked initially by a common opposition to slavery's westward extension. In mid-1861 the outnumbered Radical wing of the party, composed mainly of ardent prewar abolitionists, went along with more moderate members, chiefly of Whig and Democratic ancestry, in declaring that the war's sole purpose was to restore the Union. By December, however, Radicals refused to reaffirm that stand and began demanding more vigorous military campaigning against the South and an immediate end to slavery. Led by spokesmen like Thaddeus Stevens, George W. Julian, and Schuyler Colfax in the House, Charles Sumner, Benjamin F. Wade, and Zachariah Chandler in the Senate, Radicals urged swifter change, especially in pushing confiscation and emancipation, rigorous prosecution of the war and elimination of slow-moving Democratic generals from army commands. While Radicals had large doubts about Lincoln, the more numerous moderate Republicans were willing to follow Lincoln's cautious, plodding lead in matters relating to the war's prosecution and slavery. But on questions of economic policy Republicans of all stripes stood shoulder to shoulder.

In opposition the Democratic party was badly ruptured by the loss of its Southern wing, the death of its leader, Stephen Douglas in June, 1861, and the shift of some eminent Democrats to Republican ranks. It shuffled along under leaders like Samuel S. "Sunset" Cox, George H. Pendleton, Daniel Vorhees, and Erastus Corning in the House and under James A. Bayard, Reverdy Johnson, and Garrett Davis in the Senate. Many Democrats like Secretary of War Stanton and Senator Andrew Johnson became staunch, consistent supporters of the war and the administration. Others like

Vallandigham went into practically total opposition to all administration efforts, while the outnumbered, outvoted bulk of the party's moderates like Cox gave war measures a grudging support but denounced the administration's disregard of civil liberties and economic legislation.

In the economic field, Republicans demonstrated their familiarity with the political axiom that a political party to survive and succeed must satisfy the wishes of its constituency. Since the party's main constituents were Northern farming, manufacturing, and business interests, not surprisingly Republican leaders pushed speedily through Congress a series of economic measures favorable to farm and business interests that settled issues of long standing and injected a powerful stimulant into the already expanding economy. In 1861, as noted above, Republican votes enacted two tariff acts (February and August) that boosted rates to protect American manufacturers, especially iron-steel makers, from foreign competition. In 1862 and again in 1864 tariff revision reduced the free list and raised duties until the overall average of tariff rates stood at about 47 per cent, more than twice the prewar level. The obvious beneficiaries of this program of indirect government subsidy were Northeastern manufacturing interests, who had helped elect the party in 1860.

Another group of Republican constituents, farmers of the North, were not neglected. In 1862 the long-debated Homestead Act passed, allowing any person to obtain free a quarter section (160 acres) of government land in the public domain on condition of occupying it for five years and making specified improvements, including a dwelling, on it. In the same year the (Justin) Morill Land Grant College Act offered each state a parcel of public domain land (amounting to 30,000 acres for each of its Congressional representatives) on condition that the state establish a college offering education in agriculture and mechanical arts. Although Atlantic seaboard states already well supplied with colleges were slow to accept the Federal offer, states from New York and Pennsylvania westward responded quickly. Most of today's great state universities originated with this law. Approving wholeheartedly, Lincoln had declared farming "a field for the profitable and agreeable combination of labor with cultivated thought. . . . [Education] gives access to whatever has already been discovered by others. . . . Some knowledge of Botany assists in dealing . . . with all growing crops. Chemistry assists in the analysis of soils, selection and application of manures . . . . The mechanical branches of Natural Philosophy are ready to help in almost everything; . . . especially . . . in implements and machinery." Holding these ideas, Lincoln readily and understandably signed another act (May 15, 1862) creating the Department of Agriculture to provide farmers with sample seeds and plants and with scientific information for improving farming methods, crops, and livestock.

Not only manufacturing and farming received generous attention, but the Republican-run Congress acted swiftly on the transportation front as well.

No longer thwarted by Southern insistence on a Southern route for a transcontinental railroad, Congress in the Pacific Railroad Act of 1862 approved a central route running from Omaha, Nebraska, to Oakland, California. Since all conceded that private capital alone was insufficient for the job, Congress chartered and gave direct aid to two companies—the Union Pacific Railroad to built west from Omaha and the Central Pacific to build eastward from San Francisco Bay. Each railroad received from the government a free 400-foot-wide right of way, a gift of ten sections (6,400 acres) on alternate sides of the right of way for each mile of track built (doubled in amount in 1864), and government loans of $16,000 for each mile of track laid over level terrain, $48,000 in mountain country, and $32,000 in in-between areas. Altogether the government donated over 15.5 million acres. Little work was done while the war lasted, but in the postwar era the promoters, amassing immense fortunes from government largesse, pushed ahead rapidly, using Irish immigrants and Union war veterans as construction crews to lay the 1,086 miles of Union Pacific track and imported Chinese labor gangs to build the 689-mile Central Pacific. On May 10, 1869, the lines were finally joined in an elaborate ceremony at Promontory Point near Ogden, Utah, where Leland Stanford, a Central Pacific promoter and ex-Governor of California, hammered home the final, golden spike to "strengthen the bonds of union between the Atlantic and Pacific coasts." The feat of constructing the railroad across the broad, dry plains and over the staggering mountains was clearly an impressive, historic achievement for nineteenth century Americans.

While railroads won lavish Federal support, the nation's financial community, too, attracted Republican attention. As described above, Congress adopted the National Bank Acts of 1863 and 1864. The resulting new national banking system produced a degree of order and stability out of the banking chaos dating from Jackson's day. But its inelastic currency arrangement, tending to contract national bank notes as government bonds were redeemed and its unfair administration favoring Northeastern interests during the system's first fifty years created inequities that eventually led to a major overhaul incorporated in the Federal Reserve Banking Act of 1913.

After a temporary, brief slowdown due to uncertainties of the war's first year, the Northern economy enjoyed a boom. Little wonder, what with favorable Congressional legislation and war-generated demand for all manner of farm and manufactured goods. A wave of inflation resulted. The general price index standing at 100 in 1861, climbed to 135 by 1863, and hit 179 in 1865. How much real economic growth arose from the war is debated by economic historians. But there is little doubt that massive government spending at the rate of $2 million a day stimulated expansion and mechanization in agriculture and spurred production in industries turning out shoes, uniforms, wagons, guns, steel, and countless other products for the war machine's insatiable maw.

While demand for labor in Northern industry rose steadily and nudged wages upward, wage increases were still pitifully slow and small, dwarfed by spiralling inflation. The real wage index, indicating actual buying power, declined from 100 in January, 1861, to 89 two years later to 67 in April, 1865. The need for labor spurred efforts to stimulate immigration, which slumped from its prewar annual average of over 300,000 to only 72,000 in 1862. Federal naturalization requirements were relaxed to confer immediate citizenship upon any alien volunteering for army service. In December, 1863, Lincoln, reporting to Congress "a great deficiency of laborers in every field," urged action to encourage immigration. In response Congress enacted the contract labor law of July, 1864, permitting the importing of laborers under contract to American employers with their future wages or prospective homesteads pledged in advance to repay the cost of their migrating. In consequence the flow of newcomers jumped to 180,000 in 1865 and to 332,000 the following year. The manpower to run America's machines, mines, mills, railroads, and farms in their phenomenal postwar upsurge was gathering for the full-scale industrial revolution that would change the face of the land and the lives of virtually all Americans.

Wartime business pursuits laid the basis of individual fortunes that American businessmen like Stanford, Huntington, Morgan, Rockefeller, Mellon, Carnegie, and others would amass in the postwar years. Capital accumulation, so crucial for industrial expansion, zoomed upward as rifles cracked at Shiloh and men lay dying in the cornfield at Antietam. America's economy would emerge from the war, its face turned from an agrarian past looking toward a complex urban-industrial future. A staggering change was encompassed in a single lifetime. John D. Rockefeller, for example, born on a farm while Van Buren occupied the White House, peddling farm produce during the war, would soon hawk kerosene from a horsecart on Cleveland's streets after the war and would live to see his giant Standard Oil Company provide fuel for millions of cars jamming American cities before he died, as Franklin D. Roosevelt entered upon his second term as President.

In politics the Republicans who did so much to stimulate the revolutionary changes in America's economy and society retained their power at Washington throughout the war. Politics were not suspended as they might have been during critical junctures when the nation's very survival teetered in the balance. The shattered Democrats made a seeming recovery in the 1862 mid-term elections but still remained divided, uncertain, and ineffective. At times resorting to pointless obstructionism, they remained a critical opposition, denouncing arbitrary military arrests, resisting new economic handouts by the government, supporting military measures and appropriations but at the same time urging a negotiated peace with the Union restored to end the lengthening "brutal war." Many Democrats found themselves tarred, in many instances quite unfairly, with the label of "Copperheads" and disloyalists if not outright traitors. Many Peace Democrats, representing a throwback to the Jacksonian agrarian tradition, were concerned that Western agriculture was being subordinated to Eastern industrial-financial interests and that a traditionally state-rights Federal union was being submerged in an all-encompassing centralized nationalism. Their concerns had basis in fact.

What they proposed as an alternative reflected a wishful yearning for what had been: call a halt to fighting, hold a full-scale convention with the South included, and amend the Constitution to reinsure state rights. Thereby, they said, the Union would be rejoined and the former agrarian combination restored to rightful power. Unrealistic as the proposal was, Peace Democrats did not favor dividing the Union. Their rallying cry was "The Constitution as it is, the Union as it was." Some secret societies like the Knights of the Golden Circle and the Sons of Liberty, composed of Peace Democrats and operating mainly in the old Northwest, allegedly engaged in treasonable activities, but the evidence suggests that only a small number of Copperheads who even bordered on treason lacked the courage or skill to carry out any plans for action. More often Democrats focused their critical fire on military conscription, Lincoln's "despotism," and the Emancipation Proclamation, which changed the war's purpose from saving the Union to a crusade against slavery. Democratic newspaper editors rained a barrage of denunciation on the administration, some finding their newspapers suppressed and winding up in jail for a time, only to renew their outcry on being released from the "military bastille."

At their national nominating convention in Chicago in 1864, Democrats sought to satisfy advocates of both sides of the question. They named McClellan as the Presidential candidate to capture the "hawk" vote and included in their platform a plank calling for "a negotiated peace, with the Union restored," to win the "dove" vote. It was an ingenious approach and might well have succeeded.

Among Radical Republicans resenting Lincoln's "go-slow-on-slavery" approach and seeming softness toward the South, some got up a move to dump him in favor of Chase. When the Chase "boomlet" collapsed, a splinter group pinned their hopes on Frémont. The main body of Republicans, however, absorbing War Democrats into a Union Party, nominated Lincoln in June with Andrew Johnson as his running mate. During the summer of 1864 Lincoln found himself prodded by Greeley and others to make peace and by Stevens and others to make war more aggressively. Discouraged over the prospects, he recorded his feeling privately in August, 1864: ". . . it seems exceedingly probable that this administration will not be reelected. Then it will become my duty to so cooperate with the President-elect, as to save the Union between the election and the inauguration."

But rapidly changing events made such action unnecessary. General Sherman's capture of Atlanta on September 2 strengthened the Union Party's appeal among the voters, and Lincoln won at the polls in November. His victory, Democrats charged, was determined by Republican manipulation of the "soldier vote." Soldiers known to be Republicans were granted furloughs to go home to vote and Democratic soldiers were refused, while for states allowing absentee voting, soldiers in the field were able to obtain only Union-Republican ballots. Whatever irregularities there may have been (and Democrats were convinced these were large enough to turn the outcome), the final tally gave McClellan 1.8 million votes (45 per cent of the total popular vote), while Lincoln won 2.2 million (55 per cent) and a renewed lease on the White House.

3. The Bloody Road to Appomattox, 1864–1865

Before the election results were in, the Federal military machine had thundered into high gear. Early in 1864 General Grant, fresh from his successes in Tennessee and the west, went east to Washington and met Lincoln for the first time. The president now named Grant to the army's highest position, and as Lieutenant General, Grant took full command of all Union military operations. A less glamorous, less likely appearing military chief than Grant could scarcely have been found. Short, stubby, shy, laconic, careless of dress, eternal cigar clamped between his teeth, unseen inner tensions relieved with an occasional whiskey binge, Grant revealed none of the outward flair or conceit of the elegant McClellan. But he had guts, shrewdness, precision in planning, stubborn determination, and a direct approach. "The art of war," he observed, "is simple enough. Find out where your enemy is. Get him as soon as you can. Strike him as hard as you can and keep moving on."

Grant's overall plan for ending the conflict was simple enough—apply a giant, deadly pincer to the Confederacy's heart and crush the life out of it. Send "Uncle Billy" Sherman's western army on a wide swing through Georgia and then north into the Carolinas, while Grant rammed the Army of the Potomac south through Virginia, trapping the remaining rebel forces under Lee and Johnston in the closing jaws of the Federal vise.

In May, 1864, Sherman rolled out of Chattanooga with his 60,000-man army and steadily hammered Joe Johnston's faltering Confederates back toward Atlanta, the key rail center of the Southeast. In a series of hard fought engagements Sherman drove off the defenders and forced his way in, occupying Atlanta on September 2. A large rebel army under General John B. Hood, moving away from Sherman, shoved off on a diversionary thrust into Tennessee, only to be smashed in a crushing defeat at the hands of General Thomas's veterans at Nashville in December. By that time "war-is-hell" Sherman had bulldozed a sixty-mile-wide swath of destruction and desolation "from Atlanta to the sea," capturing Savannah as "a Christmas present" for President Lincoln. Heading his troops north into the "hell-hole of secession," South Carolina, he seized Columbia on February

17, 1865. There, a fire, whether accidental or purposely set was undetermined, broke out and gutted the city. In less than a week the ports of Charleston and Wilmington, the last major Atlantic harbors open to accommodate blockade-runners, fell into Federal hands. Without pause, Sherman's army blazed ahead, pounding Johnston's outnumbered, weary veterans, to reach by mid-March a point in North Carolina scarcely 150 miles south of Petersburg where Grant's forces were gnawing at Richmond's defenses.

Meanwhile in May, 1864, Grant's Army of the Potomac, numbering 118,000 soldiers, shoved south across the Rapidan River. Sooner than expected, they smacked into Lee's 60,000-man army in the rough terrain of the Wilderness near Chancellorsville where for two days amid a hail of gunfire and a hell of forest fire the two giants mauled each other mercilessly. Where previous Union commanders paused or withdrew after battle, Grant drove on. He hit the entrenched rebels again four days later at Spottsylvania, where at the "bloody angle" in Lee's defense line Federal assaults, firing, and bayoneting produced what one veteran called "the most terrible twenty-four hours . . . in the war." By midnight rebel lines cracked under the relentless pounding, but their resistance had cost Grant 7,000 casualties.

Again shifting eastward to flank Lee, "Butcher" Grant slugged on "hurrying young men to their deaths," hurling wave on wave of assault troops against the new rebel earthworks only to be checked again in the savage slaughter at Cold Harbor ten miles northeast of Richmond. When General Butler's coordinated offensive, repeating McClellan's Peninsular campaign of two years earlier, sputtered out, Grant swung his entire army around Lee's eastern flank to charge at Richmond from the south. But Confederate defenses held firm at Petersburg twenty miles south of the Confederate capital. At that point, as Grant settled in for a long, drawn out seige, "the spade took the place of the musket." In the preceding seven weeks Federal casualties reached 60,000 men, while Confederates lost 31,000. Although Federal losses were equal to Lee's entire army at the start of the campaign, Yankee casualties were soon replaced from the North's seemingly limitless manpower pool, while Lee's losses were irreplaceable, bringing the inevitable end closer.

"I'll fight it out on this line, if it takes all summer," Grant growled over his cigar at the Petersburg seige lines. And he did, and it did—take all summer, all fall, and winter as well. For nine dreary, messy months Federal beseiging forces probed, prodded, punched, and pounded Petersburg defense works, denting, twisting, and stretching the lines westward, bending but not breaking them, cutting two of the three rail supply lines from farther south, as the Grant stranglehold squeezed tighter.

To relieve the pressure on Petersburg-Richmond defenses, Lee resorted to the diversionary tactics that earlier in the war had worked so well under Jackson. General Jubal Early's small Confederate force was sent to the

Shenandoah Valley. After checking a Federal army there, "Jubal's raiders" made a swift dash into Maryland, actually penetrated Washington's outskirts, and gave the capital's leaders and residents a "terrible fright" before marching back to Virginia. To check such raids and to cork up one of Richmond's supply areas in the Shenandoah Valley, Grant now dispatched General Philip Sheridan with orders "to eat up Virginia clear and clean as far as you can go" so that "nothing . . . be left to invite the enemy to return . . . [and] the Shenandoah Valley [will] remain a barren waste." A few months later, Sheridan, having scourged the valley in Sherman style, reported to Grant: "A crow would have had to carry its rations if it had flown across the Valley." Early in 1865 his force rejoined Grant's for the final crunch on Petersburg-Richmond.

The combined pile-driving blows of Sherman, Sheridan, and Grant left the Confederates reeling. Sherman's march for 500 miles unopposed through the center of the South convinced many Confederates that further fighting was futile. The rate of desertion increased to such a point that in September, 1864, President Davis lamented, "two-thirds of our [army] men are absent . . . most of them absent without leave." As the Union blockade pinched tighter, and as transportation facilities broke down, common articles of consumption like coffee, tea, salt, and clothing became increasingly rare. Food riots erupted at Atlanta, Richmond, and Mobile; women at Mobile marched under banners reading "Bread or Blood" and broke into stores appropriating what they wanted. The squeeze grew even more severe after August, 1864, when Admiral Farragut, lashed to the rigging of his ship and shouting "Damn the torpedoes, full speed ahead!", gunned his way into Mobile harbor and sealed off the Confederacy's last major Gulf port.

Discontent and criticism of the Confederate regime mounted to the point where the government moved to extend the suspension of the writ of habeas corpus. In some states, like Georgia and North Carolina, governors refused to honor requisitions for supplies from Richmond and even threatened to call back to their states troops serving in Virginia and elsewhere. Desperation was reflected in Davis's recommendation and the Richmond Congress's approval in March, 1865, of emancipating slaves for service as soldiers in the army.

Peace feelers, initiated by Francis P. Blair, Sr., received an eager response from Richmond in January, 1865. President Lincoln himself went to meet with his old friend, Confederate Vice President Alexander Stephens, on board the *River Queen*, a Federal ship anchored at Hampton Roads. On one side of a blank sheet of paper Lincoln wrote his peace terms: (1) reunion, (2) end of slavery, (3) disbanding of hostile armies. Handing the sheet to Stephens, he said he would accept any other nonconflicting terms the latter wished to write on the other side. Since the Confederacy held out for cessation of fighting with other matters left open to subsequent negotiation, the conference broke up in disagreement. Lincoln went on to confer with Grant and Sherman indicating that he wished generous terms of surrender extended to the Confederates when the end came.

In the meantime Grant had stretched the rebel defense lines before Petersburg so ominously thin that his major attack on April 1, 1865, at Five Forks sixteen miles southwest of Petersburg broke through and severed the last rail line into that city from the South. In haste the Davis government fled Richmond, which Federal forces occupied on April 3. Heading westward toward Danville trudged Lee's exhausted veterans, Union troops snapping at their heels. A Massachusetts volunteer in the pursuing force wrote in his diary on April 6: we "sent a few shots after the rebs as a caution for them to hurry up and get out of our way. . . . Forward men! Double quick! . . . The battle [Sailor's Creek] was completely won. More than 300 wagons were taken—with artillery—hundreds of horses and mules and 2,000 prisoners." The next day Lee, his retreat route cut off, asked for terms. On Palm Sunday, April 9, natty in a spotless uniform, Lee met the mud-begrimed Grant in the parlor of Wilmer McClean's farmhouse at Appomattox Court House and offered his sword in surrender, which Grant graciously declined.

In accordance with Lincoln's orders, Grant allowed "the most liberal terms" permitting Confederates to "have their horses to plow with" and wishing "those people to return to their allegiance to the Union and submit to the laws." Grant, however, insisted that muskets and rifles be stacked in surrender. One North Carolina veteran of four years' fighting muttered, as he did so, "Damn me if I ever love another country!" On the other side, one Billy Yank observed the scene as General "Meade appeared on the field [to announce the surrender], the colorbearers vie with each other . . . surrounding him with a fluttering brilliancy as he rode triumphantly along the lines of his exultant troops. The deafening roar of artillery and the music of a hundred bands only added to the sounds of rejoicing," as the "air was rent by rousing cheers from 10,000 happy throats—caps hurled on high till the sky was darkened." By the end of April, Johnston had surrendered to Sherman in North Carolina. President Davis, fleeing southward, was captured by a Federal patrol in Georgia and jailed.

Five nights after Appomattox, on Good Friday, President Lincoln, attending Ford's Theater in Washington, was shot by a mad actor infuriated over the Confederacy's defeat. As his life ebbed out the following morning, only a few fellow countrymen recalled his counsel in the Second Inaugural Address to "judge not that we be not judged," and "with malice toward none, with charity for all . . . let us strive on to finish the work we are in; to bind up the nation's wounds; . . . to do all which may achieve a just and lasting peace."

Whether "a just and lasting peace" would follow remained to be seen. The haunting melancholy of Lincoln's words reflected the sadness of four, cruel years of America's agony as well as its hopes for the future. The

Grant and Lee. (Left, Library of Congress; Right, National Archives)

guns were now at last still, the Civil War over. The immediate tangible results were there for all to see: secession dead, slavery ended, the American experiment in self-government preserved, the Union still one. The nation would not again face the challenge of internal rupture by state withdrawals.

The palpable costs had been immense. More than 618,000 young Americans were dead—twice as many from infection and disease as from bullets.

Over 400,000 survivors, wounded and maimed, would carry for a lifetime the scars of war on their bodies and minds. Estimates placed at $20 billion the calculable property and financial costs of the war, but hidden, invisible, indirect costs were perhaps equally large. Incalculable human suffering and mental anguish did not end at Appomattox. Who can say what damage the war had done to the human spirit of America?

Had it been worth the cost? The postwar years would offer a partial answer.

PART III

Reconstruction, 1865–1877

During the years following Appomattox, Americans experienced a mixed blend of emotions—joy over the end of the war, elation in victory, sadness and frustration in defeat, futility and anger, hope, unselfishness, hate, greed, vengeance, and optimism. Some Americans were hopeful that the return of peace would usher in a new day, a day of fulfillment—of completing the task of freeing the American Negro from centuries-old oppression, of erasing meanness and restriction, of making practice match profession of ideals, of welcoming newly freed blacks into the American mainstream to exercise new-found rights and enjoy new opportunities to develop along with fellow Americans.

Others felt little or no concern for the freedmen but busied themselves rather with driving ahead, with amassing money, with seizing the main chance for themselves. Still others, resentful over defeat in war and determined to resist social change, struck back in a fury born of fear and frustration. Contemporary and later observers, noting this hostile spirit, spoke of "America's age of hate," even a "tragic era"; and other commentators viewed the driving vigor and ruthlessness and waste of the acquisitive spirit during the days of "the great barbecue" as ushering in a "chromo civilization" of the "gilded age." As in all American eras, the truth is a complex combination of many stories whose focus varies with the eyes, interests, and feelings of the chronicler.

But central and inescapable in America's Reconstruction era is the story of the Negro—4 million Negroes, for the first time legally released from the shackles of chattel bondage. How America responded to this release forms the core of Reconstruction's story. A revolution, begun during the war with fine idealism and high hopes, moved forward for a time with full speed and enthusiasm, then slowed and faltered. In less than a dozen years it was abandoned—with what consequences later generations of Americans would come to know all too well.

10

Restoring the Union under Lincoln, 1862–1865

1. Wartime Beginnings of Reconstruction

While the war was being fought, the main thrust from Washington was naturally to subdue Southern military forces and, as the Johnson-Crittenden resolutions of July, 1861, announced, to restore the Union. As the fighting continued, the matter of restoring the Union became tangled in related complexities. If secession was null and void, Southern states might simply quit fighting, acknowledge national authority, and resume their places. But soon intricate, emotion-charged questions intermingled with what had appeared a simple process of getting the Union back together again. These questions revolved about (1) what was to be done to the states that claimed to have left the Union and about their institutions; (2) what was to be done about Negroes who had been slaves at war's outbreak; (3) what was to be done about Southerners who had engaged in rebellion. Both Lincoln and the Congress sought to develop policies on these related questions.

Early in the war, Congress enacted legislation to deal with persons engaging in and aiding the rebellion. The Second Confiscation Act of July, 1862, authorized the seizure of rebels' property including lands and slaves. To allay Lincoln's constitutional concern about the law's validity, Congress passed "an explanatory joint resolution" that the law did not apply to acts committed prior to its passage and did not impose forfeiture beyond the life of the person in rebellion. The law, of course, could be enforced only where Federal courts were operating, and the administration, still unhappy over the procedural defects of the act, did not take vigorous steps to enforce it. One provision in the act authorized emancipation of slaves, but since all confiscated property was to be sold (a procedure clearly inapplicable to slaves), it was not clear how emancipation was to be achieved. At the time Congress was debating the bill, Lincoln decided upon his own policy of emancipation and in September, 1862, issued his celebrated Proclamation to take effect January 1 in areas still in rebellion.

With an eye to the still loyal border South, Lincoln had been pressing for gradual, compensated emancipation. On several occasions he prodded upper-South Congressmen to move their states in this direction, even proposing that Congress foot the bill for compensation. Indeed, in April, 1862, the Congressional act abolishing slavery in the District of Columbia provided compensation up to $300 per slave. Again Lincoln urged the border states to follow suit, but they took no action. The President promulgated emancipation but limited it to the still rebellious parts of the South. It was intended in large measure as an act of human justice to Negro slaves. But the question of what to do about freed slaves after emancipation roused apprehensions. Lincoln continued to press for colonization of blacks outside the United States and was supporting such schemes as late as 1864.

To others, especially the ardent abolitionist Radical Republican leaders in Congress, the question of what to do about freed slaves was easily answered. They should be welcomed to the Union's side and encouraged to aid Federal armies crush the rebellion. General Ben Butler had early used escaped slaves, whom he termed "contrabands," for fatigue duty and fortification work in eastern Virginia. In July, 1862, Congress gave half-hearted consent to employing noncombatant Negro workers in the armed forces and later authorized the active recruiting of black soldiers. Before the fighting ended, as noted earlier, 180,000 Negroes would see service.

By July some voices were raising the Negro suffrage cry, which would grow louder after 1865. Frederick Douglass declared that if the Negro "knows enough to take up arms in defense of this Government, and bare his breast to the storm of rebel artillery, he knows enough to vote." The freed Negro, said Douglass, was entitled to "the most perfect civil and political equality," and black suffrage was "the *only solid* and *final solution* to the problem before us." Wendell Phillips went along, contending: "From the possession of political rights, a man gets means to clutch equal opportunities of education, and a fair space of work. Give a man his vote, and you give him the tools to work and arms to protect himself." Few would second Douglass and Phillips in 1863, but time would convert many in the postwar years.

Meanwhile, the issues of what to do about rebels and about Negroes had become joined. In the Sea Islands along the coast of South Carolina, owners had abandoned their plantations as Federal troops invaded. These lands were taken over by the army under Generals David Hunter and Rufus Saxton. In February, 1863, Senator Sumner proposed a bill to grant ten acres of land to every Negro soldier. And about the same time Congressman George W. Julian called for adoption of "an equitable homestead policy, parcelling out the plantations of rebels in small farms for . . . the freedman . . . instead of selling it in large tracts to speculators. . . ."

What Julian had in mind was probably the land sale about to take place in the South Carolina Sea Islands area. Under an 1862 Federal direct tax law the President sent tax commissioners to assess taxes owed in occupied parts of the Confederacy and to offer for sale at public auction the lands of delinquent taxpayers. In the Sea Islands the tax commissioners put on sale at auction some 16,000 acres in March of 1863, of which 2,000 acres were bought by freedmen who had pooled their savings. From here on government policy zigzagged with dizzying effect. Of 60,000 acres held by the government, a Presidential order reserved 16,000 for purchase by freedmen. When it was pointed out that this was inadequate for the 15,000 blacks in the area to support themselves, a new order permitted a Negro head of household to preempt up to 40 acres with the expectation of buying at the minimum price of $1.25 per acre. Since the order was later rescinded after preemption claims had been entered, much confusion resulted in the tax sales of February, 1864. In many instances the tax commissioners ruled against the preemptioners, with the result that freedmen acquired only 2,276 acres at the special $1.25 per acre price. A few groups of Negroes put their funds together and bought 470 acres at $7.00 per acre in competitive bidding. One observer, disturbed by this turn of events, argued, "Every colored man will . . . feel himself a slave until he can raise his own bale of cotton & put his own mark upon it. . . ."

In other parts of the South, too, lands fell into the hands of advancing Union armies. And tens of thousands of fugitive blacks swarmed into army camps. In the North, freedmen's aid societies sprang up to provide immediate assistance to these displaced persons of the war. They raised funds and sent relief supplies and agents to the South. In some places the army brought the land and the Negro together, establishing farming operations on leased or appropriated plantation lands in areas scattered from Virginia through Kentucky and Tennessee to Arkansas and Louisiana.

Lincoln had been urged to develop a government agency specially charged with developing plans to guide "our emancipated . . . blacks from the old condition of forced labor to their new state of voluntary industry." The President drafted no plans, but legislation in 1864 directed special Treasury agents to assume control of and lease abandoned lands and to "provide in such leases . . . for the employment and general welfare" of freedmen. To the army's relief, Treasury Secretary William P. Fessenden on July 29, 1864, issued a set of regulations. Curiously, these regulations were suspended the following month, and by late 1864 the army was again in charge.

Clearly some systematic approach was needed. In March, 1864, the House passed a bill to establish a Bureau for Freedmen in the War Department. Julian in the House and Sumner in the Senate attempted to attach an amendment to extend the 1862 Homestead Act provisions to the South so that a freedman could acquire a forty-acre homestead out of lands confiscated form large planters. Repeal of the 1862 Congressional joint resolution, tacked on to the 1862 Confiscation Act, was needed, and such a repeal was passed by both houses in 1864 and again in 1865 but lost in conference committee negotiation over the precise form of the wording. By late February, 1865, six weeks before Appomattox, Congress authorized the establishment of a Bureau of Refugees, Freedmen, and Abandoned Lands, but not a confiscation-homestead policy. The Freedmen's Bureau will be dealt with more at length in a later section. A land-for-freedmen policy could probably have been made to stick had it been adopted in 1864 or early

1865 and might well have resolved many problems that later plagued the nation. Not adopted in 1865, the proposal would be revived again later, but with little prospect of approval.

Meanwhile General Sherman, following his march in late 1864 through Georgia, which brought in its wake thousands of slaves fleeing their former plantation homes, issued his field order to deal with the complex situation: "the islands from Charleston south, the abandoned rice-fields along the rivers for thirty miles back from the sea, and the country bordering the St. John's River, Florida, are reserved and set apart for the settlement of Negroes now made free by act of war." A beginning was made to implement the Sherman order but it was viewed as a temporary war measure. Whether it would become a permanent feature of Reconstruction depended upon final decision in Washington.

If Congressional action in regard to land for Negroes was fuzzy, its action regarding those who had participated in or aided rebellion was somewhat clearer. Early in the war Congress had adopted Treason and Conspiracies legislation. In order to enforce these acts effectively, the lawmakers required that jurors serving on Federal court juries take a loyalty oath. By the second year of the war Congress had specified a stricter oath that came to be called the ironclad test oath and required all Federal officials and employees to subscribe to it. The ironclad test oath came in two parts: the first section attested to the oath-taker's past loyalty—that he had not voluntarily fought against the Union nor aided nor supported the rebellion in any way; the second part provided a pledge of future loyalty.

As Federal armies moved into the South, the ironclad test oath raised peculiar difficulties for administering Federal policies. For example, the Treasury Department sought to appoint tax assessors, customs inspectors and collectors, and other officials. Since by law they had to be chosen from residents of the local district concerned, the Treasury Secretary often found it difficult to find persons who could qualify. In some instances he appointed men who took simply an oath of future loyalty, informing Congress and asking that exceptions be made in these cases. The Postmaster General encountered similar difficulties. Congress did not look kindly upon these evasions and refused to make exceptions.

In restoring the Southern states to a place in the Union, the ironclad test oath would obviously play a part. But the matter was complicated in another way. As Union armies moved into Confederate territory, President Lincoln, under his constitutional pardoning power, authorized military commanders to grant pardon to those persons who took an oath of future loyalty, as prescribed by the Chief Executive. Many peculiarities surrounded these proceedings. No one could doubt that the President under the Constitution had the power to pardon. Indeed, his power to pardon had been underscored in the 1862 legislation. But his issuing of pardons to persons not convicted of crimes raised curious questions. Just as curious, it could be argued, was

Congress's imposition of penalties on persons as a class who had not been convicted of an offense. Requiring an ironclad test oath for persons seeking to hold Federal office clearly lay within Congress's power. Whether it was wise or accomplished its purpose could be debated. And whether the test oath could be extended, as it was in January, 1865, to apply to attorneys as a class seeking to practice their profession in Federal courts would certainly be challenged.

And so matters stood when the fighting ended in April of 1865—confused. The three major issues remained unresolved. (1) Southern states: Were they still in the Union, as those who rejected secession as illegal could argue; were they out of the Union, as leaders of Southern states had been contending for the past four years? How and under what conditions were they to be restored to the Union? (2) Ex-Confederates: Related to the problem of how to restore Southern states to the Union was the question of what to do about former Confederates. Were they to be punished for having tried to break up the United States? Were penalties to be imposed equally upon rebel leaders and followers? Was some distinction to be made between them or were they to be brought back in without penalty? (3) Freedmen: Freedom, announced in the Emancipation Proclamation, was now confirmed in Thirteenth Amendment. But what did freedom mean? Was the freedman now to have land and a farm to support himself? Did freedom entitle him to equality? What equality—legal, civil, political? What rights would he have—the right to vote? to land, to schooling, to public accommodations?

2. *War's Aftermath*

The first of modern wars, the Civil War began, as would some of its successors, without a formal declaration of war. It was fought with the total society mobilized to prosecute it against soldier and civilian population alike, and it ended in unconditional surrender without a peace treaty. The war's totality was caught in a Southern veteran's comment that Northern troops "destroyed everything which the most infernal Yankee ingenuity could devise means to destroy; hands, heart, fire, gunpowder, and behind everything the spirit of hell—were the agencies which they used."

Since Federal officials viewed the war as a rebellion, there could be no terminating treaty of peace. As Lincoln phrased it three days before he died, "Unlike . . . a war between independent nations, there is no organized organ for us to treat with. No one man has authority to give up the rebellion for any other man. We must simply begin with, and mould from, disorganized and discordant elements." And so when the shooting stopped, the war ended. The vast Union army, after a grand victory march of endless columns of troops up Pennsylvania Avenue, was largely demobilized in systematic, orderly fashion by late summer, 1865. When bluecoated Johnny went marching home at government expense, he faced a hero's welcome with $235 mustering out pay in his pocket and high hopes for a farm, job, wife, schooling, or business of his own.

On the other side, Confederate forces simply dissolved. Disheartened veterans trudged wearily homeward, pausing to ask for handouts en route, "with nothing to exchange for bread save the unwelcome news of Appomattox." Upon arriving, they might find only a blackened chimney remaining of what they had once called home. It was not a pretty sight—what war left. Large areas of the South, especially in Virginia and Tennessee, had been fought and refought over by marching armies and marauding bands of armed men. Sheridan and Sherman, true to their threats, had blazed a path of devastation and ruin through Virginia's valley and across Georgia and the Carolinas. Cities like Richmond, Charleston, Atlanta, Vicksburg, and Columbia lay battered by artillery or gutted by fire. Columbia appeared to a visitor in September, 1865, "a wilderness of ruins. . . . Not a store, office or shop escaped [burning]; and for a distance of three-fourths of a mile on each of twelve streets there was not a building left."

The Tennessee valley, as seen by an English traveler, revealed "plantations of which the ruin is for the present total and complete. . . . The trail of war is visible . . . in burnt up gin houses, ruined bridges, mills, and factories. . . . The roads, long neglected, are in disorder, and . . . in many places . . . impassible. . . . Many who were once the richest men . . . have disappeared from the scene." Southern railroads, coastal cities, and river ports were largely out of commission. In places like Atlanta and Richmond, food was so scarce that Federal authorities had to distribute rations to as many as 50,000 persons. One Northern naval officer observed, "A more completely crushed country I have seldom witnessed."

The losses of Southern manpower had been staggering—perhaps as high as half of the men of military age killed or wounded. The labor of keeping home and farm going fell to the women, for even boys had run off to fight. During the war, too, the South had lost one-third of its mules and horses by death, theft, or confiscation, so that women and old men sometimes had to harness themselves to plows to get the fields planted and cultivated. Southern mills, lacking both materials and workers in many instances, fell into disrepair and disuse and were abandoned. Production of raw cotton would not again reach its 1860 levels until 1878.

Confederate leaders, now discredited, took different postwar paths. Some fearing retribution fled abroad—to Mexico, South America, and England; most notable was Judah P. Benjamin, Davis's most able cabinet officer, who now entered upon what became a distinguished career at the London bar. A few were arrested, held briefly, and released. Only Davis was imprisoned—at Fort Monroe. After two years he was freed on bail and indicted for treason, but the prosecution was soon dropped. Most leaders simply returned home and attempted to put their lives back together again, in many cases with considerable success. Robert E. Lee, after turning down

Richmond after the war. (Library of Congress)

a high-salaried offer as an insurance executive, assumed the presidency of Washington College (later renamed Washington and Lee) and served till his death in 1870. No other country's civil war had seen vanquished leaders get off so lightly.

At the war's close, few suffered more than the war's displaced persons, the ex-slaves of the South. When word of emancipation brought the long-awaited "day of jubilee," many Negroes, feeling "free as a bird," abandoned old homes, haunts, and living habits, and swarmed into Federal army camps in such large numbers as to create difficult problems of feeding and housing. A few Federal officers had confiscated land during the war and made it available to some Negroes to live on and farm on easy terms, as at Port Royal, South Carolina. Other commanders set up so-called "contraband camps," where thousands of ex-bondsmen were herded together in flimsy, unsanitary quarters. Northern philanthropy, working through the Sanitary Commission and freedmen's aid societies, sought to improve such conditions. Finally on March 3, 1865, as noted above, Congress created within the War Department the Bureau of Refugees, Freedmen, and Abandoned Lands, authorizing it to distribute "provisions, clothing and fuel . . . for destitute and suffering refugees and freedmen" and to manage such lands "abandoned" or confiscated in the South by leasing at a fair rent to any "male citizen, whether refugee or freedman . . . forty acres of such land."

The Freedmen's Bureau under General O. O. Howard's direction got off to a fine start but presently found itself so inundated with displaced persons that its full energies (to the neglect of land distribution programs) were totally absorbed in providing food and necessities to the tens of thousands of blacks who flooded centers at New Orleans, Mobile, Savannah, Charleston, Atlanta, Norfolk, Richmond, and other cities. Bureau camps were so packed with people that epidemics killed about one-third of their occupants in two years after the war's close. Southern whites were little better off. Widespread destitution and even famine were aggravated by paralysis of transportation, a skimpy 1865 harvest, and lack of any local relief arrangements. One Bureau official observed as "an everyday sight . . . women and children, . . . formerly in good circumstances, begging for bread from door to door." To the extent of its limited resources, the Bureau cared for them, too, distributing to black and white some 21 million rations in four years, 6 million of them to whites.

Military defeat left its mark in disappointment followed by despair, as most ex-Confederates faced life resentful and angry. Those young men who survived the holocaust saw a disheartening future. Many "aimless young men in grey, ragged and filthy," wandered about the countryside, having "lost their object in life." The restraints of government having dissolved, some men turned to violence, as did the James Brothers in Missouri, roaming as lawless, gun-slinging guerrillas. Economic conditions and opportunities remained limited and discouraging for years to come.

Refugee family crosses river into Union line. (Library of Congress)

Even before the war's fighting ended, as Northern troops moved southward, such governments—state, county, and local—as had remained in those areas of the Confederacy not occupied by Union troops, simply stood paralyzed. Indeed, in many parts of the South, even before the war's end, local government broke down or vanished completely. Into the resulting vacuum stepped the only agency on the spot and the only one even partly equipped to meet the emergency—the Federal army. Hence, of necessity, the first step in the Reconstruction of the South was, in effect, the establishment of military governments. And as military Commander in Chief, President Lincoln became the first architect for erecting a Reconstruction program.

3. Presidential Reconstruction: Lincoln Style

On the three major Reconstruction questions—status of the Southern states, position of ex-Confederates, position of the Negro—President Lincoln had expressed his views at least partially before his assassination. Consistently holding that attempted secession was invalid, that no state could "by its mere notion" get out of the Union, Lincoln maintained that, in theory at least, Southern states were still part of the Union although out of "their proper practical relation'' with it. Hence the chief object of what he proposed was ''to get them into that proper practical relation'' speedily and with as little fuss as possible.

As Federal armies advanced in 1862 and occupied much of Tennessee and parts of Louisiana and Arkansas, Lincoln quickly appointed provisional, military governors. In the first it was Andrew Johnson, the only Senator from a seceded state who remained loyally in the Senate at war's outbreak. The governor's initial assignment called for reestablishing in his state ''such a republican form of government'' as will meet the requirement of the Constitution (Article IV, Section 4) and enable that state ''to be protected by the United States against invasion and domestic violence.'' The first tentative steps toward restoration proceeded under this presidential directive.

By late 1863 most of Tennessee was in Federal hands, and Union control had been secured in many segments of Arkansas and Louisiana. The time seemed appropriate for some official government statement concerning restoration. On December 8, 1863, President Lincoln issued a Proclamation of Amnesty and Reconstruction that stipulated more exactly the process by which a seceded state could resume its place in the Union. Issued in the midst of war and in the face of mounting Radical Republican pressure for punishing rebels, as reflected in the Second Confiscation Act, Lincoln's ''ten per cent plan'' barred from politics all civil and military officers of the Confederacy and its states, all who had left Federal offices to become rebels of whatever rank, and other persons who might seek to re-enslave Negro soldiers captured as prisoners of war. To all other Southerners, upon their taking an oath of future loyalty to the Constitution and swearing ''to abide by all acts of Congress passed during the existing rebellion'' concerning slavery and to observe the Emancipation Proclamation, the President's plan offered pardon and return of confiscated property except slaves unless the rights of third parties had intervened. When in any state the oath was taken by a group of voters numbering at least 10 per cent of that state's 1860 electorate, they could proceed to call a convention, draft a new state constitution with slavery prohibited, organize state and local governments, and then hold elections. The Chief Executive also promised that ''any provision which may be adopted . . . in relation to the freed people, which shall recognize and declare their permanent freedom, provide for their education . . . will not be objected to'' by the President. Southerners interpreted this as an invitation to re-enact their pre-1860 ''Black Codes,'' which defined the Negro's legal position in Southern society. Lincoln readily acknowledged that under this plan the acceptance of men elected to Congress would of course be determined by Congress.

Lincoln's lenient plan went into at least partial operation in three states—Louisiana, Tennessee, and Arkansas. Indeed, under a makeshift plan administered by General Ben Butler, Louisiana had undergone a partial restoration by 1863. Two representatives, Michael Hahn and B. F. Flanders had been elected to Congress, where they were officially seated in February, 1863, and served until the end of the session. In 1864 a Louisiana state convention adopted a constitution abolishing slavery that was approved by the voters. In subsequent elections Hahn was chosen governor. Announcing his satisfaction, Lincoln treated the state as if restored to the Union and enforced the Federal conscription act there. But doubts and confusion soon developed.

In Arkansas a new constitution was also approved at the polls. But Congress later refused to recognize the state goverment and to seat the men elected to the House. In Tennessee under Andrew Johnson's direction, amendments to the state constitution ending slavery and making other changes were drafted by a convention and ratified in a February, 1865, election. Before leaving to assume office the next month as Vice President, Johnson issued a proclamation recognizing that Tennessee had met Lincoln's conditions for reconstruction. Although Tennessee had earlier (1861–63) sent some representatives to the national Congress, it had none in the 1863–65 sessions and would have none again until 1866. In Virginia a "restored government" under Governor Francis H. Pierpoint had been operating a kind of "straw government" from a capital at Alexandria since 1861. It had approved the formation of West Virginia, drawn up a new constitution declaring slavery ended, and sought full recognition at Washington, but Congress seesawed on seating its representatives.

In the face of many irregularities, frequent challenges, and confused conditions, none of these four states was recognized as a full-fledged state in the Union by the time of Lincoln's death. All except Tennessee would later travel Congress's more rigorous road to restoration.

In sum, then, in regard to the question of Southern states, Lincoln hoped for a speedy restoration with practically no conditions or penalties, other than insisting on a pledge of future loyalty by new state leaders. As to ex-Confederates, he would bar the top leaders, at least temporarily, from participating in the process of reconstruction, but those at lower levels would be freely pardoned. When Congress in 1864 passed the more stringent Wade-Davis bill that would impose penalties and restrictions, including the ironclad oath, Lincoln gave the bill a pocket veto.

In regard to the position of Negro freedmen, Lincoln's views and announced policy underwent change from 1863 until his death. In an August, 1863, letter to General Nathaniel P. Banks, military governor of Louisiana, urging that the process of restoration begin, he expressed his hope that Louisiana would "adopt some practical system by which the two races could gradually live themselves out of their old relation to each other, and both come out better prepared for the new. Education for young blacks should be included in the plan." And "the power . . . of 'contract' may be sufficient for this probationary period'' in regulating work and working conditions for Negroes, but none shall ''ever return to slavery.''

Within days after Lincoln's Proclamation of Amnesty of December 8, 1863, the Thirteenth Amendment was introduced into Congress. Passed quickly by the Senate, it stalled in the House, lacking thirteen votes for the necessary two-thirds majority in June, 1864. After the Presidential election of that year, enough House votes switched to carry the amendment in January, 1865, and send it to the states for ratification. Radical Republican Senator Charles Sumner observed that the amendment's second section—''Congress shall have the power to enforce this article by appropriate legislation''—could enable Congress to authorize Negro voting if needed to preserve Negro emancipation.

As early as December, 1863, the Negro suffrage question had been broached by Frederick Douglass in a speech to the American Anti-Slavery Society meeting. Lincoln moved cautiously and slowly and often appeared undecided in his own mind as to what the government should do about the postwar status of the Negro. During 1864 he appears to have been swinging away from his early colonizationist view toward a belief that necessary accommodation between the races could be facilitated by universal education, work contracts, and gradual extension of the suffrage. He advised Governor Hahn that Louisiana's government in process of restoration might consider ''whether some colored people may not be let in [to vote] . . . the very intelligent and those who have fought gallantly in our ranks. They would probably help . . . keep the jewel of liberty within the family of freedom.''

Lincoln made this statement against a background of events and conditions that made Louisiana exceptional. More than 18,000 free Negroes lived in New Orleans and owned property valued at $15 million as of 1860. Most coul read, write, and had proved themselves responsible residents. They had written General Banks ''asking to be allowed to register and vote.'' Getting no satisfaction they appealed to President Lincoln. The President took no action but included the above suggestion regarding a limited Negro suffrage in his letter addressed to Michael Hahn, ''first Free State Governor of Louisiana.''

To Lincoln it appeared logical that Louisiana with its advanced Negro people should grant suffrage especially to black soldiers. Louisiana's convention of 1864 thought otherwise, adopting a resolution that the legislature should not permit Negro voting. Doubtless, Governor Hahn's influence was at work when later a new resolution sought to authorize the legislature to extend suffrage to such ''citizens of the United States, as by military service, by taxation to support the government, or by intellectual fitness, may be deemed entitled thereto.'' Here was the substance of Lincoln's suggestion.

Doubtless, Lincoln was disappointed, but he did not insist on Negro suffrage as a precondition of restoration. Indeed, he seemed to sense potential black-white antagonism in a fatalistic passage of his Second Inaugural Address of March 4, 1865: "Fondly do we hope—fervently do we pray—that this mighty scourge of war may speedily pass away. Yet, if God wills that it continue, until all the wealth piled by the bond-man's two hundred years of unrequited toil shall be sunk and until every drop of blood drawn by the lash shall be paid by another drawn by the sword," we must accept; " 'the judgments of the Lord are true and righteous altogether.' " He also wrote that if God "wills that we of the North as well as you of the South, shall pay fairly for our complicity in that wrong [slavery], impartial history will find therein new cause to attest and revere the justice and goodness of God."

In not pressing the Negro question, Lincoln kept his eye on political considerations as he offered a forgiving, quick, easy path to political restoration of Southern states. As a practicing politician and former Whig, he was striving essentially to attract the remaining Southern Whigs (some of them staunch wartime Unionists in the South) into a nascent Southern wing of the Republican party. He would not therefore run the risk of antagonizing Southerners by punishing Southern leaders by inflicting harsh penalties. By such leniency he hoped to lure many Southerners to Republican persuasion. His plan, essentially procedural in nature, was to get Southern states functioning as part of the Union as rapidly as possible. Then, under established Republican direction and control in Southern states, other problems of Southern society like the place of the Negro and economic recovery could, he hoped, be dealt with more fully. Soft-pedaling on the question of Negro suffrage was an obvious necessity in this moderate, pragmatic approach. But it failed to face squarely and directly the heart of the Southern dilemma—the Negro.

In the last few weeks of his life Lincoln may have been changing, as some writers assert. Upon visiting Richmond in April, 1865, after the Confederates had abandoned it, he was likely impressed by the absence of white people and by the warm greetings he received from Negroes lining the streets as he passed by. Back in Washington on April 11 he spoke to a crowd that gathered at the White House to hail the happy news of Appomattox. In his remarks he referred to "a plan of reconstruction (as the phrase goes)" which he had offered as a possible means by which a Southern state might be restored to the Union. With some satisfaction he noted that under his "plan" Louisiana had moved well along toward restoration—"organized a State government, adopted a free-state constitution, giving the benefit of public schools equally to black and white, empowering the Legislature to confer the elective franchise upon the colored man," and ratifying the Thirteenth Amendment ending slavery. He reiterated his hope that Negro suffrage might be "now conferred on the very intelligent, and on those who served our cause as soldiers." Conceding that the Louisiana process was only an imperfect beginning, he urged the acceptance of Louisiana, with an eye to his Congressional critics, because by so doing "we shall sooner have the fowl by hatching the egg than by smashing it." To those who contended that the proposed Thirteenth Amendment needed to be submitted for ratification only by loyal states, Lincoln retorted that "such ratification would be questionable, and sure to be persistently questioned; while a ratification by three fourths of all the States would be unquestioned and unquestionable."

On the final day of his life, Lincoln discussed reconstruction with his cabinet. Secretary Stanton submitted a draft of a plan for unified military government for Virginia and North Carolina looking toward the reestablishment of national government functions such as mails, customs collections, Federal courts and attorneys, and ultimate reorganization of government, with the possibility of eventual Negro suffrage. Secretary Welles raised some objections, especially relating to the plan's disregard of the Pierpoint government in Virginia. Lincoln instructed Stanton to rework the plan, making it apply separately to the two states. Various participants received differing impressions of the President's future intentions. Seward later stated that Lincoln was considering a proclamation similar to that issued May 29, 1865, by President Johnson. But Attorney-General James Speed concluded that the President was moving closer to the Radical Republican position on the basis of Lincoln's conceding that he "had perhaps been moving too fast in his desire for early reconstruction."

Whether Lincoln would have modified his views, shifted tactics, pushed new proposals for dealing with the triple problem of restoration, ex-rebel leaders, and Negroes in the South is impossible to say. His death by assassination six days after Lee's surrender at Appomattox leaves unanswered the question of what change and how much he might have made in the postwar atmosphere. He could not help being aware that complications in his dealings with Congress, already visible, would become more difficult in the postwar era.

Long before Lincoln's death, his reconstruction plan appeared inadequate to many. Among his critics stood Radical Republican leaders in Congress who believed that nothing short of a full-scale social revolution in the South would fulfill the promise and sacrifices of the war. Some contended that Southern states, by seceding and making war on the United States, had surrendered their statehood, forfeited any claim to lenient consideration, yielded all rights, and in effect assumed the position of territories. As such they could be admitted to the Union only on the conditions that Congress alone chose to set. While not opposing "constitutional" reconstruction of the South by the President, they believed that the process belonged properly in the hands of Congress and that the President could act only under direction and authorization by Congress. Especially after the end of hostilities, they felt that the President's extraordinary wartime powers should contract and no longer be used.

Radical leaders thought Lincoln's plan moved too precipitately in flinging open the door for immediate Southern return to statehood. They did not share his concern about reviving Southern Whigs as converts to the Republican party; instead, they were opposed to trusting ex-rebels immediately with political power and fearful that rejuvenated Democrats might gain control in Washington. As ardent prewar abolitionists, some leaders held the interests of the Negro close in their hearts and wanted to see some assurance that the Negro would obtain his legal rights and his legitimate economic, political, and social position in Southern society, in accordance with the ideals of the Declaration of Independence. Power-wielding politicians, many were also idealist reformers. At times they may have appeared obsessed with exercising only political power and wreaking vengeance on the "prostrate South," but the underlying humanitarian feeling of many of them cannot be overlooked or dismissed.

Congressional Radical Republicans viewed Lincoln's 10 per cent plan of reconstruction as weak and inadequate. Not only was it soft on rebels, but it also moved Southern states too easily and rapidly back into the Union and thereby posed a threat to consolidating the ends for which the war had presumably been fought. They had been uneasy over Lincoln's Proclamation of Amnesty of December 8, 1863, and had chafed as steps were taken under it to restore Louisiana and Tennessee. Earlier they had pushed the ironclad test oath as the only true test of loyalty. Only loyal men, as measured by that oath, could be trusted with the job of reestablishing government in the South. By July 4, 1864 (the last day of the session), they had mustered strength enough to drive the Wade-Davis bill through Congress. Under this reconstruction proposal the South would be held under military occupation until a *majority* of citizens, not just 10 per cent, took the ironclad test oath—swearing not only future loyalty to the Union (as Lincoln's oath required) but swearing that they had been consistently loyal in the past and had not voluntarily aided the Confederate cause—a provision that of course ruled out the vast majority of Southern whites, who had adhered to the Confederacy. If and when a majority of loyal oath takers was obtained (which seemed impossible at the time), then loyal voters could choose conventions to make new state constitutions that must abolish slavery, disfranchise ex-Confederate officials, and repudiate state debts incurred in support of rebellion. This bill, Radicals hoped, would commit the Republican party to the stricter course of reconstruction when it appeared before the voters in the 1864 fall elections.

But Lincoln responded by letting the bill die without his signature. Privately, Lincoln said he disapproved of an oath requiring a man to swear he had not done wrong in the past, adding: "It rejects the Christian principle of forgiveness on terms of repentance. I think it is enough if the man does no wrong hereafter.'' Publicly he indicated that he would have no objection to Southern states returning via the Wade-Davis route if they voluntarily chose to do so. Infuriated, Congressional Radicals denounced the President's veto as allowing him to manage ''the electoral votes of the Rebel States'' for ''his personal ambition'' in the coming election. ''A more studied outrage to the legislative authority had never been perpetrated. . . . He must understand . . . that the authority of Congress must be respected . . . and he must leave . . . political reorganization to Congress.''

In the 1864 Presidential election Radicals gave Lincoln grudging support, lacking any enthusiasm but required by the necessity of keeping in power the Republican party, which the Radicals hoped soon to control. In January, 1865, final House passage of the Thirteenth Amendment buoyed the Radicals' spirits. In the following month, Radical pressures blocked the seating in Congress of members elected by Louisiana, which Lincoln had earlier pronounced ''reconstructed'' under his 10 per cent plan. To deal with Negro affairs that had been neglected by Lincoln, Congress created the Freedmen's Bureau on March 3, 1865, the day before its adjournment. A full showdown between Lincoln and the Radicals had been averted—for the time being. They would return to Washington in December, 1865, more determined than ever to push their Southern strategy. But the same President would not be there to meet them.

11

Congress Makes a New Start, 1865–1866

In 1866 the revolution that was begun with the war became enmeshed in the explosive battle between Congress and President Andrew Johnson. Congressional Radicals, whether motivated by idealistic or political considerations, grew increasingly determined not to lose the fruits of military victory by giving away the peace settlement. They courted and won over additional Republican allies in their fight to oppose Presidential reconstruction. Not united at first on a program, Republicans became more and more anxious over distressing developments in the Southern states under "Johnson governments." As a result, they joined together in insisting upon at least minimal protection for Southern Negroes through legislation extending the Freedmen's Bureau and authorizing Federal protection of civil rights.

When the proposed Fourteenth Amendment sought to push the revolution a notch further by insuring Negro rights and imposing penalties on ex-Confederates, the President fought back. Taking his case to the electorate, Johnson sought to secure a Congress that would support his program. He lost disastrously in the 1866 mid-term elections.

1. Presidential Reconstruction: Johnson Style

When Lincoln died on April 15, 1865, Andrew Johnson, fifty-six years old, became President. With much political success behind him, Johnson was in many ways uniquely prepared to tackle the problem of restoring the South to the Union. Having bootstrapped himself from extreme poverty in his early days as a tailor's apprentice, self-taught, he climbed Tennessee's political ladder by dint of vigor, persistence, and popular appeal. Town alderman of Greenville at the age of twenty, he rose to mayor to state legislator to Congressman, Governor, and Senator. A Jacksonian Democrat, he adhered to the principles of states' rights and a strict construction of the Constitution. Although he had come a long way, he had never developed close ties with the national Democratic party nor had he cultivated close friendships or associations with other leaders. In contrast to Lincoln, he exhibited little flexibility or shrewdness in political matters, falling back for the most part on fixed abstractions rather than attempting to think political problems through rationally or to calculate the effects of his political judgments or actions.

He was justly proud of his emergence from plebeian origins and seemed compelled to refer constantly to his humble beginnings. As a recent writer has observed, "Unlike Lincoln, whose 'humility' was sustained by the odd arrogance of a superior man's self-knowledge, Johnson lacked assurance. He tended to hesitate in full realization of his own shortcomings." That he exhibited personal courage and determination few could doubt, but it seemed at times that his determination swelled into a mulish obstinancy reflecting a fixed pattern of thought. His frequent references to adhering to the Constitution and accepting the people's will caused difficulty and confusion when the Constitution's meaning was subject to conflicting interpretations and the people's voice was not clear.

His directness and independence made him extremely popular with ordinary voters in Tennessee, who elected him time and again to office. His very success maay have molded him into a kind of lone wolf without ties and without connections. In his elevation to high office, it was his very independence in refusing to go with his seceding state that made him appealing. In 1862 Lincoln appointed him military governor of Tennessee, and for three years he wrestled sturdily and bravely with the problems of restoring civil government there. His good record of encouraging Unionism impressed Republican leaders, who with Lincoln's approval tapped him as Vice Presidential candidate for the National Union Party in 1864 in an effort to appeal to a broad spectrum of voters beyond the strict Republican ranks. Johnson, although a Unionist cooperating with Republicans, remained a Democrat with states' rights predilections. He continued, as one historian notes, "an outsider," not fully accepted by national leaders of either the Republicans or Democrats, although both would seek to sway him to their views on Reconstruction. He would remain independent—or courageous or inflexible or stubborn, depending on the observer's viewpoint.

And so when Johnson assumed the Presidency in mid-April, 1865, he stood in a unique position. He brought to the office an exceptionally broad experience with reconstruction problems in his home state. He had much promise, and much was expected of him. Pressures on him mounted quickly. Radical Republican leaders made no effort to hide their pleasure over the change at the White House. On the day Lincoln died, Indiana Congressman George W. Julian noted: "Aside from Mr. Lincoln's tenderness to the Rebels . . ., his views on the subject of reconstruction were as distasteful as possible to radical Republicans." Even before Lincoln's burial, Radical hopes were expressed by Michigan Senator Zachariah Chandler, who pronounced Johnson "as radical as I am and fully up to the mark." Ohio's Senator Ben Wade was almost ecstatic: "Johnson, we have faith in you. By the gods, there will be no trouble now in running the government." Especially pleasing to Radicals was Johnson's clear hostility to Southern planters. "Treason is a crime," he declared, "and must be punished. . . . The traitor has ceased to be a citizen . . . has become a public enemy." To which he added, "traitors must be punished and impoverished. Their great plantations must be seized, and divided into small farms, and sold to honest and industrious men. The day for protecting the lands and Negroes of those authors of rebellion is past."

Thus in the first flush of post-Appomattox passion, Johnson and the Radicals seemed to harmonize neatly. Forgotten were Johnson's sentiments of 1863 when he expressed his hope "that the President [Lincoln] will not be committed to the proposition of States relapsing into territories and held as such." By May, 1865, Johnson was saying, "there is no such thing as reconstruction. These States have not gone out of the Union. Therefore reconstruction is unnecessary."

During his first few weeks in office, as pressures mounted, Johnson parried them by seeming to agree with those who talked with him. At times he appeared almost all things to all men. In Lincoln's fashion he listened to all men who proffered advice, and for the time at least did not turn them off. Many went away with the impression that Johnson would adopt their suggestions, even though the President had remained noncommittal.

To Senator Sumner who called at the White House to urge Negro suffrage as "the great essential," Johnson reportedly replied, "On this question there is no difference between us." "His manner," Sumner reported jubilantly to friends, "has been excellent, and even sympathetic," adding that Johnson was "well-disposed, and sees the rights and necessities of the case [Negro suffrage]." A Pennsylvania delegation headed by Thaddeus Stevens listened while the President exclaimed that traitors who "attempted to destroy the life of the nation" deserved "the severest penalties." But a few weeks later Stevens, developing an uneasy feeling that Johnson might rush too fast in restoring the Southern states, wrote the President "to suggest the propriety of suspending further reconstruction until the meeting of Congress." Clearly Stevens, the House's most powerful member, wanted Johnson to consult on reconstruction policy with Congressional leaders, if not call an early special session before Congress's regular meeting seven months off in December. But Johnson took no heed. Stevens would not forget the slight.

Seward, Gideon Welles, and other Republican moderates urged Johnson to continue Lincoln's lenient policy and restore the South with a minimum of restrictions. Northern Democrats hoped the President would ease the Southern states smoothly back into the Union. Prominent Southerners, too, pleaded with him to extend executive clemency.

Although no one in the early weeks knew for sure what course the new administration would follow, Johnson perhaps tipped his hand when he retained Lincoln's cabinet in April. In early May he recognized the Pierpoint regime as Virginia's legitimate government. As to Tennessee, Louisiana, and Arkansas, he gave every indication of considering them properly restored under governments created in conformance with Lincoln's plan. To have done otherwise for Tennessee would have been to negate his own labors there.

But outwardly Johnson remained silent for the moment as to his policy. Perhaps it was the circumstances of being suddenly thrust into executive power. Perhaps it was a defect of temperament. In appearance, with his massive head, wide face and firm jaw, set upon a sturdy body, he gave visitors the impression of firmness and determination. His sharp eyes seemed to penetrate an interviewer. But his extreme seriousness and reserved aloofness suggested a coldness stemming from insecurity, which set him apart and made close relations with fellow politicians impossible. For a President by political accident, who represented no major interest and commanded no cohesive political following, the situation demanded an astute gauging of public opinion, winning of political allies, subtle wielding of Presidential instruments of persuasion. Needing Republican support (Northern Democrats having no place else to go), he could have courted moderate Republicans in Congress who were inclined to follow his lead. Instead, within a year's time following his accession, he managed to alienate and drive them into close cooperation with the Radicals.

On May 29, Johnson initiated his own Southern policy by issuing two proclamations. One, a proclamation of amnesty, resembling Lincoln's earlier one, required an oath of future loyalty of all who wished pardon and "restoration of all rights of property, except as to slaves." Classes of high ranking Confederates were still "excepted" from amnesty; to these were added all persons owning property worth more than $20,000. He thereby excluded wealthy planters, who he believed had pushed the South into breaking up the Union. But a special application for pardon could be made directly to the President by any person in the "excepted" classes.

The second Presidential proclamation of May 29 outlined his plan for restoring North Carolina to the Union. A provisional governor, native Unionist William W. Holden, appointed by the President, was authorized to set rules for electing a convention of delegates by the loyal men of the state to amend the state constitution. Secession and slavery were both to be repudiated by the convention, which was also to set the qualifications for future voters and office holders. Within six weeks Johnson issued similar proclamations for the six other "unrestored" states—Alabama, Florida, Georgia, Mississippi, South Carolina, and Texas. A provisional governor, too, was appointed for each state.

Provisional governors proceeded with their work speedily and systematically. During what was viewed as an interim period, they used their appointive powers to fill state offices with those who took the loyalty oath, as prescribed in the amnesty proclamation. State and county courts, where they existed, resumed operations. And elections and preparations for the conventions were made. Side by side, a military governor, appointed by Johnson for each state, commanded Federal occupying forces and administered martial law where required.

Federal wagons going into captured Petersburg. (Library of Congress)

Southerners who had been apprehensive over possible penalties and punishments for their part in the war breathed easier upon learning of Johnson's lenient terms. Since the amnesty proclamation offered forgiveness, all that remained for most Southerners was to take the oath of future loyalty as restoration proceeded. Those Confederates who had held high civil or military posts would have to apply directly to the President for pardon. During the summer and early fall, many of these men beseiged the White House seeking clemency. Johnson appears to have enjoyed watching proud Southern leaders and wealthy planters figuratively prostrate themselves in seeking forgiveness from the former humble tailor's apprentice. He was not slow to respond in exercising his power. Although a few petitions for pardon were denied, most were granted swiftly. By September, they were being granted at a rate of 100 per day, and by the year's end some 13,000 had been issued.

Still, many Southerners had the feeling that military defeat required some acknowledgement of guilt and atonement beyond the pardoning process. When on numerous occasions they inquired of the President, he repeatedly assured them that the Executive was in full charge, that restoration not reconstruction was all that was needed and on doubtful points "let the Constitution be our guide." Since the Constitution was subject to varying interpretations, Southerners could hope that the strict constructionist view would prevail. And they were not to be disappointed.

When the question of suffrage arose, Johnson informed Mississippi's provisional governor that the convention might "with perfect safety" grant suffrage to well-qualified Negroes, with education or Federal military service, so as to "completely disarm the adversary." And "the adversary" was identified as "the radicals who are wild upon Negro franchise" and who thereby "will be completely foiled in their attempt to keep the Southern states from renewing their relations with the Union by not accepting their senators and representatives." Encouraged by the President to defy Radical leaders in Congress, Mississippi even so made no move toward Negro suffrage. Neither did South Carolina's convention, when Johnson informed the governor, "It must be left to the Legislature of each State to decide who shall be allowed to vote. . . ."

Johnson's views on Negro suffrage reflected his own ambivalent feelings. In October, he told a Negro regiment, "This is your country as well as anybody else's. . . . This country is founded upon the principle of equality." He added that the great question was whether the Negro "race can be incorporated and mixed with the people of the United States—to make a harmonious and permanent ingredient. . . . Let us make the experiment, and make it in good faith." At another time, he observed that in Tennessee "I should try to introduce Negro suffrage gradually; first those who had served in the army; those who could read and write; and perhaps a property qualification for the other, say $200 or $250." Possibly if Johnson had been more persistent in prodding Southerners to provide a qualified Negro suffrage and to avoid choosing high ex-Confederates to office, the subsequent Congress might have been more willing to accept his handiwork.

During the summer and fall of 1865 Southern state conventions met operating under a virtual carte blanche from the President. For the most part the few steps prescribed by the President were followed. Changes in state constitutions eliminated references to slavery; the Thirteenth Amendment was ratified; state debts incurred because of the war were repudiated. A few states balked, fearful that the Thirteenth Amendment's second section "Congress shall have the power to enforce this article by appropriate legislation," would lead to Federal interference. Mississippi in fact did not ratify the amendment. South Carolina failed to repudiate its debt.

Despite this recalcitrance, Presidential agents sent south to observe conditions there reported Southern good faith in carrying out the President's terms for restoring government. General Grant, after a two-month tour, noted, "the mass of thinking men in the South accept the present situation in good faith." To a New York *Times* reporter it seemed that "the South—the great, substantial, prevailing element—is more loyal now than it was at the end of the war." A discordant note was sounded by Carl Schurz, a Presidential observer in the South, who reported "an *utter absence of national feeling* . . . and a desire to preserve slavery . . . as much and as long as possible.

. . . The emancipation of the slaves is submitted to only'' out of necessity. When Johnson brushed aside this report and its recommendation for a Congressional investigation, the Senate at Sumner's insistence published the report.

State elections resulted in putting into office—local, state, and Federal—many men who had been prominent Confederate officials or army officers. Even a few who had not yet received Presidential pardons were chosen. This thwarted Johnson's hope that Southerners would have the good sense to elect only Unionists or reluctant Confederates. Many state legislatures in the fall proceeded to enact ''Black Codes'' that denied any political rights to freedmen and imposed economic and social restrictions on their freedom. Some states called for immediate removal of Federal troops and elimination of the Freedmen's Bureau agents.

As each Southern state completed the process, the President announced through Secretary Seward official, legal recognition of the new state government. So far as Johnson was concerned, the task of restoring Southern states, both as to their own governments and as to resuming their place in the Union, was now complete. It remained only for Congress to give formal confirmation. But Congress was not so sure the process was complete. Among the men who presented themselves at the opening of Congress in December, 1865, were ex-Confederate leaders, including Georgia's new Senator, Alexander H. Stephens, only eight months earlier Vice President of the Confederacy, and four Confederate generals, eight colonels, and a host of lesser officers seeking to take seats in the House.

2. Congress Checks President Johnson

The immediate response of Congress, upon convening, was to exclude from the initial roll call and thereby to deny seats to all Senators or Representatives sent from the eleven former Confederate states. The rejection was based on several considerations. First, for staunch Unionists to welcome back with open arms rebels who for four years had tried to destroy the Union was to expect too much of human nature and would have required the forbearance and forgiveness of a saint. Second, many in Congress resented the President's having proceeded on his own without so much as having consulted Congress on reconstruction policy. Third, the party that won the war wanted to enjoy the political prizes of victory. As Radical Thaddeus Stevens put it bluntly, ''Let all who approve our [principles] tarry with us. Let all others go with copperheads and rebels.'' Further, many were convinced that genuine, not superficial, changes were needed to reform Southern society and eradicate any vestiges of slavery. For some, this meant moving fully to implement the principle of equality in political, economic, and social matters for the Negro.

On the three major questions—restoration of Southern states, what to do about ex-Confederate leaders, the postwar status of the Negro—the views of Congressmen were far from unanimous in December, 1865. Democrats from Northern and border states, plus some conservative Republicans, favored swift restoration of Southern states and no action to penalize Southern leaders or to change the Negro's position. Most conservative and moderate Republicans generally did not object to a quick return of Southern states but believed ex-Confederate leaders could not be trusted with political power and hence should be barred from political participation at least for the time being. They were willing to have the Federal government assume some obligation to protect the freedman in his newly-won freedom. Hence, although they could approve part of Johnson's work, they were distressed over Southern responses, which appeared unrepentant. Radical Republicans rejected all of Johnson's labors and especially resented Southern conventions' reluctance in repudiating secession and rebel state debts, Southern legislatures' adoption of repressive Black Codes and election of ex-rebels to state offices and to Congress. So, at the outset, although there was no Congressional consensus as to what was to be done, most agreed that the President's action had been hasty and ill-advised, that there was no need for such haste, and that Congress should deliberate and determine reconstruction policy, perhaps incorporating parts of Johnson's work, modifying parts, rejecting parts.

Having refused to seat Southern representatives, Congress then voted to create a Joint Committee on Reconstruction, composed of nine Representatives and six Senators, to investigate the whole reconstruction problem and recommend policy. Moderate Republican Senator William Pitt Fessenden, who became chairman of the committee, declared that "calm and serious consideration" of the whole question of restoration was "an imperative duty" of Congress. Moderates and Radicals agreed with Fessenden.

Reflected in Committee members' feelings was four-years of pent-up Congressional resentment against Presidential wielding of almost unlimited power. Congress, irritated by wartime executive intrusion on its sphere of power, was becoming increasingly determined to set the conditions for the South's return to the Union. Thaddeus Stevens expressed the mood of many when in December he told Congress, "Dead states cannot restore their existence. . . . [Their] future condition . . . depends on the will of the conqueror. . . . Congress must create states and declare when they are entitled to be represented" or it would "deserve and receive the execration of history. . . ."

News from the South disturbed many Congressmen. Former Confederates appeared to be acting as though there had been no war and no defeat and no change in the position of the Negro. At least a dozen meetings of blacks in scattered Southern cities reported numerous cases of Negroes being victimized. They asked Congress and the President for protection and for the vote. Wendell Phillips commented: "The rebellion has not ceased, it has only changed its weapons. Once it fought; now it intrigues; once it followed Lee in arms, now it follows President Johnson in guile and chicanery."

Where Radical Republicans had hailed Johnson the previous April, rising animosity toward him now labeled him as anti-Republican, "an irresolute mule . . . devil-bent upon the ruin of his country." Quickly it became clear that the Radicals and Johnson had little in common so far as reconstruction goals went. They agreed upon reunion and the end of slavery, but beyond that they were worlds apart. Indeed, some opponents now argued that, since Johnson came from a state that had seceded, his legitimacy as President was in doubt.

As 1866 began, the situation in Washington was not hopeless. The President still had support in Congress and in the North. Had he played his cards skillfully and used his leverage adroitly, he might still have succeeded in salvaging part of his program. Instead, by incredible ineptness and by failing to restrain his penchant for blunt, intemperate speaking, he managed in the first four months of 1866 to weaken his own position, upset his own followers and antagonize the large body of moderates whose support he needed to carry the contest with Congress.

In facing the President, Republicans were far from united in attitude or in agreement on policy in dealing with the South. On the party's right, conservatives like Senators James R. Doolittle, James Dixon, and Representative Henry J. Raymond provided support for speedy restoration of the Southern states without imposing any major social changes. To the left stood the Radicals, Thaddeus Stevens, Charles Sumner, Ben Wade, Julian, Henry Wilson, Zach Chandler, James M. Ashley, George S. Boutwell, and others, who wanted a substantial recasting of Southern society and politics. In the center, a large group of moderates, including Senators John Sherman, William P. Fessenden, James W. Grimes among others, were at the outset willing to go along part way with the President's plan. It was to this large middle faction that Radical leaders directed their appeals—primarily in terms of the political necessity of delay in restoring Southern states and readmitting Democratic leaders to the nation's councils in order to preserve Republican party control. Obviously Radical leaders were moved by mixed motives—idealistic, humanitarian, emotional, political, and economic. They won over some cohorts by arguing that determining reconstruction policy was a power belonging to Congress not to the President, who by launching such a program had overstepped his proper authority. They called for preserving Republican unity to ensure that the victors would not be robbed of the fruits of of victory, and they labeled the President as untrustworthy.

The Joint Committee, not originally dominated by Radicals, did much to nudge moderates, and even conservatives, toward a more advanced position on reconstruction policy. Over a period of months, the committee gathered evidence from a stream of witnesses showing that Southerners accepted little change as a consequence of the war.

President Johnson himself helped consolidate the opposition in Congress. On February 22, responding to a Washington's birthday group of serenaders who called at the White House, he bitterly assailed the Joint Committee as an "irresponsible central directory" usurping the powers of government and seeking to destroy the President. "I fought traitors and treason in the South," shouted Johnson, "now when I turn around, and at the other end of the line find men—I care not by what name you call them—who will stand opposed to the restoration of the Union of these States, I am free to say to you that I am still in the field." The crowd demanded to know who the Northern traitors were. "You ask me who they are?" replied Johnson. "I say Thaddeus Stevens . . . is one; . . . Mr. Sumner of the Senate is another; and Wendell Phillips is another."

Such an intemperate, violent outburst and personal abuse by the President shocked moderates in Congress. Many now moved closer to the Radicals. When Congress voted to extend the life of the Freedmen's Bureau, Johnson returned the bill with a strong veto message contending that the bill was an unwise, unconstitutional invasion of the internal affairs of the states. Congress sustained his veto on February 21. It would prove to be a hollow success for the President. Senator Lyman Trumbull's Civil Rights bill, passed by Congress, was also vetoed by the President March 27. Two weeks later Congress overrode the veto, and the bill became law. Within a few months Radicals generated enough strength to pass the Freedmen's Bureau extension over the Presidential veto. The break between Congress and the President was virtually complete, as the spring of 1866 melted into summer.

3. Radical Republicans Gain Allies

The Republicans in Congress who blocked President Johnson's reconstruction program in the spring of 1866 were a mixed crew. Classifying them into groups is not easy. Labeling them as conservative, moderate, or Radical Republicans may be of some help. But the qualifier must be understood as describing their respective views on the three major issues of the Reconstruction era—restoration of the Southern states, status of the Negro newly freed from legal bondage, and status of ex-Confederates in the new postwar era.

Those called Radical Republicans were themselves a varied lot. Generalizing about them is risky and can be misleading. Shot through with a strain of Puritan fervor, many of them believed that wrong-doing and rebellion required the repentance and contrition that the righteous might properly exact from sinners. Southerners should be made to pay for their sin of rebelling. Most of them had been schooled in the reforming zeal of the prewar antislavery drive. It was a religious crusade. Evil had been beaten down, the cancer of slavery now cut out by the sword. Convinced that the ideals of democracy should become practice as well as profession, some now sought to carry the revolution through to the logical extension of liberty, equality, and justice to the newly emancipated Negro. Many would change the system by pushing Federal intervention and control into areas formerly thought to be solely the domain of the states. If the Constitution threw up barriers to such action, the Constitution itself must yield or be changed.

Some Radicals, as hard-headed, practicing politicians for many years, had developed much skill at their trade. Having formed the Republican party as the instrument of moral reform, they were sure that only their party, the savior of the Union in war, could be trusted to secure the peace. Some had business interests and connections that affected their feelings and views. Others operated as lone wolf independents loosely associated with the party. Still others were outright opportunists. Differing in attitudes on many public questions, they shared a common inclination, though far from exact agreement, on policy relating to Reconstruction's major questions—readmission of Southern states, treatment of ex-rebels, status of the Negro. The revolution begun in the war was not to be thwarted by a strict constitutionalist in the Presidency and a Southerner at that. The revolution must be advanced.

Prominent among the Radicals stood seventy-four-year-old Thaddeus Stevens of Pennsylvania. During a long career as attorney-politician, Stevens had battled for causes he believed in—public education, protective tariff, abolition of slavery. Astute, hard-driving, incisive of mind, brief but caustic in speech, he had by diligence and ability worked his way to preeminence in the House where as chairman of the powerful Ways and Means Committee he influenced the fate of new legislation. Viewed by some as an eccentric bachelor, addicted to gambling and profanity, Stevens exhibited a curious blend of political realism and humane idealism. A shrewd lawyer, successful in practice, he had invested in an iron works near Gettysburg, which had been destroyed by Confederate invaders in 1863. Some ascribe to this loss his postwar hostility to the South. But undoubtedly he would have urged his strongly held convictions anyway. All his life Stevens championed the Negro, advocated Negro suffrage in Pennsylvania, treated his female Negro servant as a household equal (some enemies said as a mistress), insisted ultimately upon being buried in the only nonsegregated cemetery in Lancaster, Pennsylvania, and provided in his will that blacks be admitted equally with whites to the trade school at Lancaster which was endowed by his will.

In appearance Stevens struck observers as forbidding and somewhat odd—limping along on his club foot, his penetrating eyes glinting with fire, stern face topped with a black wig often askew, his tightly drawn mouth with "underlip defiantly protruding," speaking with "remarkable . . . argumentative pith and sarcastic wit" and disclosing an "absolutism of opinion with a contemptuous scorn for adverse argument." A figure not easily overlooked, a voice not readily dismissed nor forgotten. In his own mind, he saw clearly what had to be done: "The whole fabric of southern society must be changed. . . . The Southern states have been despotisms, not governments of the people. It is impossible that any practical equality of rights can exist where a few thousand men monopolize the whole landed property. . . . If the South is ever to be made a safe republic let her lands be cultivated by the toil of the owners or the free labor of intelligent citizens." Since conditions in the South were extreme, the remedy must be extreme. As Stevens put it, "reformation must be effected; the foundations of their [Southerners'] institutions—political, municipal and social—must be broken up and relaid or all our blood and treasure have been spent in vain." The revolution must go forward.

In the Senate the most distinguished Radical spokesman was fifty-four-year-old Charles Sumner of Massachusetts. Handsome, eloquent, polished in manner and appearance, Sumner had from the first maintained that the war must eradicate slavery. Now that the Negro was freed, full justice should be done to the freedman. "If all whites vote, then must all blacks," he reasoned, adding that "without them the old enemy will reappear, and in alliance with the Northern Democracy put us all in peril again."

Ranged with Sumner and Stevens in the forefront of the Radical drive opposing Johnson's Southern policy stood others in both houses. "Bluff Ben" Wade, veteran abolitionist from Ohio whose gruff manner and ribald jokes irritated many, Zachariah Chandler of Michigan, and Henry Wilson of Masaachusetts pushed Radical views in the Senate, while George W. Julian of Indiana, James M. Ashley of Ohio, George S. Boutwell of Massachusetts, William D. Kelley of Pennsylvania, James F. Wilson of Iowa, and John M. Broomall of Pennsylvania joined with Stevens in the House. All had been prewar abolitionists and had criticized Lincoln for not prosecuting the war more aggressively and for not moving more swiftly and decisively to end slavery. Now that the war was past, they wanted to let Southern states wait while Congress insured protection for Negroes and the Republican party consolidated its political power. To act too fast in restoring Southern states to the Union might endanger these goals.

In time the Radicals would pick up strength with new allies in Republican ranks, as moderates and conservatives found Johnson's intransigence and insults too much to stomach. But at the beginning of 1866 they formed only a minority of Republicans in Congress. The best they could accomplish then was the blocking of immediate restoration. They could not foist any new policy on the country unless they won support for it. A combination of political circumstances, the President's ineptness, and developments in the South pushed many Republicans to adopt a Radical stance.

Earlier, the Radicals had criticized Lincoln as slow on slavery and soft on the South. They viewed Lincoln's 10 per cent plan of restoration as weak, inadequate and entirely too lenient on rebels. Resenting the President's wartime dominance, they drove through Congress on July 4, 1864 (the session's last day) the Wade-Davis bill, which proposed to hold the South under military control until a *majority* of a state's 1860 voting population (not just 10 per cent) evidenced loyalty to the Union. In order to participate in political restoration, men were to swear not only future allegiance but that they had been consistently loyal in the past as well—a condition that of course ruled out the vast majority of Southern whites who had supported the Confederacy. If a majority of loyal oath-takers could be found (which seemed impossible), the new state constitutions they would then be authorized to make must abolish slavery, disfranchise ex-Confederate officials, and repudiate state debts. This bill, Radicals hoped, would commit their party to the Radical approach for the 1864 campaign and election. Parenthetically, its provisions resembled closely those ultimately adopted by Congress in 1867.

Lincoln let the bill die without his signature, but he indicated that Southern states might return to the Union via the Wade-Davis route if they chose to do so. Infuriated, Congressional Radicals struck back with the Wade-Davis Manifesto denouncing the President. As noted above, the Radicals gave only perfunctory support to Lincoln's reelection in 1864. In January, 1865, they cheered the final passage of the Thirteenth Amendment; in February, they blocked Congressional seating of members from Lincoln's "reconstructed" Louisiana; and in March they got the Freedmen's Bureau established.

After Johnson's accession to the executive chair, Radicals became increasingly hostile as the new President proceeded to sponsor a Lincoln-like program for reestablishing governments and then pronounced Southern states restored, as described in the preceding sections. And so when Congress met in December, 1865, the President's work was stymied as Congress barred members-elect from Southern states and created the Joint Committee on Reconstruction to investigate conditions in the South and to recommend policy regarding the rebel states.

Such an investigation gave Congressional leaders time to deliberate on what policy to pursue. Radicals viewed it as a holding action, hoping to win more converts to their position. No general agreement existed even among Republicans on either policy or theory regarding the South. All Americans, both North and South, held the Constitution in high reverence. No action could be taken without constitutional sanction for it, men agreed. Several theories had already emerged as to the South's status. Lincoln and Johnson rested their approach to reconstruction on the theory that since secession was a nullity Southern states could not leave the indissoluble Union, hence were still part of the Union and had only to be brought into their proper operating relation to it. This, they believed, could be done most simply and directly by Presidential action, and they acted upon that theory.

In contrast, Stevens advanced the doctrine that the Southern states had in fact left the Union, as they claimed, and waged war as a foreign power against the United States. When the fighting ended in their defeat, they were in the position of conquered provinces and were therefore subject to the will of Congress, unrestrained by the Constitution, which would not apply to conquered territory. Thus Congress would determine the conditions of restoration, including political, social, and economic terms for the South. Senator Sumner would have Congress follow the theory that Southern states had by rebellion committed political suicide, but since their territory still lay within the borders of the United States, their society was subject to the power of Congress, which should now adopt civil rights and Negro suffrage legislation.

No one of these theories commanded broad support in Congress, where the restraining hand of the Constitution gave members pause over adopting internal reform and property confiscation legislation. All agreed, however, that the Constitution authorized Congress to insure that each state had a republican form of government. On this basis, a theory advanced by Representative Samuel Shellabarger of Ohio in January, 1866, held that, while secession was null, the attempted rebellion so altered the relation of rebelling states to the Union that they forfeited their rights and powers and hence were subject to Congress's power to guarantee a republican form of government within them. The forfeited rights theory, avoiding mention of conquest, suicide, or property confiscation, appealed to many congressmen. With its ring of constitutionality, it became in effect the theory followed. It allowed Congress to suspend decision on seating Southern representatives while it investigated the nature and validity of Johnson-sponsored state governments and examined conditions prevailing in the South. Moderates and conservatives found this approach acceptable, and Radicals went along. Policy could be decided upon after investigation.

Although some conservative Republicans at the start of 1866 were willing to support the President's program, a growing number of the party' numerous moderates were developing misgivings. For one thing they were disturbed by reported developments in the South in the closing months of 1865. Southern foot-dragging on ratifying the Fourteenth Amendment, reluctance to repudiate state debts, resolutions of repeal rather than outright repudiation of secession, talk of compensation for freed slaves, and disregard and abuse of freedmen all were irritating if not alarming tendencies.

The fifteen-member Joint Committee on Reconstruction, established in January, 1866, under the chairmanship of moderate Senator William P. Fessenden, was not dominated by Radicals at the outset. Sumner, for example, was denied a place on the committee, which he wanted badly, and although Stevens expounded his strong views as a committee member, Fessenden kept the proceedings under fair control and wrote the final report himself. From January to May, committee hearings in Washington and other cities gathered a massive array of evidence from 142 witnesses, including 8 Negroes, 57 Southern whites, and 77 Northerners residing or sojourning in the South. Many witnesses were army officers, like Grant, or Freedmen's Bureau officials or Southern loyalists, but newspapermen and former Confederates like Lee and Alexander Stephens also testified.

What emerged from the testimony was a picture of the postwar South where whites, while resignedly accepting the legal end of slavery, were bent on keeping Negroes in a servile-dependent social, economic status without political rights. Southern Unionists were being proscribed, and clearly the "Johnson governments," dedicated to white supremacy, had no intention of altering conditions to make room and opportunity for the newly freed Negro.

The evidence of this situation, in Northern eyes at least, was exhibited in the "Black Codes" of laws adopted in 1865–66 by most, but not all, Southern state legislatures. Such legislation sought to define the new status of the Negro after release from slavery. The provisions in the codes were drawn from various sources—army and Freedmen's Bureau regulations of freedmen, Northern state laws, as well as Southern prewar codes. Their spirit was most pointedly exemplified in the Mississippi Code's preamble, which proclaimed: "Under the pressure of federal bayonets, . . . the people of Mississippi have abolished the institution of slavery. . . . The Negro is free, whether we like it or not. . . . To be free, however, does not make him a citizen, or entitle him to social and political equality with the white man. But the constitution and justice do entitle him to protection and security in his person and property, both real and personal."

Black Codes in most states conceded Negroes the right to sue, give evidence in court subject to certain restrictions, as in cases where a white was party to the suit, have marriages regularized, and go to school. Some states allowed blacks to hold such jobs as they could obtain. Other codes restricted them to farm labor unless they secured special licenses as mechanics and artisans. Owning or leasing land was forbidden in some states. Purchase and possession of firearms and liquor were prohibited. Penalties for certain offenses were in some instances heavier on blacks than whites. Some apprenticeship laws assigned under-eighteen Negroes whose parents could not care for them to work for an employer who supplied room and board in lieu of wages. Vagrancy laws provided that persons "wandering about in idleness" could be fined $50 or sentenced ten days or longer as vagrants to be put to work on state chain gangs or more often bound out to employers without wages until earnings were sufficient to reimburse employers for what had been paid in fines and upkeep. In some instances a Negro vagrant was returned to work for his previous master on the very plantation he came from. Some states placed restrictrictions upon moving about (except by special permit), place of residence, assembling in public meetings, and making labor contracts. By such laws the Negro was being relegated to an inferior social and economic status, which to outward appearances resembled that of his former servitude.

Such Southern action disturbed many in Washington. Carl Schurz saw the Black Codes as embodying "the idea that although the former owner has lost his individual right of property in the former slave, the blacks at large belong to the whites at large." Secretary of the Navy Gideon Welles, a supporter of Johnson's policy, observed, "The entire South seems stupid and vindictive. . . ." And in Congress moderate Republicans like Lyman Trumbull were deeply disturbed by "Black Laws" that submerged Negro rights.

While Joint Committee hearings continued, a stalemate loomed as Johnson in January, 1866, insisted on the legality of "restored" Southern state governments and their "right" to representation in Congress. Congressional leaders just as firmly denied such legality and rights. Faced with evidence gathered by the Joint Committee, many Congressmen, including moderates who still thought compromise with the President possible, expressed growing concern over the condition of the freedmen. On January 11 the able, scholarly Senator Lyman Trumbull of Illinois introduced two bills —one to extend the life of the Freedmen's Bureau, the other a civil rights bill.

The Freedmen's Bureau, since March, 1865, had been providing many essential services in the war-wracked South. It distributed rations, supervised wage contracts, relocated freedmen, established schools and hospitals. An arm of the War Department, it even ran its own courts to settle disputes over labor contracts, land holding, and similar problems. Its life, limited by law to one year after the close of hostilities, would presumably end in late April, although some argued that the war had not yet ended. Trumbull's bill proposed to extend the bureau's life until terminated by law and to enlarge its judicial jurisdiction to cover all cases of discrimination against persons on account of race, color, or previous servitude. Appearing to be a logical extension of the Thirteenth Amendment and appealing to the sense of fair play of the moderates as well as of Radical Republicans, the bill passed both houses handily.

Many Republicans, including Trumbull and Fessenden, were sure the President was willing to support this measure of protection for the freedmen. On February 19, Johnson's sharp veto of the Freedmen's Bureau bill came as a shock. Johnson refused his approval on constitutional and practical grounds. The bill was needless, he said, since with the Union virtually restored, the Federal civil courts were again beginning to function in the South. These courts could better handle any cases that might go to the bureau courts, which, he argued, were a costly and unnecessary enlargement of Federal bureaucracy. Congress had no authority under the Constitution, said Johnson, to intervene in a state's domestic affairs, and besides it was unfair to adopt such legislation when the eleven states most affected by it were unrepresented in Congress. The well-argued message had considerable impact in the Senate, which could not at once muster a two-thirds vote to override it.

However, three days later Johnson's incredibly gross verbal attack on Radical leaders, branding them as traitors during his Washington's birthday speech, alienated many moderates who until now had been willing to sustain the President and seek an accommodation with him. From this point on, they moved closer to the Radicals, who capitalized on every Johnson misstep and tactless outburst. The Chief Executive undercut his own already weakened position. From now on he could not guide affairs; he could only drift with the tide, attempting now and then in vain to slow its momentum. Radical leaders moved swiftly to destroy remaining Presidential influence. Sumner referred to Johnson as "an insolent drunken brute," while Stevens dismissed him as "an alien enemy of a foreign state." During the months to come, newspapers and magazines in the North, formerly sympathetic or at least impartial toward the President, turned harshly critical, some editors elaborating the myth of Johnson "the inebriated moron."

By mid-March Congress approved Trumbull's Civil Rights Bill by 3–1 margins in both houses. The bill declared all native-born persons to be citizens of the United States, stipulated that citizens "of every race and color" had the right to sue, give evidence in court, own property, and have "full and equal benefit of all laws and proceedings for the security of person and property, as is enjoyed by white citizens." Depriving citizens of equal rights was punishable in Federal courts, which had exclusive jurisdiction, and the use of the full power of all Federal agencies, including the armed forces, was authorized to insure enjoyment of equal rights by all.

Jacksonian Democrat that he was, Johnson returned the bill to Congress with his veto message on March 27. Sticking to the traditional constitutional view that civil rights derived from state citizenship, the President maintained that recognition and protection of civil rights lay entirely within the province of each state to determine. For the United States to intrude in this area would radically undermine the states, overturn the historic Federal division of authority between center and parts, and require a vast and frightening increase in Federal agents to enforce the proposed legislation. Such a departure Johnson considered not only unnecessary but harmful.

This veto, enlarging the rift, succeeded in driving additional moderate Congressman away from supporting the President. Within two weeks they rallied in concert with the Radicals to drive through the Civil Rights Act of 1866 over the veto. Later, Congress shattered the Presidential veto barrier again by voting into law, in slightly revised form, the Freedmen's Bureau extension bill.

4. Congress Takes Command: The Fourteenth Amendment and the Critical Election of 1866

Another jolt hit the President on April 28 when the Joint Committee reported to Congress. Southern states were not entitled to representation in Congress, the committee asserted, because the President did not have authority to establish governments in the South. Southern states would be barred from political participation until ex-Confederate leaders were banned from political affairs and rights for Negroes were recognized and protected.

On this much, Congressional leaders were agreed, because by late spring of 1866 the dangers of immediately readmitting Southern states were acknowledged by all Republican factions. The prospect of larger Southern representation in Congress was a clear threat. Now that slavery was ended, the three-fifths clause of the Constitution was no longer valid, which meant that all, not just three-fifths of the blacks would be counted. Some calculated that the South would have at least fifteen more House seats than in the pre-1861 era. Combined Southern-Northern Democratic strength, many believed, would menace Republican control in Washington, undermine civil rights guarantees, return the Negro to virtual bondage, and even threaten repudiation of the national war debt. Why reward rebellion? Even cautious Republican Senator John Sherman vowed that "never by my consent shall these rebels gain . . . increased political power and come back here to wield that power . . . against the safety and integrity of the country."

Both moderate and Radical Republicans could readily agree on this much. Beyond this, views diverged. To insure Negro rights, was it necessary to authorize Negro suffrage? Would such a proposal be acceptable in Northern states, most of which denied the vote to Negroes? How could Republican ascendancy be insured, Southern Democrats be barred from regaining influence in Washington, Negro rights be protected, and payment of the war debt be guaranteed?

Sharing Sherman's concern, many Republicans were convinced that the logical results of the war had to be locked into the Constitution. The Joint Committee was wrestling with the dilemma when Stevens proposed an amendment, initially prepared by reformer Robert Dale Owen, calling for (1) protection of civil rights of all persons, (2) no payment of the rebel debt or compensation for slaves, (3) no denial of suffrage to Negroes or ex-Confederates after July 4, 1876, but before that time any state's representation in Congress would be reduced in proportion to the number of its citizens denied the suffrage. This proposal, after some revision by the Joint Committee, was adopted by the House but encountered opposition in the

Senate. There, changes were made, adding a definition of citizenship, prohibiting office-holding by certain ex-Confederates, and guaranteeing payment of the national debt. After weeks of debate the Senate passed the amendment on June 8; the House approved five days later.

The Fourteenth Amendment proposed to push the revolution, unleashed by war, a notch further. The first section of the amendment (an effective rejection of the Dred Scott ruling on citizenship a decade earlier) declared "all persons born or naturalized in the United States" to be citizens of the United States and of their state of residence. It thereby constitutionally conferred citizenship upon American-born Negroes. States were forbidden to abridge "the privileges and immunities" of citizens of the United States nor could a state "deprive any person of life, liberty, or property, without due process of law, nor deny to any person within its jurisdiction equal protection of the laws." This section, on top of the 1866 Civil Rights Act which many feared might be held unconstitutional, provided a sweeping revolutionary change in Federal-state relations by essentially placing civil rights under Federal protection. It would over the years become the most litigated clause in the Constitution, as men sought to clarify the meaning of the abstract phrases, "due process," "privileges and immunities," and "equal protection of the laws."

The first section was largely the handiwork of Republican Representative John A. Bingham of Ohio, a long time abolitionist who in prewar years had persistently advanced in Congress "the great democratic idea that all men, before the law, are equal in respect to those rights of person which God gives and no man or state may rightfully take away." Bingham contended for recognition of "the absolute equality of all" and "the equal protection of each [in] those sacred rights which are universal and indestructible," as he phrased it in an 1859 speech. As a Joint Committee member, Bingham defended Section One in a February 27 speech as "simply a proposition to arm the Congress . . . with power to enforce the Bill of Rights" so "that all shall be protected alike in life, liberty and property" and in "all privileges and immunities of citizens" and so that no state can "deny equal protection to any human being." Bingham and other Radical spokesmen succeeded in persuading Congress to adopt this position.

Section Two of the amendment ingeniously sought to introduce Negro suffrage by indirect means in facing Southerners with the distasteful choice of allowing Negroes to vote or having their state's Congressional representation reduced in proportion to the number of adult male citizens denied the suffrage. In a state where the black population ran close to 50 per cent, for example, the state stood to lose a substantial number of its seats in the House if voting rights were denied to Negroes. The third part of the amendment barred all Confederates who in prewar years had taken an oath to support the Federal Constitution from holding state or Federal office (but not from voting). This disability, designed to solidify Republican control, could be removed only by a two-thirds vote of Congress. In effect it counterbalanced the President's power to pardon Confederates. Finally, payment of the Federal debt was guaranteed, while Confederate war debts were canceled.

The Fourteenth Amendment, proposed by the Joint Committee and modified and approved by Congress, now became the crucial test. Did Americans want to secure the one major goal of their Civil War? Did the war generation genuinely wish to move ahead toward the ideal of equality of rights that the Founders glorified in the Declaration and the Jacksonians praised so glowingly? The first section of the amendment in effect wrote into the Constitution what Americans had been saying they believed since 1776. Granted, the constitutional, Federal system that had evolved up to this point had left matters of citizenship and civil rights in the hands of the states. Could Americans lift the heavy hand of the Constitution in order to move closer to implementing the ideals of their Declaration? True, the phrasing of the amendment was as vague as it was idealistic. Could it be made to mean in practice what its framers intended? The answers lay in the future.

For the present—1866—views on Reconstruction policy still remained divided. Many moderates expected that the amendment would be "the final condition of reconstruction." Southern acceptance of it would end Reconstruction. But some Radicals believed the amendment did not go far enough. For example, Sumner insisted that the Negro should be given the right to vote immediately. Stevens had been urging distribution of land to Negroes and a change in "the whole fabric of southern society." Some stand-patters thought the amendment too extreme, too revolutionary. President Johnson opposed the amendment, contending that no constitutional change could be properly made while eleven states were still out of the Union and unrepresented in Congress. He advised the states not to ratify it. The showdown on the critical test began as the amendment went out to the state legislatures in the summer of 1861.

During discussion of the Fourteenth Amendment several events underscored the confusion resulting from Congress's failure to set a fixed Reconstruction policy. The result was a strengthened belief that Federal protection for Negroes in the South was needed. During the war, an Indiana Copperhead, Lambdin P. Milligan, had been arrested, tried, and convicted by a military commission in Indiana where civil courts were operating. His appeal for a writ of habeas corpus reached the Supreme Court, which in April, 1866, ruled that he was entitled to the writ because the military commission had no authority to try him. Formal written opinions were deferred until a later Court term. But the immediate effect of the *Milligan* ruling was to cast doubt upon using Federal military courts for law enforcement in the South where civil courts were already reopened.

In late April at Memphis, sidewalk jostling incidents involving Negro soldiers of the Federal garrison there and local whites erupted into wild violence. Local police joined a white mob to invade the city's Negro quarter, burning and killing indiscriminately. After three days (April 30 to May 2), General George Stoneman's troops intervened and restored order. The toll stood at forty-six Negroes killed and eighty wounded, four churches and twelve schools of the blacks destroyed. Stoneman's report to Washington that Negroes did nothing after the first day except "be killed and abused" was confirmed by a Congressional investigating committee. Its report concluded that the white mob acted out of fierce hatred of Negroes.

Two months later another outbreak produced a similar massacre in New Orleans. The affair arose from the tangled skein of Louisiana politics. One group of Radical Republicans, fearful of losing political control, reconvened the state's adjourned 1864 convention members. Both the governor and the mayor opposed the move and called out the police. On July 30 a procession of Negroes from outside the meeting hall cheered the delegates in hopes that Negro suffrage would be adopted. Suddenly police closed in. Rocks were thrown. Police guns blazed as marchers tried to gain sanctuary by entering the hall. Policemen and white toughs then fired through the windows and shot and beat those seeking to escape by a rear door. Federal troops raced to the scene to find 37 Negroes and 3 white supporters dead and more than 100 wounded. General Sheridan reported that "nine-tenths of the casualties were perpetrated by the police and citizens stabbing and smashing in heads of many who had already been wounded or killed by policemen." It was not a riot, he concluded, but "an absolute massacre . . . a murder which the mayor and police . . . perpetrated without the shadow of necessity." The whole affair might have been prevented, but the Federal military commander's telegram to Stanton asking instructions had inexplicably gone unanswered.

The impact of the Memphis and New Orleans outbursts upon feeling and opinion in the North was enormous. Whether a majority of Southern whites approved or deplored the violence was immaterial. In Northern eyes, all Southern whites were guilty of brutality designed to force blacks back into bondage and thereby nullify the North's victory in the war. Radical newspapers gave large play to these developments. The New York *Tribune* cried out: "The hands of the Rebels are again red with loyal blood" and added: "Johnson's statesmanship [has] again raised the Rebel flags in New Orleans." Many Northerners concurred with Senator Chandler's judgment that "the same [rebels] are alive today . . . who have only changed their leaders, and their tactics. . . . They mean to overthrow the government." The *Independent's* editor called upon voters to "rebuke at the ballot-box the outrages which the President has abetted at New Orleans. . . . How long will the Conservatives be blind to the mad career of Andrew Johnson? . . . [He] abetted the New Orleans mob . . . The President's policy is bloodshed. . . . He has turned treason into loyalty. . . . He is co-head of the rebellion.'' In view of local failure, the charge against Johnson was unfair, but it was widely believed in the North.

Here sounded one major Radical theme for the upcoming midterm Congressional campaign of 1866. Along with it ran the debate over the Fourteenth Amendment. Within six months, governments in all ex-Confederate states, except Tennessee (which ratified and was readmitted by Congress in July), rejected the amendment, appearing to follow the President's negative advice. Along with rejection by Delaware and Kentucky, the total showed twelve states not ratifying out of thirty-seven states in the Union. To meet the Constitutional three-fourths requirement, ratification by twenty-nine states was needed. Some raised the question whether the ex-Confederate states, since they were not yet fully restored to Union membership, had a right to act and had to be counted; but Congress had signaled that they should be.

As debate over the amendment went on, so did the political campaign. In mid-August a National Union Convention at Philadelphia brought together notable Democratic and conservative Republican spokesmen, like Postmaster General Alexander Randall, Senators James R. Doolittle and Edgar Cowan, General John A. Dix, and New York *Times* editor Henry J. Raymond who was also a Congressman. After featuring an ''arm-in-arm'' entrance of a pair of Massachusetts and South Carolina delegates as a symbol of the reunited Union, the gathering endorsed Johnson's Reconstruction program and urged voters to support Congressional candidates who backed Johnson's policies.

Seeking to rally popular support, President Johnson himself took to the hustings on a ''swing around the circle'' from Philadelphia, New York, and Albany west to Cleveland, Chicago (where he dedicated a monument to Stephen A. Douglas), Indianapolis, Cincinnati, and Pittsburgh. In the rough and tumble manner of a brawling Tennessee stump speaker, Johnson loudly harangued his audiences, denounced the Radicals, and praised the Constitution. Often taunted by hecklers in the crowd, Johnson abandoned Presidential dignity and descended into direct shouting matches. One went like this: Heckler: ''Why don't you hang Jeff Davis?'' Johnson: ''Why don't you?'' Johnson: ''Congress is trying to destroy the government.'' Heckler: ''It's a lie!'' Johnson: ''They are ready to impeach me, just let them try.'' Heckler: ''Too bad they don't.'' It was too much when Johnson compared his persecution to Christ's and pledged his willingness to die for country and Constitution. Such harangues did neither the President nor his cause any good. Indeed, in the eyes of many he appeared the ''ludicrous boor'' and ''drunken imbecile'' that some Radical papers pictured him. Support for pro-Johnson candidates melted away rapidly.

Republicans, Radical and otherwise, fought back. In September they sponsored a convention of Northern and Southern loyalists in Philadelphia. Dubbed by foes as a ''black and tan'' convention, it featured Albion W.

Tourgée, an Ohioan now living in North Carolina, and noted abolitionist-editor Frederick Douglass, along with talk of Negro suffrage, which the meeting failed to endorse. Radical speakers on the campaign trail, including Stevens, Sumner, Ben Wade, Carl Schurz and John A. Logan, pounded away at Johnson's ineptness. They magnified his mistakes, pictured him as a "tyrant," compared him to Judas, Benedict Arnold, and Vallandigham, charged him with allying with the rebels to rob the North of the fruits of victory. Northern businessmen were warned that the return of unreconstructed rebels would jeopardize high tariffs, hard money, government bonds, and railroad subsidies. Appeals were directed to Union veterans, just then organizing the Grand Army of the Republic for its first national convention to meet at Indianapolis, calling on them to "vote as you shot" to save at the polls the victory achieved in battle. As long as Johnson's policies operated, the South would give no sign of "repentance" nor could there be any security for the Union.

With the Fourteenth Amendment hanging in the balance, Republicans sought a major success at the polls. In November they got it. They swept to victory in all Northern states, amassing large majorities in the East, winning narrower victories in the West. The new Senate would have 42 Republicans to 11 Democrats, the House 143 to 49—much more than the two-thirds majorities needed to override Presidential vetoes. Whatever voters may have meant by their votes, many Radical leaders were convinced that the election was a mandate for the South to accept the Fourteenth Amendment and beyond that for Congress to extend the revolution begun by the war.

12

Revolution at Full Speed, 1866–1868

Following the 1866 mid-term elections, Radical Republicans quickly took full charge of Reconstruction policy. They shunted the President aside and came close to ejecting him from office. Potential interference by the Supreme Court was forestalled. New legislation in 1867 required Southern states under military supervision to accept the Fourteenth Amendment and to revise their own state constitutions allowing place and opportunity for Negroes before restoration to the Union. In a year and a half's time, with all opposition swept aside, the Congressional Radical program moved into operation. By then new state constitutions were adopted, the Fourteenth Amendment ratified, and new state governments established largely under Radical control. All but three ex-Confederate states were formally pronounced as restored to the Union. In the national election of 1868 voters seemed to approve the program by elevating Republican Ulysses S. Grant, now a Radical cohort, to the Presidency.

1. Radical Reconstruction at Full Throttle

When the new Congress met on December 3, 1866, leaders brushed aside the President's message which argued that the stated purpose of the war to restore Southern states to the Union was accomplished, that restoration had been achieved, and that Congress in justice and in accordance with the Constitution should seat Southern elected representatives. This, Congress was not about to do, although Radical spokesmen were far from agreement on what remained to be done. News from the South was troubling; the states of Alabama, Arkansas, Florida, Georgia, North and South Carolina, and Texas had rejected the Fourteenth Amendment (and the other three unrestored rebel states would turn it down in early 1867).

Some Republican leaders like Wade, Sherman, and Bingham believed that Southern states' acceptance of the amendment should be the final condition for full restoration. Others like James G. Blaine of Maine thought Negro suffrage should be required. Stevens and others supported this position.

At its winter term, 1866–67, the Supreme Court added a complicating factor that Radicals would have to reckon with. Limitation on the number of justices on the Court had already been set by an 1866 act of Congress approved by President Johnson. Now the Court, with five members speaking through Justice David Davis, issued its opinion supporting the already announced ruling in the *Milligan* case. A civilian, said the Court, could not be held by the government and tried by a military court in areas where civil courts were functioning and where there was no actual war and fighting. "The Constitution . . . is a law for rulers and people, equally in war and peace," declared the Court, which ventured further its opinion that neither Congress nor the President had legal power to institute military courts to try civilians in nonwar zones, at least in the nonseceded states. Shortly, the Court proceeded also to strike down the requirement of its own earlier rule that attorneys practicing in Federal courts must swear to past loyalty by taking the ironclad test oath (*ex parte Garland*). At the same time in *Cummings* v. *Missouri* the court voided the provision in Missouri's 1865 Radical-inspired constitution requiring voters, ministers, attorneys, and candidates for office to swear to past loyalty. Thereby the Court cast a doubt on action contemplated by the Radicals to establish military rule in the South, indeed made dubious Johnson's use of the military in his restoring process, and placed the Freedmen's Bureau courts in a similarly dubious position.

Despite the Court, Congress's big guns opened fire early in 1867. Thad Stevens began it by offering a reconstruction bill which he supported with a powerful speech that struck directly at the core of the situation. Southern rebels, he argued, had demonstrated that they could not be trusted. Not only had they tried to tear the Union apart, but since the war they had acted as "barbarians . . . murdering loyal whites daily and daily putting into secret graves not only hundreds but thousands of colored people." To meet these actions, the government must use drastic measures: Johnson governments to be declared illegal, ex-Confederate military and civil leaders to be stripped of citizenship for at least five years, and military control to run the South until Southern state constitutions were revised to provide Negro suffrage. Enfranchising blacks was necessary for several reasons. First, Negroes could then protect themselves and loyal whites from being "oppressed, exiled, or murdered." Second, "it would insure the ascendancy of the Union party" upon which "depends the safety of this great nation," and without "impartial suffrage" Southern states would send "a solid rebel representative delegation to Congress" and with "their kindred Copperheads of the North . . . always elect the President and control Congress." Further, as a matter of justice, insisted the old Pennsylvanian, "every man, no matter what his race or color . . . has an equal right to justice, honesty, and fair play." Let Congressmen have the courage to make real the Declaration's aim "to secure these rights" for all men, lest history "magnify their meanness." Seldom had Stevens been more direct, incisive, and eloquent.

Some leaders still turned away from Stevens's path, holding that acceptance of the Fourteenth Amendment would suffice to readmit the South. But the Radical drive gained momentum. Sumner's bill to enfranchise Negroes in the District of Columbia was enacted over a Presidential veto. Congress provided also that the new session would start on March 4 rather than in distant December. When Stevens's bill bogged down in committee, George Julian won House acceptance for his bill to extend military rule throughout the South. The Senate balked as conservatives and moderates objected. To break the stalemate, as February dragged on, a party caucus produced a committee under John Sherman's lead to mold the Julian bill into the final form in which it passed both houses. A Johnson veto was beaten down overwhelmingly, 138–48 in the House and 38–10 in the Senate. The First Reconstruction Act became law on March 2, 1867.

Declaring ten Southern states to be without legal government, the act divided the South into five military districts, each under the command of a general authorized to use the army to maintain order and enforce the law. Each commander was to supervise elections of delegates to state conventions to draft new constitutions and organize new governments. All adult males, black and white, could vote except those disfranchised for participation in rebellion. The new constitutions must include similar suffrage provisions. When a state's voters approved its new constitution and ratified the Fourteenth Amendment (thereby eliminating any Black Code), and when the state's new constitution received Congressional approval and the Fourteenth Amendment had actually become part of the United States Constitution, Congress would readmit the state and seat its representatives.

The Radical Reconstruction program, embodied in this act, expressed the Radicals' prime concern over the Negro, who was, after all, the central figure of Reconstruction and whose bondage had been a major cause of the war itself. Negroes had already demonstrated that they could work, but few had had an opportunity to become literate or to compete in the economic-political realm. The Radical program now conferred civil rights and the franchise, in expectation that with political rights the Negro could make a successful transition to living as a free man.

But political participation alone, on paper, in law, would prove insufficient to secure the Negro his fair place in American society. Thaddeus Stevens saw this more keenly than his fellows when he urged an economic base to undergird the Negro's new political place. "In my judgment," he observed in 1866, "we shall not approach a measure of justice until we have given every adult freedman a homestead on the land where he was born and toiled and suffered. Forty acres of land and a hut would be more valuable to him than the immediate right to vote." Congress should set aside all public lands in the seceded states, confiscate the 394 million acres held by the "chief rebels" and give each head of a Negro family 40 acres of land. Beyond the amount needed for this revolutionary redistribution, the surplus proceeds from the sale of excess confiscated lands would yield a government fund from which subsidies, pensions, and buildings could be provided to new Negro landowners.

Here was the logical and practical extension of the Civil War's revolutionary thrust, if the Negro was truly to escape servitude and achieve a solid position to stand on his own economic feet. George Julian seconded the proposal. But Stevens and Julian could not convince other Republicans, even Radicals, who, though willing enough to support human rights, drew back in fright at tampering with property rights by so extreme a measure as full confiscation. Failure to enact Southern land reform spelled ultimate defeat for the whole Radical program and opened the way to eventual peonage for sharecropper and tenant farmer. Given land and ballot—economic and political underpinning—the Negro might have more readily moved into the nineteenth century's social-economic mainstream, and the American dilemma of the twentieth century might have been partially mitigated if not averted.

But land reform proposals aside, Congress acted to make sure that its program would not be thwarted. The Army Appropriations Act (March 2, 1867) shaved the President's authority by requiring that he issue all military orders through the General of the Army, U.S. Grant, whose headquarters must be in Washington where Congress could keep close tabs. The Tenure of Office Act, passed the same day, required the President to secure Senate consent before dismissing any executive officer whose appointment had been confirmed by the Senate. Seeking to prevent Johnson's use of the patronage, this law would later be used to keep in the cabinet Secretary of War Stanton, who was sympathetic with the Radical program. A Second Reconstruction Act (March 23, 1867) and a Third (July 19, 1867) spelled out details for implementing the program, required prospective voters to swear to the ironclad test oath, gave military commanders full authority to bar voters and to discharge officials in Southern states.

In the two years that had passed since the fighting ended, there had been confusion, uncertainty, and misunderstanding over how the Southern states were to be reconstructed. Now the uncertainty was resolved, the confusion dispelled, as Congress set the terms for Southern states to meet. Some men might condemn the severity of the terms, while others might praise their humanity toward the Negro. But none could doubt the intentions of the Radical framers of the new Reconstruction legislation. For the sins of slavery and disloyalty Southern secessionists must now do penance, while loyal men, black and white, might at last garner their just rewards—if they could.

For all but one of these acts, which form the basis of the Congressional Reconstruction program, Presidential vetoes were overturned by Congress. Johnson, resenting legislative usurpation of executive control of the army, might understandably have undercut the Congressional program, which he thought unconstitutional, by naming as commanding generals in Southern military districts men sympathetic to his views, such as William T. Sherman, Lovell H. Rousseau, and Winfield S. Hancock, or by creating a military Division of the South to supervise the work of department commanders.

But if he was tempted, Johnson restrained himself. The district commands went to Generals John M. Schofield, Daniel E. Sickles, John Pope, Edward O. C. Ord, and Philip H. Sheridan.

But if the President did not try to stymie the program, Southern leaders did. Initial response to Congressional decrees was stunned disbelief by former Confederates. The next reaction was an attempt to obstruct the new acts by appeal to the courts. Mississippi sought an injunction to block Johnson from enforcing the acts, but in April, 1867, the Supreme Court refused to intervene on the ground that it had no power to prevent the President from executing the laws. Georgia then tried to enjoin Stanton, Grant, and Pope (the district commander), to which the Court responded that it could not rule on a "political question." Later in the year when a Mississippi editor, William McCardle, was brought to trial before a military commission for libeling General Ord, McCardle sought a writ of habeas corpus from a Federal district judge. Failing there, McCardle's lawyer, former Attorney General Jeremiah Black, a current close adviser to Johnson, carried an appeal to the Supreme Court. But by the time the appeal was scheduled, Congress exercising its constitutional power had shaved away the Court's appellate jurisdiction over habeas corpus cases arising under the new Reconstruction legislation, and the Court acquiesced, dropping the case.

Meanwhile the process prescribed by Congress began in the South under military auspices. The already existing "Johnson governments" continued for the time being in anomalous fashion, although the generals did remove governors and some lesser officials in Virginia, Georgia, Louisiana, Mississippi, and Texas. Where local officials, like registrars were removed, replacements were usually drawn from army officer and Freedmen's Bureau ranks, including a few Negroes. Even with fewer than 20,000 soldiers in ten Southern states, quartered at camps usually far from population centers, the army could and did exert substantial influence in Southern political affairs.

Registration of voters proceeded during the summer under the supervision of local registrars. The overall results showed 627,000 white and 703,000 Negro voters. White registration was held down not only by the required loyalty oath, but by the losses during the war and by the outright refusal of many to participate. In the five lower Southern states black registrants outnumbered white, but because of the concentrated nature of the Negro population, every state had more counties with white majorities. Before 1867 ended, delegates were elected to the new constitutional conventions in all states but Texas.

Many former Confederates viewed the proceedings as illegal, unwarranted, and intolerable. Most distressing to them was the fact that Negroes did vote, while ex-Confederate leaders were banned. When hope of intervention by the Supreme Court faded, some former plantation owners.

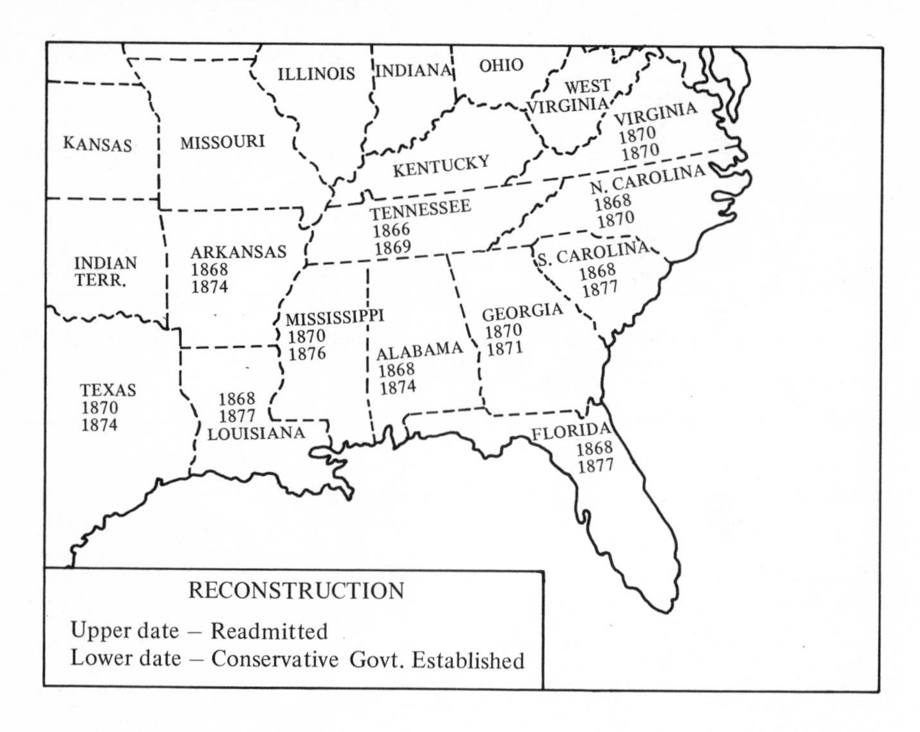

believed their best hope lay in seeking to control Negro voters. Others consoled themselves in the knowledge that the economic power of white Southerners was their ultimate weapon in determining farms, houses, jobs, pay, credit, and goods.

2. *Fight for Negro Rights*

During the period of registration, constitution-making, and the elections of 1867 and 1868, the central question was what kind of a new order was to be produced. Intimately related was the question of what part the Negro would play in helping to create the new order and what his new status would be. Since the Negro was entitled to register and vote, clearly he not only could play an active part in the political process, but as the registration figures showed, over 700,000 Negroes out of a total population of 4 million qualified as voters. Some few were eminently well prepared by virtue of intelligence, education, and background for political action. But unfortunately, most Negroes, having just emerged from bondage, were, as John Hope Franklin observed, "without the qualifications to participate effectively in a democracy." In this respect they were not very different from hosts of fellow illiterate Southern whites or recently arrived immigrants in Northern cities. Many Southern Negroes readily agreed with the comment of Beverly Nash, an illiterate former slave elected to the South Carolina convention. He remarked, "I believe, my friends and fellow-citizens, we are not prepared for this suffrage. But we can learn. Give a man the tools and let him commence to use them, and in time he will learn a trade. So it is with voting. We may not understand it at the start, but in time we shall learn to do our duty."

Ready help in using the "tools" of politics came from two sources. Freedmen's Bureau agents, often military men, were relied upon by the army in getting Negroes registered and in helping them get to the polls. Also the Union League, organized initially in 1862 in Philadelphia to bolster morale in support of the war effort, had sent agents southward after the fighting ended. Extending its social club format, the League often provided teachers for Negro schools, advocated Negro suffrage, and devoted its efforts to building the Republican party. Establishing secret lodges, League organizers attracted many Negro members with an elaborate initiation ritual, nocturnal meetings with oaths, pledges, handshakes, passwords, songs, high-sounding titles, and ceremonies featuring the four *L*s—Liberty, Lincoln, Loyal, and League. In consequence, the League did much for the political education of Negroes, especially in molding a nucleus of Republican party branches throughout the South. On this basis Negroes were able to play an active political part early in the reconstruction of their section.

Joining with Southern Negroes in molding the Republican party of the South were a considerable number of Northerners. Their migration southward had started with the war. Union soldiers, having observed Southern communities at first hand during the war, chose to return after discharge seeking the main chance for wealth or power—and often finding it. It is impossible to estimate how many millions of dollars Yankees invested during the postwar years in buying land cheap, setting up cotton gins, mills, shops, mercantile and other businesses. Former Federal officers like Willard Warner and John T. Wilder launched iron and coal operations in Tennessee and Alabama; others set up law practices, like New Hampshire native Clinton Cilley in North Carolina, or newspapers, like New Yorker B. H. True in Georgia. These men became permanent residents, remaining the rest of their lives and contributing much to the growth of the new South. Others, however, more numerous perhaps, deserved the name carpetbaggers, having come with their few possessions stashed in a carpetbag and looking for a quick killing. Still other Yankees served as teachers, Freedmen's Bureau agents, and Union League organizers. But in the minds of staunch Confederates all these were lumped indiscriminately and disparagingly together as carpetbaggers. Actually, they were a mixed crew, including in their ranks many idealists who came to serve, establishing schools, hospitals, and other useful agencies. Others were outright opportunists, seeking only their own advantage and a fast buck.

A third element (scalawags), merging with Negroes and Northern newcomers in the new Republican party of the South, were native Southerners of assorted backgrounds. Some were former Whigs left stranded in the party's breakup a decade earlier, men of standing as planters, merchants, business or professional men, including such prominent leaders as James Longstreet and James Orr. Others were sturdy Unionists from the mountain counties of Tennessee, North Carolina, and Virginia. Still others were simply unprincipled men who sought their own advantage. Some joined with Republicans in hopes of controlling Negro voters and the course of Reconstruction policy. Labeled derogatorily as scalawags, this group's views varied widely from full radicalism, accepting legal and social equality of Negroes, to tight conservatism holding that Negroes were not citizens and not entitled to hold office and urging segregation. Many who found it expedient for the moment to cooperate with carpetbaggers and Negroes would in time move over to the Democrats as the latter gained strength as a political force.

Opposing the Republicans stood conservative Democrats, comprising former Confederates, Whigs, and Constitutional Unionists of diverse backgrounds and views. That they could participate in politics at all depended on whether they could take the ironclad oath. In June, 1867, President Johnson, acting on the basis of an opinion by the Attorney-General, had opened the door slightly by instructing military commanders that each oath-taker was to be the judge of his own truthfulness in taking the oath. Some conservative Democrats hoped to win political control by appeals to freedmen to follow their natural leaders of prewar days. When this tactic failed, many resorted to boycotting and later to threat, intimidation, and even violence.

Although there is no easy, accurate way to determine the relative strengths of the above groups in influencing political Reconstruction, a glance at the membership figures for the state constitutional conventions of 1867–68 offers a partial clue. Those accounts that picture Negroes and Northern carpetbaggers as running the whole show are misleading. Only in South Carolina did Negroes form a majority (76) of the convention's 124 members, while Louisiana's conclave numbered 49 blacks and 49 whites. The figures for Alabama show 18 Negroes and 31 Northerners out of a total of 108; for Georgia, 33 and 9 respectively out of 170; for Mississippi, 17 and 54 out of 100; for North Carolina, 15 and 18 out of 118; for Virginia, 25 and 47 out of 80. Scarcely can it be said that the conventions were "Africanized" or "Northernized."

The state constitutions hammered out in the conventions of 1867–68 eliminated many archaic prewar practices and moved Southern states forward into the mainstream of nineteenth century American political practice. Property qualifications for voting and office-holding, still lingering on in a few states, were abolished. Reapportionment of legislative and Congressional districts secured a more equitable system of popular representation in government. Imprisonment for debt and similar outdated social practices were at last eliminated where they had persisted. New social welfare institutions were authorized to provide for "the poor, unfortunate, and orphans," the insane, and the deaf and dumb. Although some conventions discussed the question of land, none made any provision for its redistribution. Negro hopes for a firm economic base for advancement went glimmering as the revolution that was begun in the war sputtered futilely on this obstacle.

On the questions of political franchise and education, the conventions were more decisive. Universal manhood suffrage was specified in most new constitutions. A few included provisions reiterating the Federal disfranchisement of classes of ex-Confederate leaders, although some Negro delegates urged the speedy lifting of such disabilities.

The most significant gain was provision for adequate public schools. Immediately after the war's end, Northern church groups had sent teachers south to establish schools for Negroes. The Freedmen's Bureau attempted to provide elementary grade instruction in many places. Both efforts, welcomed almost ecstatically by blacks hungry for schooling, had been resisted by Southern white extremists, who in some instances as noted in Carl Schurz's 1865 report harrassed teachers and students and burned down such schools. Under new constitutions, public education for all children was given high priority. Typical was Alabama's provision: The state Board of Education shall "establish throughout the State, in each township . . . one or more schools at which all children of the State between the ages five and twenty may attend free of charge." Other states had similar requirements. In Louisiana and South Carolina, integrated schools were specified, although most constitutions ignored, skirted, or evaded the integration issue.

In practice the drive for schooling accelerated rapidly, as an almost totally illiterate, deprived Negro people eagerly grasped educational opportunity. "This great multitude," wrote a Freedmen's Bureau officer, "rose up simultaneously and asked for intelligence." Schools mushroomed, and in a few years demands for trained teachers, coupled with Northern philanthropy, helped create colleges and universities like Fisk, Howard, Hampton, Atlanta, and Meharry. "It was a whole race trying to go to school," observed Booker T. Washington. "Few were too young, and none too old." Evening classes opened for adults to satisfy "the great ambition of older people to learn to read the Bible before they died." And many did achieve not only that but more. By 1877 more than 571,000 Negroes were in school. The door of educational opportunity was swinging open.

Political opportunity, too, was opening for Negroes. As noted, many blacks played dignified, responsible roles in constitution-making at the Southern state conventions. When submitted to the voters, the constitutions met varying fates. White Conservative Democrats were determined to defeat the constitutions by any possible means. Their opposition was aimed at Confederate disfranchisement but even more at universal Negro suffrage, which one Floridian denounced as "a curse which should sink this infamous document beneath the detestation of every white man." In Alabama, white voters boycotted the election in numbers sufficient to prevent ratification by a majority of the registered voters. Congress quickly responded with a law that a majority of the votes cast, which had approved, was adequate for ratification. When Mississippi's constitution lost by an 8–7 vote, Congress required ratification of the newly proposed Fifteenth Amendment and a new vote on the constitution. In the resubmission, a large majority approved the constitution, although disfranchisement provisions were beaten. Texas, having delayed calling a convention, and Virginia, postponing the ratification election, remained under military rule. The other eight states approved constitutions, organized governments, ratified the Fourteenth Amendment and, with the exception of Georgia, had their Congressmen seated in the summer of 1868. More than three years after the war's end, Radical Reconstruction had pushed the gears of revolution a notch further. Whether the ratchet would hold remained to be seen.

During the entire process—registering of voters, electing conventions, making and ratifying constitutions, electing and installing new state and local officials—Federal military forces operated, and indeed supervised, throughout the unreconstructed South. Much has been made of the so-called "military occupation" of the area, leaving the impression of beastly Yankee soldiers stomping on poor, defenseless Southerners. It is true that military commanders did issue regulations governing the proceedings according to the provisions of the Reconstruction acts, that troops were used to supervise elections where needed, and that some persons were tried before military tribunals. But the total number of troops in the South was relatively small. In many cases Southerners found the soldiers friendly and even favoring whites over Negroes. Military supervision continued until the restoration process was completed and new civil governments were established and accepted by Congress. Even so, most troops remained at regular army forts and barracks except on election days. By late 1869, except in Texas, Federal troops had declined to less than a thousand in each of the other states.

The speedy dwindling of Federal troops, the increasing Republican factionalism, and the rising native opposition threatened to topple new Radical governments. In consequence, new governors, like Powell Clayton in Arkansas, realizing that conservative Democrats might soon overthrow their regimes, quickly called upon Congress to repeal the Federal law forbidding former Confederate states to maintain state militias. By 1869 Congress lifted the ban for six states, later for all. New state militias were rapidly organized and armed. Enrolling large numbers of blacks and often called Negro militias, they were used by governors to combat increasing Ku Klux Klan activity, and intimidation and interference at the polls designed to undermine Radical Republican regimes.

3. Radicals and the Presidency, 1868

Meanwhile at the nation's capital the continuing war between the Radicals and the President took a new turn. Radical legislators had pretty well manacled Johnson in the 1867 legislation. Resentful over his intemperate denunciations and persistent vetoes, some Radical leaders now determined to humiliate him. Early in 1867 Congressman James M. Ashley called for an investigation of the "high crimes and misdemeanors" of "acting President" Johnson, including a charge of implication in Lincoln's murder. Despite a committee recommendation favoring impeachment, House members remained unconvinced and voted it down.

A new crisis soon erupted over the prickly Secretary of War, Edwin M. Stanton. Upon his accession Johnson had retained Lincoln's cabinet. Those members who disagreed with the President's Reconstruction policy resigned, except for Stanton who moved closer to the Radical position and became increasingly opposed to Johnson. Stanton's personality—cold, dogmatic, austere, self-righteous—had repelled many people, but his monumental services in managing the war effort perhaps made Johnson hesitate to fire him while it was still possible. In March, 1867, the Tenure of Office Act required Senate consent to the dismissal of an executive appointee previously confirmed by the Senate. In August, 1867, with Congress out of session, Johnson suspended Stanton and named Grant as *ad interim* Secretary of War. Johnson believed the Tenure of Office Act an unconstitutional attempt by Congress to prevent a President from controlling his own administration. Johnson said he hoped to get a court test of the law's constitutionality and thought he had Grant's promise to hold the *ad interim* appointment until such a court test. Meanwhile the President shifted Generals Sheridan and Sickles in their Southern commands and later removed General John Pope. This action seriously disturbed Grant because of its seeming evasion of the law.

In January, 1868, the Senate, back in session, rejected Johnson's reasons for suspending Stanton and declared him reinstated. The affair that followed did none of its principal actors credit. Grant yielded the office to Stanton, despite a promise three days earlier to deliver possession of the office only to the President. Johnson called Grant before the cabinet and stubbornly forced him to admit that he had violated their "understanding." Curiously, Grant soon suggested that the President issue an order that "we of the army are not bound to obey the orders of Mr. Stanton as Secretary of War." But the breach between President and General was now irremediable, and in consequence, Grant moved into the waiting, open arms of the Radicals.

Johnson now charged ahead defiantly. He issued an order dismissing Stanton. After failing to get Sherman to accept, he appointed as *ad interim* Secretary the semi-retired General Lorenzo Thomas, known more as a dandy and buffoon than a man of action. Thomas boasted he would batter down the Secretary's door and have Stanton ejected by force. Stanton had Thomas arrested. But on release a few hours later, Thomas quaffed a glass of whiskey in the office of Stanton, who remained Secretary of War.

The Thomas fiasco jolted Congress into action. On February 24, 1868, the House approved John Covode's resolution, "That Andrew Johnson, President of the United States, be impeached of high crimes and misdemeanors in office." The party-line vote showed 126 for and 47 against, even though the resolution carried no specific charges. Factors other than the Stanton row operated in the background. In September, 1867, Johnson had granted amnesty to thousands of ex-Confederates and was reportedly urging that they be registered to vote. His stand against Negro suffrage was strengthened by the rejection of such proposals in Ohio, New Jersey, and Maryland and by the Democratic election victories in Ohio, Pennsylvania, and New York. Consequently, Johnson reiterated his stand in his December message to Congress. And, finally, his veto of Colorado's proposed admission as a state irked Radicals.

Impeachment offered a chance to humiliate the President. After hearing Stevens's plea to remove "the great malefactor" who was "tangled in the meshes of his own wickedness" and thereby to restore democratic government to "a free and untrammeled people," the House promptly approved eleven articles of impeachment. The first nine formed variations of the charge that Johnson had "unlawfully" attempted to remove Stanton from office. The tenth charged him with seeking to bring Congress "into disgrace, ridicule, hatred, contempt, and reproach" by public "intemperate, inflammatory, and scandalous harangues . . . and loud threats and menaces. . . ." The catch-all eleventh article asserted that the President had, by removing Stanton, sought to devise means of obstructing execution of the Reconstruction acts and thereby was "guilty of a high misdemeanor in office." The White House took no public notice and made no immediate response.

The impeachment trial began in the Senate on March 5 and ran until May 26. Chief Justice Chase presiding over the Senate insisted on judicial impartiality. But many, including Ben Wade, who as the Senate's president pro tempore would be President upon Johnson's conviction, viewed the affair as strictly political and counted on every Republican to do his duty. Stormy, cagey Ben Butler, the nation's toughest criminal lawyer, headed the prosecution presented by the House managers. Moving swiftly beyond the alleged breach of the Tenure Act, he lambasted the President for verbal attacks seeking to overthrow Congress and for stirring Southern resistance to Reconstruction laws. In melodramatic illustration Butler waved a bloodstained nightshirt that he announced belonged to an Ohio carpetbagger who had been flogged by Mississippi toughs. Thereafter, "waving the bloody shirt" became the tactic often used by Republicans running for office or urging larger Federal powers in the South. Other prosecutors proceeded in similar fashion, including old Thad Stevens who, despite deteriorating health, warned fellow Republicans to convict Johnson or suffer self-torture "on the gibbet of everlasting obloquy."

Johnson's legal defense was well conducted by a team of top-flight lawyers led by forceful William M. Evarts of New York and Henry Stanbery who resigned as Attorney General to defend his chief. Given but ten days to prepare the case, the defense argued that since Stanton was still holding the War Office, Johnson had not in fact removed him and hence had not violated the Tenure Act. Further, as a Lincoln appointee, Stanton was removable by Johnson even under the act. Johnson's effort to get a test case in court was not illegal. And finally, setting aside personalities and party politics, the defense warned of serious damage to the government's functioning if a President were ousted for political reasons. It was a persuasive argument and may possibly have convinced a few, who came to share Lyman Trumbull's concern that "no future President will be safe who happens to differ with a majority in the House and three-fifths of the Senate."

Most Senators' minds were probably made up from the start. Nine Democrats and three administration Republicans would probably vote for acquittal. Conviction or acquittal rested with moderate Republicans. Public pressure on them mounted unbearably as the big guns of the Radical press and even the Methodist Church annual conference bombarded them with threats of retribution. Even so, Johnson was acquitted by the narrowest of margins. Seven Republicans, including Trumbull and Fessenden, voted "not guilty" along with the twelve pro-Johnsonites, as against thirty-five votes for conviction—one vote shy of the needed two-thirds.

Everybody recognized the trial as a political spite-fest. Even before it started, Johnson had been shorn of any power to block Reconstruction policy. Indeed, in a sense, the trial backfired and roused some sympathy even in the North for the discredited, badgered President. Even before the trial ended, battle lines for the coming Presidential campaign were shaping up.

Among early Republican hopefuls stood Salmon P. Chase, whose record as abolitionist and advocate of Negro suffrage had earlier attracted Radicals. But he lost their support by his impartial handling of the Johnson trial and was reduced to looking expectantly toward the Democrats. Indianan Schuyler Colfax, House Speaker since 1863, appeared most available. But when the convention met in Chicago in late May, delegates turned unanimously to Grant. The general's appeal, in the absence of any notable qualifications, rested on his impressive war record. Second spot went to Colfax. The platform denounced Johnson and his works, praised Congressional Reconstruction policies, called for Negro suffrage in the Southern states, pensions for Union veterans and their widows, and repayment of the national debt.

Democrats, meeting in New York in July, faced an abundance of aspirants. Chase, Johnson, and General McClellan all had a scattering of backers. But former Congressman "Gentleman George" Pendleton, whose inflationary "Ohio Idea" called for large new issues of greenbacks to pay off national bondholders and aid farmers with higher prices in the difficult postwar economic readjustment, won wide support among Western delegates. On the first ballot he carried one-third of the convention's vote. But Eastern opposition stiffened and ultimately thrust the nomination on reluctant Horatio Seymour, New York's wartime governor. Former Congressman Francis P. Blair, Jr., of Missouri was named his running mate. The platform condemned Congressional Reconstruction as "unconstitutional, revolutionary and void," urged an end to military rule and to the Freedmen's Bureau, a return to the states of suffrage matters, amnesty for all, and adoption of the "Ohio Idea."

During the campaign both Grant and Seymour remained silent and largely out of sight. But Republican speakers denounced Seymour for disloyal foot-dragging during the war, while lauding Grant's superb generalship. Democrats were painted as unreliable in economic matters, notably the national debt, and untrustworthy in preserving the gains won by war. Democratic responses, ranting against military despotism, were often drowned out in counter charges of disloyalty, while Thomas Nast's cartoons in *Harper's Weekly* lampooned the Democrats mercilessly. In the outcome, Grant won by a wide electoral margin, capturing all but eight states. But in many areas the race was close, the popular count showing Seymour with a surprising 2.7 million total to Grant's 3 million votes. An informed estimate indicates that 450,000 Negroes voted for Grant; 50,000, for Seymour. Without Negro votes, Grant would still have won, but his total would have fallen 100,000 votes short of his rival's. Nevertheless, the electoral system had spoken, and Radical leaders could look forward to a more congenial occupant in the White House.

The year 1868 had been a decisive one. New governments in Southern states (all but four) came into operation, and their representatives were seated in Congress. One condition for readmission had been approval of the Fourteenth Amendment. Some raised the question of whether a state not legally in the Union had the legal capacity to ratify any amendment to the Constitution. The total number of states, including the Confederate South, was thirty-seven, necessitating twenty-eight ratifications to make the required three-fourths. As ratification notices reached Washington, Secretary of State Seward was in a bit of a quandary. On July 20, 1868, he announced that the amendment had been ratified by twenty-three Northern legislatures and by six assemblies that called themselves legislatures in the South. Although the New Jersey and Ohio legislatures had passed subsequent resolutions rescinding approval, Seward stated his assumption that their original action was valid, and he certified the amendment in force.

By joint resolution, an unsettled Congress sought to clarify the situation. Considering only the fully reconstructed Southern states as members of the Union (making a total of thirty-three), the resolution stated that twenty-seven ratifications were sufficient to meet the Constitution's amending requirement and directed Seward to promulgate it. He did so, issuing on July 28 another certification listing all states that had ratified and those that had rescinded. Although the process was a bit sticky, the Fourteenth Amendment was now officially part of the Constitution.

Meanwhile, on July 4, Johnson extended amnesty to additional groups of ex-Confederates. And on Christmas day he issued a general, unconditional amnesty for most of the remaining proscribed Southerners.

Again the President had raised the hackles and fears of Congressional Radicals. Political participation by Confederates who had received amnesty might, it was feared, erase black suffrage in Southern states. When Congress met, the House swiftly adopted a resolution for a manhood suffrage amendment. After some changes made by the Senate, both houses agreed on its provisions. In February, 1869, the proposed Fifteenth Amendment was submitted to the states. The still unreconstructed states of Virginia, Georgia, Mississippi, and Texas were required to approve it before readmission. Despite opposition by Democrats generally, who viewed the proposal as a move to insure Republican political ascendancy, three-fourths of the states gave approval. In March, 1870, the Fifteenth Amendment officially added to the Constitution the provision that the right of citizens to vote "shall not be denied or abridged by the United States or by any State on account of race, color, or previous condition of servitude."

13

New Road in the South, Distractions in the North 1869–1873

By late 1868 the new order decreed by Congressional Reconstruction measures was moving into operation in most parts of the South. Ex-Confederate leaders were mostly barred from political participation. Negroes, while participating substantially, did not dominate Southern politics. High hopes were held out that the Fourteenth Amendment would secure Negro rights. As new state governments moved into operation, legislation brought changes—new schools, public works, economic endeavors. Conservative white resistance to changes, sometimes accompanied by violence, produced countermeasures of more stringent Federal legislation and renewed military intervention at points.

But disastractions elsewhere—in the North, in Washington, in economic pursuits, in foreign affairs—shifted much of the nation's attention away from Southern problems.

Conservative white Southerners, growing increasingly insistent as the 1870's advanced, took to direct action as well as more subtle pressures to wrest from carpetbagger-scalawag-Negro hands the control of local and state governments. Northern objections, formerly swift and loud, were now muted. Washington showed less inclination to intervene. The tide of revolution was ebbing rapidly.

1. The South Starts on a New Path

In June, 1868, Congress determined that the prescribed conditions for readmission had been met by seven states—Arkansas, North and South Carolina, Georgia, Florida, Alabama, and Louisiana. Except for Georgia, representatives and senators were duly seated and the states now stood formally restored to the Union. In Georgia the legislature denied seats to twenty-seven elected Negro members and seated some ex-Confederate leaders, contrary to Congressional Reconstruction policy. Congress refused to seat Georgia's representatives, rescinded acknowledgement of the state as restored, and authorized the Federal military commander to take control again. He did, eliminating ex-Confederates and compelling the seating of Negro legislators. A new condition, ratifying the Fifteenth Amendment, was stipulated. And when Georgia complied in July, 1870, her Congressmen finally assumed their places in Washington. Sharp controversy over the disqualifying of former Confederates, among other factors, delayed action on Mississippi, Texas, and Virginia, which did not gain readmission until early 1870.

Contention, too, accompanied the launching of new governments under the newly adopted constitutions in Southern states. In opposition, native white conservative Democrats used flexible tactics. After trying in vain to win control of Negro votes, they engaged in diversion and delay at times, sometimes cooperated with Republican carpetbaggers and scalawags on given measures to gain specific ends as in Georgia's case, and at other times resorted to outright obstruction.

In the entire process of creating new constitutions and governments, Negroes played a considerable part. But despite their numerical preponderance in early Reconstruction days in some states, they did not dominate the political arena. To picture Southern states as pressed down under Negro rule and dominated by black politicians and office holders is sheer distortion. Working in cooperation with other Republicans, they voted and held office in an effort to insure their own rights and to secure their own interests, difficult as this was in face of ingrained prejudices against them. In a way, they resembled the newly enfranchised voters of the Jackson era or the recently arrived European immigrants in the later nineteenth century who were often herded to the polls by political machines. Although most were illiterate at the outset, they sought as rapidly as they could to overcome this handicap.

Senator Blanche Kelso Bruce of Mississippi, an escaped Virginia slave who studied at Oberlin and later owned a plantation. (Library of Congress)

Among the Negroes appeared a remarkable number of leaders, able and often cultured, who did hold responsible offices at various times. Many had been ministers of the gospel before the war, a few were lawyers and teachers. For instance, Francis L. Cardozo, a New Haven clergyman educated in Great Britain, became a school principal in Charleston after the war and then rose to be South Carolina's secretary of state and later state treasurer. Massachusetts-born Robert B. Elliott, having studied at Eton College, was elected to the national House from South Carolina. So, too, from Alabama was James Rapier, who had studied and traveled widely in the North and in Canada. Dartmouth alumnus and Presbyterian minister Jonathan C. Gibbs served effectively as Florida's secretary of state, and later as superintendent of public instruction, he did much to improve that state's school system. In Mississippi the exceptional John Roy Lynch, having struggled in slavery times to educate himself, gained office and handled the Speaker's gavel so skillfully in the state legislature as to win general approval and election to Congress. Later he would serve as temporary chairman of a Republican national convention and still later record his astute observations in an impressive book, *The Facts of Reconstruction*. Pennsylvanians James W. Hood and Jonathan J. Wright, a prewar attorney, became respectively assistant superintendent of public instruction in North Carolina and a judge on South Carolina's state supreme court.

In no state was a black chosen as governor. But in South Carolina, Mississippi, and Louisiana, Negroes were elected as lieutenant governors, holding the office in the last state from 1868 to 1876. Louisiana's P. B. S. Pinchback served several weeks as acting governor, as did Alexander K. Davis in Mississippi. Some fourteen Negroes occupied seats as national Representatives at various times during the Reconstruction: six from South Carolina, three from Alabama, and one each from Florida, Georgia, Louisiana, Mississippi, and North Carolina. Joseph H. Rainey of South Carolina enjoyed the distinction of being the first to serve in the House. Mississippi's legislature sent two notable Negroes to the United States Senate. Hiram Revels (1822–1901), a Methodist minister educated at Knox College, after laboring to advance Negro education in Mississippi, went to the Senate where he impressed many by advocating removal of political disabilities from Southern whites. The remarkable Blanche K. Bruce, born a slave in Virginia, escaped during the war and went in 1869 to Mississippi where he speedily rose from sheriff to county school superintendent. In 1875 he won a full term in the Senate where he urged "a more enlightened policy toward the Indians [and] . . . interracial harmony." In 1881 he was prominently mentioned for a cabinet post, but missing that, he became a Federal civil servant for the next seventeen years.

In only one state legislature did Negroes form a majority, and that was in South Carolina's lower house from 1868 to 1874, though the state senate held a white majority. In Mississippi, where black population exceeded white, the first Reconstruction legislature with 115 members contained but 40 blacks. In local governments Negroes held many offices, ranging from sheriff, assessor, and justice of the peace to school superintendent and supervisor. Their records, like those of most of their contemporaries, were of mixed quality. On this point a leading historian offers this assessment: ". . . as governments go, that supplied by the Negro and white Republicans in Mississippi between 1870 and 1876 was not a bad government. . . . Negroes who held county offices were often ignorant, but under the control of white Democrats and Republicans they supplied a form of government which differed little from that in counties where they held no offices. . . . Those in the legislature sought no special advantages for their race, and in one of their very first acts they petitioned Congress to remove all political disabilities from the whites. With their white Republican colleagues, they gave to the state a government of greatly expanded functions at a cost that was low in comparison with that of almost any other state."

Negroes might well have taken out on whites long-standing resentments bred of years in slavery. But instead, in most states they sought in forgiving fashion to have Congressionally-imposed restrictions on whites removed. Ironically this action, stemming in part from alliance with white politicians and perhaps in part from taking a broader veiw of affairs, would ultimately lead to disabilities imposed on Negroes by the very class of men for whom they sought lenient treatment.

Radical carpetbagger-Negro governments in the South have often been characterized as ineffective and excessively dishonest, corrupt, and extravagant. Careful examination of the evidence suggests that such a view is much exaggerated and distorted. The new governments launched into a variety of activities. Much needed to be done, after years of neglect, to repair or rebuild public buildings, roads, bridges, and other public works. To get new and expanded public schools functioning required a generous infusion of state funds. Since only Louisiana and South Carolina made an effort at integrated schools, dual systems in the others greatly increased the expense.

In the economic field, Congress did enact a law, sometimes called the Southern Homestead Act, in June, 1866. Applying to 46 million acres of Federal public lands in Alabama, Mississippi, Louisiana, Florida, and Arkansas, it enabled an applicant to acquire an eighty-acre homestead by paying a $5 filing fee and meeting the conditions of occupancy. Limited at first only to persons of established loyalty, it was intended to provide Negroes with the opportunity of buying a farm. The land office in Florida issued patents to some 3,000 blacks in its first two years of operation. In other states the lands available and number of applicants were much smaller. But the whole process was discouraging. Much of the land was marginal. The costs of moving and securing tools and equipment made it difficult for a poor Negro family to move, and hostile white neighbors added further obstacles. Although by 1876 2,012 Negroes in Florida had homesteaded 160,000 acres of the state's 19 million public acres, the number declined by half in three years. In other states the story was similar, and in 1876 Congress rescinded the act.

Some states appointed land commissioners to aid impecunious persons in buying land. A few adopted modified homestead legislation. Some set up immigration bureaus to attract newcomers. Some created industrial commissions that sought to stimulate business investment and industrial enterprises. All Southern legislatures made major efforts to encourage railroad building, which was equated with progress. All groups—Radical Republicans, carpetbaggers, scalawags, Negroes, conservative Democrats—agreed that the construction of rail lines was essential to economic advance for their states. State legislatures eagerly granted subsidies to railroad promoters by issuing state bonds or guaranteed rail corporation bonds, by stock purchases, or even direct grants of money or land. Much of the pushing, tugging, and hauling of Southern political infighting of this era revolved about railroad promotion and financing. Indeed, in some states, like Virginia, politics was dominated by struggles between railroads competing for state favors. Unscrupulous promoters like carpetbagger Milton S. Littlefield and scalawag George W. Swepson in North Carolina bilked state treasuries of tens of millions of dollars.

Extravagance in spending public funds, waste, corruption, dishonesty, and graft were undeniably common. Examples could be multiplied many times over, as was done in the writings of contemporary journalist James S. Pike and of many historians since that time. Often the misdeeds and corruption were blown up and distorted for partisan ends. Stealing and graft were undeniably common throughout the United States at the time—in Washington, New York City, and other cities and states. Not that this justifies dishonesty in Southern states, but rather it suggests that standards of morality did not differ greatly from one part of the Union to another. The "Great Barbecue" plundering fed upon itself. And to whom did the stolen funds go? Not all went to public officials, who probably received a minor share. Often they went in the form of bloated contracts to printers for state printing, to construction contractors for exaggerated costs of public buildings, roads, and other public works or to railroad promoters, as noted above. Influence peddling and political favoritism were probably not greatly different in these postwar years than they have been in other political generations.

The great increase in public outlays, the mushrooming of bonded indebtedness, and the spiraling of taxes brought cries of protest and resistance. Changes in tax assessment enlarged the burden of landholders, whose prewar taxes had been minimal. Taxpayers' protest conventions and tax-resisting associations sprang up in an effort to check tax increases in many

Southern states, but they had little success at first. Many native Southern whites became convinced that other means must be used to shake off the detested carpetbag-scalawag-Negro political control.

2. *Southern Whites Fight Back, and Congress Answers*

Radical regimes, at the beginning at least, attracted support from a fair number of native white Southerners. In most instances these were loyal Union men of Whig antecedents who had opposed secession in 1861, who could truthfully swear they had not voluntarily aided the rebellion, and who wished to regain a measure of political influence. Originally supporters of "Johnson governments" in 1865–66, they soon became Republican allies even though they did not share Radical views on Negro rights. Some were willing to concede Negro suffrage in the expectation that black voters could be controlled, as noted above. They participated in Radical regimes, often holding prominent posts. For example, wealthy planter and former Whig James L. Alcorn became the first Republican governor of Mississippi. Estimates suggest that in 1868 some 25–30 per cent of native white voters labored within Republican ranks. In some instances they cooperated with former rebels and thereby made themselves suspect in Radical eyes. Their growing resentment of Union League efforts to organize black voters and the rising prominence of Negro Republican officeholders weakened their allegiance to the Republican party. In time they deserted the party, tried to form a third party, and failing that, gradually moved into alliance with Democrats as the Reconstruction era wound down. This ultimate surrender reflected perhaps a resignation to the vehement response of other Southern whites to Radical measures and regimes.

From the beginning, large numbers of Southern whites resented the Radical program, forced upon the South, as they saw it, at Federal bayonet point. Having fought for the "lost cause" of Southern independence, they conceded when Appomattox came that they had lost the war fairly (although later recollection through the magic mists of memory would view even this in a different light). Having lost, they believed they had made every conceivable concession that a vanquished "nation" (as many still saw themselves) should have to make—the South had laid down its arms, rejected secession, repudiated war debts, and accepted the Thirteenth Amendment ending slavery. They were, after all, the first Americans to experience military defeat. Why should they, they asked, be required to make more concessions? Was this not enough? Most ex-Confederates shared this attitude, many strongly enough to resist by force the Radical efforts.

Military occupation by Yankee troops, whom they had hated and fought for four years, was bad enough. But when Yankee opportunists descended upon the South in seeming locust hordes, local tempers boiled. Freedmen's Bureau agents appeared to stir formerly docile Negroes with notions of getting land, schooling, and equality. Union League organizers, molding black voters to Republican partisan purposes, seemed to threaten total "Africanization" of the region. To grant freedom from slavery was enough; to deny suffrage to ex-Confederates and place the ballot in black hands was going too far. Such a revolution would turn Southern society upside down. To concede equal rights was intolerable. Changes were being forced with bewildering speed. One Southern editor shuddered at "the galling despotism that broods like a nightmare over these Southern states . . . to degrade the white man by the establishment of negro supremacy." He spoke the feelings of many fellow whites.

As Radical regimes geared up, providing black suffrage and equal rights for Negroes, the smoldering resentment of many native whites reached the flammatory point. Even though Negroes did not in fact dominate state or local governments, many whites feared that such a prospect might become a reality, and for them, such a disaster was to be fought off by any means.

Carpetbagger-scalawag broadside. (Brown Brothers)

"Hang, curs, hang! * * * * * *Their* complexion is perfect gallows. Stand fast, good fate, to *their* hanging! * * * * * If they be not born to be hanged, our case is miserable."

The above cut represents the fate in store for those great pests of Southern society—the carpet-bagger and scallawag—if found in Dixie's Land after the break of day on the 4th of March next.

The genus carpet-bagger is a man with a lank head of dry hair, a lank stomach and long legs, club knees and splay feet, dried legs and lank jaws, with eyes like a fish and mouth like a shark. Add to this a habit of sneaking and dodging about in unknown places—habiting with negroes in dark dens and back streets—a look like a hound and the smell of a polecat.

Words are wanting to do full justice to the genus scallawag. He is a cur with a contracted head, downward look, slinking and uneasy gait; sleeps in the woods, like old Crossland, at the bare idea of a Ku-Klux raid.

Our scallawag is the local leper of the community. Unlike the carpet-bagger, he is native, which is so much the worse. Once he was respected in his circle; his head was level, and he would look his neighbor in the face. Now, possessed of the itch of office and the salt rheum of Radicalism, he is a mangy dog, slinking through the alleys, haunting the Governor's office, defiling with tobacco juice the steps of the Capitol, stretching his lazy carcass in the sun on the Square, or the benches of the Mayor's Court.

He waiteth for the troubling of the political waters, to the end that he may step in and be healed of the itch by the ointment of office. For office he 'bums' as a toper 'bums' for the satisfying dram. For office, yet in prospective, he hath bartered respectability; hath abandoned business, and ceased to labor with his hands, but employs his feet kicking out boot-heels against lamp-posts and corner-cars, while discussing the question of [illegible]

Carpetbag regimes seemed bent on running the states into financial ruin, as graft and extravagant waste appeared the obsession of men running state houses and county courthouses. Self-preservation alone, many became convinced, demanded that they act.

The means were close at hand. Night-riding patrols that in prewar days had insured peace in the countryside were now revived as vigilance committees under various names—Home Guards, Knights of the Rising Sun, Pale Faces, White League, Sons of '76, and Knights of the White Camellia. What became the largest, most notorious of all was the Ku Klux Klan, born in Pulaski, Tennessee, as a frolicking veterans' secret social lodge in the fall of 1865. Secret fraternal orders were nothing new in nineteenth-century America, as the Masons and Oddfellows lodges testified. But the Ku Klux Klan pushed the secret society to its extremes—both in organization and in violence. Spreading haphazardly but rapidly into Alabama and then across the South, Klan organizations soon sprouted in each Southern state, known as a "realm" under the rule of a Grand Dragon aided by eight Hydras. Several counties, each called a "province" headed by a Grand Giant and four Goblins, were grouped together in a "dominion" with a Grand Titan and six Furies in charge. The overall "invisible empire" was ruled by the Grand Wizard, former slave trader General Nathan B. Forrest, assisted by ten Genii. A local lodge or "den," run by a Grand Cyclops and two Nighthawks, composed of members known as "Ghouls," was open to any white male over eighteen who took the oath of obedience and secrecy and vowed to oppose Negro equality, Union Leaguers and Republicans.

Aiming, of course, at white supremacy the Klan had no scruples about the means to accomplish its purpose. It played upon superstitions and fears of Negroes, carpetbaggers, and scalawags. Between 1867 and 1870 bands of hooded, white-sheeted men roamed the countryside and at times raided private houses and settlements. At first using silent midnight rides, threats, and intimidation, Klansmen soon resorted to whippings, mutilations, and murder. In the name of law and order, they burned dwellings and public buildings, assaulted and drove carpetbaggers, scalawags, and Negroes out of the community or county. Raw, vigilante violence shortly engulfed the terrorist outfit as members sometimes took out private grudges under Klan disguise. As revulsion set in, the more respectable members left the organization, which Forrest declared formally disbanded in 1869. But despite the official pronouncement, white supremacy organizations persisted into the 1870's.

The Klan did not succeed in its attempt to overturn Radical rule in the South. Its actions were too overtly criminal, and Northern opinion still supported a strong Radical policy in the South. Militia outfits, sometimes called the "Negro militia," were beefed up in some states to counter the raw violence. And Congress, aiming at the Klan and similar outfits, responded with the first of a series of enforcement acts, often labeled "force acts," on May 31, 1870. This law was designed to protect Negro voting rights. It set heavy fines and jail sentences for interfering with such rights and placed the trial of such offenses in the hands of Federal courts. By another act, Congressional elections, too, were brought under Federal regulation, and election abuses and irregularities became Federal offenses.

The laws proved relatively ineffective. Southern Democrats gained additional Congressional seats in the 1870 elections. By 1871, governments in Virginia, North Carolina, Tennessee, and Georgia were under the control of white supremacists, known as "Redeemers." Believing these changes the result of intimidation and violence, Congress adopted the Ku Klux Klan Act in April, 1871. Under this law, Federal courts were assigned original jurisdiction over such Klan (and kindred organization) activities as forming conspiracies, resisting Federal officers, appearing in public in disguise for the purpose of terrorizing or intimidating voters. Such acts were declared crimes, carrying heavy penalties. The President was authorized to suspend the writ of habeas corpus in terrorized communities and to impose martial law under Federal troops where necessary.

Within a short time some 7,000 Southerners were charged under the law. Few were ever brought to trial; fewer still, convicted. But for the time being, white political terrorism was curtailed. President Grant placed nine Klan-terrorized counties of South Carolina under martial law in October, 1871. Under the impact of subsequent prosecutions, some 82 persons were jailed or fined as the Klan was effectively muzzled.

Federal action against the Klan came at a time when many responsible Southern whites viewed the Klan, which was strongest in the up-country South, as filled with "drunken and lawless vagabonds." To cultivated Southerners the Klan appeared as an assault by lower-class whites to eliminate the Negro as an economic competitor. Some testified to this effect in the lengthy investigation of the Klan by Congress in 1871. The resulting thirteen-volume committee report, published in 1872 under the title *The Ku Klux Conspiracy*, offered extensive though selected testimony of lawlessness in the South. The conclusions that were drawn varied with the views of readers. The Klan was dead, said some; Southern resistance was still very much alive, said others, noting the difficulty of getting a Southern jury to convict in Federal violation cases.

But if the Klan's blatant violence was checked, Southern conservative Democrats found other means to weaken or dismember the carpetbagger-scalawag-Negro political combine where it still held on to power. Devices were developed to confuse the Negro voter and to wean him from Republican allegiance by assuring him that his interests would be better cared for by native Southerners than by Republican outsiders. Since whites continued to own most of the farm land and the businesses, the black tenant, laborer, or share-cropper could be squeezed with economic pressure, threatened loss of land or job, to get him to abstain from voting or to shift to the Democratic camp. In town, prices charged by merchants, fees by doctors, pay offered to domestics could be adjusted to apply added pressure. The Negro who continued to support Republicans paid heavily in economic consequences. Often rather than lose his job or land he quietly quit politics or became a Democrat. In many communities such tactics produced a shift of control into the hands of native white-supremacist "Redeemers."

Where political appeals and economic pressure failed, a new approach employed threat of punishment and direct action but avoided the secret feature of the Klan that earlier aroused Northern ire and stirred Congressional reprisal. The "Mississippi Plan," devised in 1874, fostered the open organizing of local rifle companies manned by red-shirted whites. No secret lodges, these companies drilled and marched in a town's main square or main street and engaged in target practice—all out in the open. Such companies aimed to make clear that local whites were united in opposing continued Republican rule, scalawag cooperation with Republicans, and Negro participation in public affairs. In Mississippi's 1875 campaign, Republican rallies were broken up by red-shirted horsemen. Negroes and others working with Republicans were threatened or beaten by toughs. Governor Adelbert Ames attempted to quell the violence, but to no avail. When the ballots were in, Democrats had garnered majorities in both houses of the legislature. Trumped-up impeachment charges were initiated against Ames, who resigned and promptly left the state. Similar actions produced similar results in other states. This time the Federal government made no move to intervene.

3. Northern Distractions Dim the Spotlight on the South

While the struggle for change in the South was being fought, pitting Radical against Redeemer, "red shirts" and "white hoods" against "black and tan" Republicans, the nation's attention was being diverted from the Southern question by distractions elsewhere. A variety of developments—political, economic, diplomatic, social—drew popular attention and concern that formerly focused on the South. Northern reform societies like the abolitionist groups tended to lose interest, especially after the Fourteenth Amendment was adopted. In 1870 the American Anti-Slavery Society dissolved itself. Religious denominations in the North, like the Methodists and Quakers, while still interested, were less absorbed than earlier in the cause of the Negro. Yankee "school marms" headed south less frequently than in the early days of Reconstruction. The Freedmen's Bureau was winding down most of its activities in the early Grant years.

With General Grant's accession to the Presidency, the Republican party itself was beginning to undergo substantial change. The idealistic, humanitarian concern of Radical leaders to open opportunities for Negroes to make their own way had already begun to fade. Stevens' death in 1868 and Wade's defeat for the Senate that fall were followed by Julian's failure to win renomination in 1870 and Sumner's decline in prestige. In their places men like Ben Butler, Roscoe Conkling, Schuyler Colfax, Oliver P. Morton, and James G. Blaine moved to the forefront, where they showed greater concern for the interests of manufacturers, railroaders, and financiers and for offices and political patronage than for the status of the Negro in American society.

A certain irony surrounds Grant and his career. Paradoxically, the general who won the war became the President who would lose the peace—in the sense that peace involved extending and protecting the rights of Negroes made legally free by war. By training, experience, and temperament, Grant was unfitted to be President. A blunt, lethargic man, with no previous experience in politics, he exhibited scant vision or capacity in dealing with political and social problems. Where he was sharp and decisive in military action, the Presidency seemed to paralyze his will and dull his judgment of subordinates' abilities and honesty. Having failed in an early business enterprise himself, he became awed and almost worshipful of successful business entrepreneurs. He wanted to appoint as Secretary of the Treasury A. T. Stewart, a department store magnate who had bought a Philadelphia house for Grant and contributed heavily to his campaign. Even when shown that Federal law prohibited an export-import businessman in the Treasury, Grant tried obstinately but in vain to get an exception made of Stewart.

Almost blindly, President Grant allowed himself and his office to be used by assorted promoters, speculators, and unsavory schemers. He often accepted social invitations from Henry Cooke, brother and Washington agent of Jay Cooke who ran the nation's largest banking firm. He traveled to the Saratoga horse racing season in Cornelius Vanderbilt's private railway car. He showed no compunction over being entertained by speculator Jim Fisk and his shady sometime partner Jay Gould. At the same time Fisk and Gould were engaged in a brazen speculative scheme to corner the nation's gold market. Using inside Treasury information they drove the price of gold up from $133 to $163 before unloading, pocketing a tidy profit and leaving in the wake of "Black Friday's" (September 24, 1869) disaster a flurry of bankrupted New York merchants and importers.

In the executive branch Grant's appointments left much to be desired. Military men were a common sight. White House staffers included such former army associates as General Horace Porter as the President's private secretary and Colonel Orville E. Babcock as appointments secretary. Controlling access to their chief, these men were also influential in the inner circle of advisers. Generals James A. Rawlins and Jacob D. Cox served in the cabinet briefly. With the notable exception of Secretary of State Hamilton Fish, most cabinet officers were ineffective nonentities.

The Federal patronage, still large from its wartime expansion, was dispensed lavishly to include family relatives, old neighbors like Elihu B. Washburne of Galena, Illinois, and cronies who attached themselves to the President. In paying little heed to the qualifications of his appointees and much heed to suggestions of his less than competent advisors, Grant succeeded in alienating Republican Senators Trumbull, Schurz, and Sumner who wanted to reform the Federal civil service by introducing the merit principle. Political chieftains, not happy over the patronage distribution, nonetheless rallied to block Congressional efforts at civil service reform.

American foreign affairs, too, became ensnared in the ambitious schemes of promoters seeking private gain with the government's active assistance. The Caribbean republic of Santo Domingo won the attention of Massachusetts and New York speculators, who persuaded the Grant regime to respond to the Dominican president's offer to sell the country to the United States, provided the latter would pay off that republic's debts. Grant became so obsessed with this project that he sent Babcock to investigate on the spot. With an eye for a naval base at Samana Bay, Babcock proceeded quite irregularly to draft an annexation treaty. When the Senate killed the treaty on June 30, 1870 Grant denounced Foreign Relations Committee chairman Sumner for killing the treaty and had him removed from the chairmanship. Doggedly pursuing the project, Grant sent a three-man commission to the island. Its report recommended annexation, suggesting among other things that here was a possible haven for the resettlement of Southern Negroes. A joint Congressional resolution again ran afoul of Senator Sumner who, privately seething against Grant, that "colossus of ignorance," once more thwarted the wretched scheme. By 1871 the project was dead. Veteran Radical Sumner spent his last four years in the Senate in bitter opposition to the administration.

Of greater significance than the Dominican affair were the settlements of other foreign problems. In the immediate postwar years Johnson's administration had achieved notable diplomatic successes with France and Russia under the skilled hand of Secretary of State William H. Seward. Shortly after Appomattox, Seward pressed gently but firmly against Napoleon III's continued maintenance of French troops in Mexico to prop up the sagging regime of imported Emperor Maximilian. To this, further pressure was added by sending troops to the Rio Grande border in a menacing gesture. By 1867 Napoleon, facing the rising power of Bismarck's Prussia in Europe, backed away from the Mexican venture and pulled out the remaining French forces thereby abandoning Maximilian to his fate at the hands of a firing squad.

In the same year Seward eagerly seized upon a surprise Russian offer to sell Alaska to the United States for $7.2 million. The purchase treaty ran into resistance from Senate Radicals who resented Secretary Seward for his loyalty to President Johnson. But the Senate gave approval after being persuaded by its Foreign Relations Committee chairman Sumner. At first unimpressed, Sumner became convinced after study of Alaska's potential value, which he set forth eloquently and persuasively in a powerful three-hour speech. The House remained unconvinced. Only after the Russian minister distributed a reported $200,000 to key newspapers, lobbyists, and probably key Congressional leaders did the appropriation pass.

Still left over from the Civil War were outstanding issues with Great Britain. Most complex of these was the American claim for reparations for damages caused by Confederate raiding vessels built in British shipyards during the war. These "Alabama" claims had become further complicated by other Anglo-American controversies. Before Appomattox, escaping Confederate prisoners of war had slipped into Canada, from which base they mounted small-scale raids across the border to such points as St. Johnsbury, Vermont. Such sorties had of course stopped with the close of the war, but Americans were again reminded of the British presence in Canada in 1866 when the Fenians, a New York-based Irish-American society, began a series of attacks across the border in the exaggerated hope of seizing Canada and bartering with Great Britain for the independence of old Ireland. The Johnson administration, though recognizing the power of the Irish vote in Northern cities, nonetheless, took strong measures to enforce neutral conduct along the frontier. While England held back, Secretary Seward was pressing proposals for settling the "Alabama" claims. Some angered Americans suggested unleashing the Fenians to bring England around, a suggestion Seward refused to notice. Finally in January, 1869, apprehensive over Germany's growing strength on the continent, England signed the Johnson-Clarendon convention to arbitrate all outstanding differences between the two nations.

What seemed an opening on the road to settlement now bogged down in the Senate. Some voices objected to the failure to include an apology by England in the agreement. Senator Sumner led the Senate in an overpowering 54–1 rejection of the agreement and then proceeded to launch his own proposal to compel England to pay "indirect damages." These, by Sumner's calculation, included the costs of two additional years of war, since the Senator attributed the prolonging of the war to sea raids on Union shipping by the British-built Confederate cruisers. In lieu of monetary payment, Sumner suggested Britain's withdrawal from the North American continent, which of course would make Canada available for American annexation. Such talk did nothing to smooth the path of diplomatic negotiation.

At this point the Grant administration assumed power in Washington. Fortunately Grant himself, except for the Dominican imbroglio, showed little interest in foreign matters, leaving the "Alabama" affair in the capable hands of the ablest secretary on his cabinet, Hamilton Fish. Growing British concern over a united Germany arising from the Franco-Prussian war, coupled with Sumner's elimination as Foreign Relations Committee chairman, led to the signing of the Treaty of Washington by the United States and England early in 1871. Under its terms each nation's claims were to be submitted to a five-member arbitration panel, which included Charles Francis Adams as its American member. Meeting at Geneva from December, 1871, to September, 1872, the tribunal heard evidence reviewing the questions of secession, Britain's recognition of the Confederacy's belligerence, the "escape" of the Confederate ships from British shipyards, and America's contention of "indirect" as well as direct damages stemming therefrom. The Geneva body threw out the "indirect" claims, ruled that England had failed to exercise "due diligence" to preserve its neutrality in regard to three Confederate cruisers, and awarded a $15.5 million indemnity to the United States. On its side, the United States was to pay $1.9 million to satisfy claims of British subjects whose ships had been subjected to illegal blockade procedures during the war.

4. Economic Expansion Moves Ahead

Meanwhile, at home in the United States, economic expansion was rolling ahead at full speed. Although expansion was not uniform, the war itself had spurred particular industries, especially those that supplied uniforms, shoes, blankets, rifles, guns, wagons, and heavy equipment for the army and the navy. But while the advance of the economy was uneven, individual entrepreneurs harbored their capital and at war's end stood ready to launch into broader, greater production.

Of such promoters, Andrew Carnegie and John D. Rockefeller provide notable examples. The latter, a Cleveland fruit and produce merchant during the war, put his accumulated savings at war's close into a local oil refinery, receiving crude oil discovered a half dozen years before in the nearby Pennsylvania fields. Within five years he had consolidated all the city's refineries under his control. In 1870 he organized the Standard Oil Company of Ohio, which expanded swiftly into direct oil drilling and production and wholesale and retail marketing of kerosene and oil lubricants. By the 1880's his newly formed Standard Oil Company of New Jersey, the nation's first trust, virtually dominated the oil industry; in another twenty years it stood poised for even greater expansion geared to the imminent automobile revolution of the twentieth century.

Scottish immigrant Carnegie, from a prewar start as a telegraph operator on the Pennsylvania Railroad, went to Washington in the war years with Tom Scott, the rail company's president. In the postwar era Carnegie's firm, the Keystone Bridge Company, supplied heavy steel for railroad construction, with the Pennsylvania Railroad as a permanent customer. As railroad building boomed, so did Carnegie's business. In 1871 he organized the Carnegie Steel Company, gained control of nearby coal fields, and rapidly became the dominant producer in Pittsburgh, the nation's steel-making center.

Besides oil and steel, other industries zoomed forward under the impact of new technology, new processes, new inventions. Standardization of sizes with mass cutting of materials and speedy sewing machines revolutionized the clothing and shoe industries and so changed Americans' buying habits that local tailors and shoemakers would become a vanishing breed. Industries related to agricultural production resumed their steady westward push. Chicago, Milwaukee, Minneapolis, St. Louis and Des Moines experienced rapid growth as new industries moved in. Slaughtering and meat packing, under the rising flow of beef cattle from the western plains and the introduction of refrigerated rail cars, flourished in Chicago and lesser cities. Other businesses, like flour milling, watch making, farm implement manufacturing, furniture making, firearms, wire and hardware production, and food processing, experienced similar growth. The opening of new sources of coal supplies and the phenomenal Mesabi range in Minnesota with its high quality iron ore helped stimulate the growth of iron-steel production in the Cleveland-Youngstown, Detroit-Toledo and Chicago-Northern Indiana areas.

Other factors, too, helped fuel the business expansion. For one, the high protective tariff enacted during the war, secured from external competition a matchless domestic market of vast extent. And this market continued to expand as heavy immigration and a high native birthrate sent the nation's population rocketing upward—from 31 million in 1860 to 38 million ten years later to 50 million in 1880—a fantastic jump of 61 per cent in twenty years. Basic raw materials for industrialization—coal, lumber, iron, petroleum, copper, and other minerals—lay in abundance waiting to be used. Improved technology exploded a bewildering array of devices to speed production—the Bessemer-Kelly blast furnace followed shortly by the open-hearth steel-making process, steam driven machinery, farm tractors, and typewriters would be followed by the electric dynamo and countless other machines.

Another spur to economic production came from the rapidly enlarging labor force. To the army of war veterans seeking jobs after the war were added armies of immigrants who came after Appomattox and continued to come in a swelling tidal wave. The yearly average rose to over 300,000 by 1870, the total reaching 3.2 million newcomers in the ten years following 1865. By the 1880's the annual flow topped 600,000, the usual Irish and Germans now joined by Scandinavians, southern and eastern Europeans, and on the Pacific slope, Chinese workers who had been imported to build the transcontinental railroads. Busy seeking jobs and often facing native resentment, this immense mass of newcomers, with few exceptions, showed little interest in politics, let alone the national Reconstruction policy or Negro rights. In fact, their very arrival in such numbers tended to distract the attention of many Northerners from the Southern question.

As the labor force grew in size and makeup and as economic enterprises grew larger, more complex, and impersonal, so the position of workingmen changed as well. In prewar years a man had a fair prospect of rising from laboring status to become a master craftsman or to own his own shop or business. In the Postwar industrial complexities, such prospects dimmed. The odds increased that he would remain a wage worker for his lifetime. In such circumstances, labor unions appeared more appealing. Railroad workers began joining the newly formed railroad brotherhoods, while iron workers joined the moulders union. Under the impact of the terrorizing tactics of the Molly Maguires, unemployed coal miners were reported on the rampage in Pennsylvania's anthracite fields. The Knights of Labor, formed in 1871, hoped to bring all workers under its umbrella and to reform society as well. Unions and workingmen generally showed little concern for the Negro, other than to resent him as a possible job competitor, and even less concern for Reconstruction policy.

Farmers in the Midwest grew increasingly distressed. After enjoying a heavy wartime demand that yielded high prices, they now faced declining prices, high fixed interest rates, steep railroad charges, marketing and deflationary problems. Determined to fight back, many farmers joined the newly organized Patrons of Husbandry, more familiarly called the National Grange. They pushed into politics, gained control of some Midwestern state legislatures, and enacted "Granger laws" to regulate rail shipping and storage charges. Pressing economic matters close at hand left little time for thinking about the South or the Negro.

Farther west, the Plains Indians, under growing pressures from cattle and sheep raisers and from homesteaders, found themselves ruthlessly swept aside by Federal troops and onto unwanted reservation lands. Still farther west in California newcomers from China, numbering over 100,000 by the mid-1870's faced resentment and hostility that erupted at times into violent outbursts and outrages against them. The prevailing attitude of many, whether in Colorado, California, Connecticut, or the Carolinas, held that persons who looked different or who had skin of a different color were somehow less worthy of consideration and fair treatment. The attitudes of southern whites toward the Negro were perhaps not so different from those of their fellow Americans in other parts of the land.

Northern entrepreneurs, raising capital, organizing corporations, building plants, grabbing raw materials, managing production, had no absorbing interest in national Reconstruction policy or the Negro's assimilation into society. So far as politics went, they concerned themselves with securing such favors as government could bestow—tariffs, land, subsidies, franchises, contracts. Beyond these, businessmen simply wanted government to leave them alone, unimpeded in acquiring profits. Negro rights and Reconstruction affairs in the South left them unmoved and uninterested.

Most visible of the postwar economic thrusts was the railroading phenomenon. Railroad mileage, spanning 35,000 miles in 1865, grew to

49,000 in 1870 and 87,000 ten years later. Following the initial federal land and money grants to the Union and Central Pacific companies in 1862, Congress, annually besieged by new proposals, had generously granted to railroads by 1871 over 160 million public domain acres with an estimated value of $335 million. Beneficiaries included the Northern Pacific, Kansas Pacific, Missouri Pacific, Santa Fe, Atlantic and Pacific, and scores of lesser lines. On May 10, 1869, two months after Grant took office, the final golden spike was hammered home near Ogden, Utah, to mark completion of the Union and Central Pacific tracks. Fittingly presiding at that ceremony was Leland Stanford, California's governor, who with Collis P. Huntington, Mark Hopkins, and Charles Crocker would soon expand their operations in California and inland through another profitable promotion, the Southern Pacific Railroad.

Railroad construction and operation became the mania of the postwar generation, attracting the varied talents of such men as Charles Francis Adams, Jr., George B. McClellan, Robert Todd Lincoln, Cornelius Vanderbilt and his son William, Thomas Scott, and Jay Gould. And a lucrative pursuit it was, yielding enormous profits. Again the nation's attention was diverted from pushing fully the Reconstructive policies begun by the Radicals.

How lucrative railroading could be was revealed in the Congressional investigation of the Credit Mobilier scandal. This construction company, organized to build the Union Pacific, spread its favors (usually free shares of company stock) among selected Congressmen through Representative Oakes Ames of Massachusetts in hopes of getting even larger Federal grants. Altogether Credit Mobilier collected $73 million for doing $50 million worth of construction, the surplus being divided among promoters serving as directors of *both* companies. Meanwhile, war veterans and Irish and Chinese immigrants, whose backbreaking labors had sweated the tracks into place received barely a subsistence wage for their work.

Such devious schemes of thievery, though occurring before 1869, did not come to light until 1872. In that year, too, Congress voted itself a $2,500 pay raise and by making it retroactive for two years thereby conferred a $5,000 bonus on each member. The resulting public outcry compelled the next Congress to repeal the "salary grab." But the "grab" was soon overshadowed by disclosures of incredible fraud and graft within the Grant administration. War Secretary W. W. Belknap, it appeared, had been accepting bribes from traders at army-run Indian posts. He quickly resigned, but even so was impeached, tried and acquitted. Post office contracts, it was discovered, were being awarded to carriers who paid the highest kickbacks. The "Whiskey Ring," including hundreds of distillers, escaped taxes by buying off internal revenue men thereby defrauding the government of millions. Deeply enmeshed in this fraud was Grant's own private secretary Orville Babcock, whom the President unbelievably saved from prison by a legal deposition made in the subsequent trial. Although Grant himself was clear of any dishonesty, his judgment of lieutenants was undeniably bad.

True, stealing and bribery were not the monopoly of the national administration nor of Republicans, as disclosures of immense graft by New York City's notorious boss William M. Tweed and his "Ring" of cronies made plain. But Grant in giving offices and seeming Presidential sanction even to some crooks and rascals substantially undermined public confidence in the Chief Executive. Once more, national attention drifted away from Southern affairs.

Although most administration scandals did not surface until Grant's second term, some Republicans were early disenchanted with Grant and his cohorts. Midterm Congressional elections saw an upsurge of Democratic strength that undermined the Republicans' two-thirds margin in Congress. An anti-Grant faction springing up in Missouri under Republican leaders B. Gratz Brown and Carl Schurz revolted against the local Grant chieftain, who later proved to be the "Whiskey Ring" boss. Success at the polls made Brown governor and Schurz United States Senator, while the state's legislature proceeded to remove political disabilities from Missouri's ex-Confederates. In May, 1872, Congress, too, adopted a general amnesty act that lifted political restraints from all but about 500 former Confederate leaders.

From Missouri the movement fanned into other Northern states where demands to end the spoils system and corruption in high places and to end all Southern disabilities were sounded by publicists Horace Greeley, A. K. McClure, and others. Old line antislavery Republicans like Lyman Trumbull, Charles Sumner, and George W. Julian joined with Francis P. Blair, Jr., Charles Francis Adams, and ex-cabinet member Jacob D. Cox to back the movement. Editors Murat Halstead of the Cincinnati *Commercial*, George W. Curtis of *Harper's Weekly*, and Edwin L. Godkin of *The Nation* lent support.

Unable to crack the regular Republican organization, these men allied with others in a Liberal Republican convention at Cincinnati in May, 1872. Hopes for a man of the stature of Adams, Lincoln's minister to London, or Supreme Court Justice David Davis, acclaimed for his 1866 *Milligan* decision, faded fast. The convention compromised by naming as the Liberal Republican candidate editor Horace Greeley, who had earlier been an ardent abolitionist, followed the hard Radical line for a time, then helped post bail for Jefferson Davis, and more recently urged forgiveness for other eminent Confederates.

The Democrats followed suit by also nominating Greeley in their subsequent convention at Baltimore—a bizarre choice since Greeley had long denounced Democrats, reportedly asserting at one point, "Not all rascals are Democrats, but all Democrats are rascals." The regular Republicans

A Nast cartoon looks at Horace Greeley during the election of 1872. (Culver Pictures)

renominated Grant. And the nation was treated to what appeared to General Sherman as the weird spectacle of a contest between longtime Republican Greeley running for the party he had despised and prewar Democrat Grant carrying the Republican standard. Greeley, cruelly caricatured as a befuddled incompetent in the press, especially in Thomas Nast's devastating cartoons in *Harper's Weekly*, succeeded by his personal eccentricities and erratic campaigning in alienating many voters who had hoped for a change in Washington. Many Democrats, unable to swallow Greeley, simply stayed away from the polls on election day. Greeley himself commented that from what was being said about him in the campaign he could not tell whether he was running "for the Presidency or the penitentiary." And he suffered the crushing blow of his wife's death late in the campaign. The November voting gave Grant all but six states (in the South and the border) and a popular majority of 753,000 votes (or 55.6 per cent of the total) for the most decisive Presidential triumph since Jackson. Facing the prospect of four more years of Grantism, the country would have concerns other than the problems of the South or the Negro to think about.

14

Revolution Abandoned, 1873–1877

In 1873 a stunning economic slump plunged the economy into a prolonged depression and turned Northerners' energies to simply keeping afloat financially at home. A sharp drop in farm prices sent farmers into revolt. Labor disturbances multiplied. Renewed cries for the easy panacea of increasing the supply of inflationary greenbacks won thousands of adherents clamoring for monetary relief. The economic distress plus disgust over the corruption in Washington brought on a Democratic resurgence that lessened national concern with the South and the Negro.

Under the impact of these forces, the tide of revolution that had already turned in the early seventies now ebbed more swiftly. The climactic Presidential contest of 1876 brought further dispute, discord, and threats of renewed clash. In its resolution, moderate counsels prevailed. And the reuslting Compromise of 1877 spelled the final abandonment of all efforts to realize the promise of the revolution.

1. Business, Panic, and Politics

The business and financial interests of the North were of course pleased with the Republican party's continuance in power in Washington. Manufacturers knew who their friends at the capital were, and paid lobbyists representing scores of manufacturing interests swarmed the legislative halls wining, dining, cajoling, and persuading representatives and Senators. For the most part, the high protective tariff rates, imposed during the war, held firm. Democratic attempts at reduction were steadily thwarted by well-heeled lobbyists representing woolen manufacturers and steel makers. Although a few minor reductions were accepted in 1870, Congress rejected the recommendations for sweeping reductions and reform of the tariff made by special commissioner of revenue David A. Wells, who argued against the tariff's inequities and monopoly-fostering tendencies. When Congress finally acted in 1872, it cut rates by an unscientific, across-the-board 10 per cent reduction that was fully and easily restored three years later.

Along with manufacturers, railroad promoters remained happy over the huge Federal grants and subsidies, described previously. Generally they succeeded in blocking drives to compel repayment of government loans (until much later) and to introduce government regulation of railroad rates, except for the relatively ineffective "Granger" laws passed by a few Midwestern states in the 1870's. Bankers in the Northeast, satisfied with the national banking legislation enacted during the war and the elimination of state bank notes, saw no reason for change.

On monetary-currency questions opinions were divided among businessmen as well as among Republican spokesmen. To generalize here is risky. Controversy continued over Federal bond issues left over from the war, and greenbacks, the inconvertible paper money issued during the war. Treasury contraction of the volume of greenbacks was stopped by a politically sensitive Congress in 1868. In addition to debtors, some businessmen, especially those whose firms had large corporate bond issues outstanding, favored expanding the supply of greenbacks, hoping thereby to pay their creditors in "less expensive" dollars. Federal bondholders, apprehensive over Pendleton's "Ohio Idea," were reassured by an act of Congress in March, 1869, that government bonds would be repaid "in coin or its equivalent," which the Treasury interpreted to mean gold. A refunding act the following year allowed bonds to be redeemed at par or exchanged for long-term, lower-interest, new bonds. This meant that wartime bonds, carrying 5 and 6 per cent interest rates, were traded in for thirty-year, 4 per cent bonds. This action, providing a considerable saving for the government, carried assurance that the bondholder would receive interest and principal in gold, not depreciated greenbacks.

The status of greenbacks remained questionable. Were they, as the 1862 and 1863 acts authorizing their issuance provided, legal tender for payment of private debts? Did a creditor have to accept them, when offered by a debtor in discharge of a debt? Even the Supreme Court reversed itself on this issue. In its *Hepburn* v. *Griswold* decision of 1870 the Court held that Congress could not make greenbacks legal tender in payment of debts incurred before 1862. Chief Justice Chase thus negated a policy he had presided over as Lincoln's Secretary of the Treasury. The decision left unresolved a number of related questions. By coincidence, two vacancies existed on the Court bench. To fill these, Grant named two former railroad attorneys, Joseph P. Bradley of New Jersey and William Strong of Pennsylvania. In two new legal tender cases of 1871, the Court by a 5–4 decision reversed its previous judgment and held valid the 1862 and 1863 legislation making greenbacks legal tender in payment of private debts.

But the monetary issue continued to rouse tempers. The $450 million of wartime greenbacks had been reduced by the time Grant took office to $356 million outstanding with their value in gold calculated at about 73 cents per paper dollar. At first Grant resisted efforts to resume specie payments allowing the exchange of greenbacks for gold on a one-to-one basis. Debtors and inflationists called for larger greenback issues. "Sound money" men, like Senator John Sherman of Ohio, spurned such proposals and urged specie resumption, which would raise paper money to a par with gold. Later, in 1873, Congress adopted the Coinage Act, which set a 25.8-grain gold dollar as the accepted, standard monetary unit and omitted silver dollars from the coinage, an action that inflationists and silver mining interests soon labeled the "Crime of '73."

On the monetary-inflation question, counsels were split. So, too, was the business community, mercantile and banking interests generally calling for "sound" money and resumption, while iron, coal, oil, and railroad businessmen urged a measure of inflation. Laborers and Southern and Western farmers pushed for monetary relief in the face of depressed wages and prices. Congress's bill to increase greenback volume to $400 million met a Grant veto. In a compromise, the government settled on $382 million of greenbacks. Following this, Congress in January, 1875, adopted the Specie Resumption Act. The law authorized the chartering of many additional national banks and removed limitations on the volume of national banknote currency—thereby meeting some of the previous complaints of Western and Southern men over the scarcity of paper currency. The resumption feature of the act called on the Treasury to arrange to redeem "in coin" (interpreted to mean gold) all legal tender notes as of January 1, 1879. Thereafter, the differential between paper and gold would disappear. "Sound money" men were happy with the prospect. Some inflationists and silverites would resume the battle. The Bland-Allison Act of 1878, passed over a Presidential veto, restored the silver dollar, which pleased silverites but did little for debtors by way of increasing the supply of silver money.

Resumption of specie payments by the Treasury in 1879 marked the close of the era of Civil War finance. The war debt had been reduced and refunded. National banks and their bank notes became permanent. Greenbacks continued to circulate and in their convertible state were "as good as gold."

Meanwhile economic disaster struck the nation. In September, 1873, the large banking firm of Jay Cooke and Company failed, its main office shut tight. Immediately, the New York Stock Exchange announced a suspension of securities trading. A wave of paralyzing fear washed over the financial community. The economy, which had been forging ahead rapidly since the war's end, showed signs of flagging in 1872 when over 4,000 businesses failed. Now in the face of the Cooke collapse and Wall Street suspension, business froze. Railroads stopped projected construction, and many defaulted on interest payments. Factories, mills, mines, offices, and shops closed down. Almost half of the nation's factory workers were laid off within a year's time. Farmers, too, suffered as prices tumbled—wheat from $1.57 a bushel to 77 cents—and mortgage foreclosures mounted. The Panic of 1873 ushered in a grinding depression that stretched into years of disheartening distress.

Undoubtedly, overextended borrowing, excessive railroad building, extravagant speculation, watering of stock, and an inflexible money and banking system had something to do with the economic crash. Some observers pointed to the tariff cut; others blamed contraction of European markets, erosion of business confidence, corrupt government, and lack of public controls of economic excesses. Still others said it was simply the normal business cycle at work.

Whatever the causes of the depression, its effects rumbled through the political forum of the nation. As in other depressions, the party in power caught most of the blame. A Greenback Labor party sprang up demanding an increase in the money supply. The response from Congress has been noted above. Organized farmers, notably acting through the Grange, pushed through legislation in some Midwestern states to regulate rates charged by railroads, grain elevators, and warehouses. The economic distress diverted still more attention from the South. Businessmen facing bankruptcy, farmers fighting to save their farms from foreclosure, workers seeking jobs gave little heed to the South or the Negro.

The economic slump sharply affected voting patterns in the 1874 elections. Continuing disclosures of corruption in Washington drove additional voters into breaking from Republican regularity. The Congressional elections that year produced what observers called a "Democratic tidal wave." For the first time since prewar days, the next Congress would have a Democratic majority of seventy in the House, while the Republican edge in the Senate would be paper-thin. Southern conservatives could take comfort.

Already Southern Conservatives had increased their power in their home states. Contrary to popular legend the Radical-carpetbag rule did not dominate the Confederate South for the full twelve years after Appomattox. In most, it did not begin until 1868. Virginia never experienced it after readmission in 1870. Conservative Democrats took control in North Carolina and Tennessee that same year, in Georgia the next year, in Texas in 1873, in Arkansas and Alabama in 1874, Mississippi in 1875. By then, Conservative Democrats remained out of power only in South Carolina, Louisiana, and Florida.

Many factors contributed to this result. As already noted, distractions elsewhere blurred the focus on the South. Southern Conservatives successfully played upon Northern attitudes in several ways. Mistreatment of the Indians and the Chinese immigrants in the West and of European immigrants in the East suggested that racial attitudes did not differ greatly among Americans on either side of the Mason-Dixon line. Southern Democrats won a hearing both at home and elsewhere by pinning the exaggerated label of corruption on Radical regimes, pointing to high taxes and extravagant waste and urging honest government. Their call for economic progress, for developing the South's resources, for opening new mines, mills, railroads, and investment opportunities perked up the ears of Northern businessmen. The latter became convinced that they could safely share in Dixie's obvious economic treasure only if the troublesome Radical regimes ceased. At home, Conservatives labored steadily to undermine Republican party unity. Native white Republicans were urged openly and subtly to shun their alien allies. Even Negro voters and leaders were wooed by such leaders as Georgia's Benjamin H. Hill and South Carolina's Wade Hampton, and occasionally a black was even placed on the Conservatives' ticket, as in the case of D. P. Penn in Louisiana.

Meanwhile, the Supreme Court undertook to say what the war and all the Reconstruction enactments meant in concrete cases. The resulting series of decisions perhaps reflects the cautious nature of the justices, skeptical of too many changes too fast. Perhaps these decisions mirrored the changing sentiment in the nation. In its *Texas* v. *White* decision (1869) the Court examined the nature of the "indestructible" Union and insisted that secession was legally impossible. Consequently, Texas having never left the Union was still a state.

In 1873 the *Slaughterhouse* cases gave the Supreme Court its first chance to speak on the meaning of the Fourteenth Amendment. A Louisiana statute that for health protection granted in effect a monopoly of butchering to one slaughterhouse was challenged by the excluded slaughterers as a violation of their rights under the Fourteenth Amendment's provision that "no state . . . shall abridge the privileges and immunities of citizens of the United States." While observing that the Fourteenth Amendment was designed to protect Negroes not businessmen, the Court made a distinction between those rights and privileges deriving from national citizenship and those stemming from state citizenship. The latter rights and privileges, such as engaging in business and most civil rights, "belong to citizens of the state as such, . . . [and] are left to the state governments for security and protection, and [are] not placed [by the Fourteenth Amendment] under the special care of the federal government." Clearly, the Court was not about to disturb the traditional relationship between Federal and state governments by interpreting the Fourteenth Amendment, as its framers probably intended, as placing most civil rights under Federal protection as against state action. A dissenting opinion, opening future possibilities, urged that the amendment's "due process" clause did limit a state's power to regulate private business.

In 1875 the Court heard an appeal by a Missouri woman in *Minor* v. *Happersett* that her right to vote under the Fourteenth Amendment was violated by state law providing only male suffrage. The justices rejected the claim declaring that "the United States has no voters in the States of its own creation" and the suffrage is a right deriving from state citizenship and therefore subject to state regulation and restriction. The implication for continuing black suffrage was ominous.

The Court soon dealt further with voting questions. In *United States* v. *Reese* (1876), the Court pointed out that the Fifteenth Amendment did not "confer the right of suffrage on anyone" but merely prohibited states from denying the suffrage on the grounds of race, color, or previous servitude. The states could still determine qualifications for voting, and two sections of the Federal Enforcement Act of 1870 were ruled unconstitutional for reaching beyond the scope of Federal authority. *United States* v. *Cruikshank* (1876) and *United States* v. *Harris* (1882) voided other parts of Federal enforcement legislation on the grounds that the Fourteenth Amendment in placing limits on states did not empower the Federal government to act against individuals who interfered with the rights of other individuals, even if they used intimidation and violence. By Grant's last year in office, Supreme Court rulings had eroded the meaning of the Reconstruction amendments and enforcing legislation to the point that Negro civil rights and suffrage rested largely in the hands of states and private citizens. In so doing the justices seemed to reflect the trend of affairs and public opinion. The process would be pushed still further in the 1880's.

One other aspect of the Fourteenth Amendment drew the Court's attention in 1877 when an Illinois "Granger law" regulating grain elevators was challenged. In *Muhn* v. *Illinois* the judges upheld the state's power to regulate "a business invested with a public interest." But Justice Stephen J. Field's dissenting opinion that unreasonable public regulation of business violated the Fourteenth Amendment's "due process" clause would within a dozen years become the controlling view—a view that the framers of the amendment could scarcely have anticipated for a provision designed to protect black freedmen.

By the mid-seventies, then, growing Northern weariness and indifference to political affairs in the South was apparent in many ways. The Liberal Republican uprising of 1872, in which former Radical Horace Greeley had urged North and South to "forget that we have been enemies," had been followed by the devastating depression. Some Northern businessmen saw violence and disorder in Radically-dominated Southern states as frustrating their hope of developing profitable enterprises there, and they looked hopefully forward to improved opportunities under "Redeemer" regimes. When Grant was considering requests for Federal troops in Mississippi at election time in 1874, his Attorney General advised him "The whole public are tired of these annual autumnal outbreaks in the South." Ohio leaders protested that sending troops would lose Republican votes in their state. The President did not order troops to intervene.

In the wake of the 1874 "Democratic tidal wave," Republican leaders in Washington faced a troubling dilemma. To be sure of winning the forthcoming Presidential contest in 1876, some Southern votes had to be held. A new enforcement bill was introduced in Congress to authorize use of troops during the balloting. Encountering resistance from some Republicans as well as the solid Democratic contingent, the bill lost.

At the same time, early in 1875, Congress adopted what might be termed the last gasp of the revolution—of the humanitarian crusade that was begun by the abolitionists, nurtured by the Civil War, and brought to fruition by the Radicals as the "first Negro revolution" in the vigorous measures of 1867–68. A new Civil Rights Act, introduced by veteran crusader Charles Sumner before his death in 1874, rolled through Congress in the closing weeks of the session and was signed by President Grant on March 1, 1875. Some saw it more as a personal tribute to honor Sumner than as a practicable measure. The law recognized "the equality of all men before the law" and set stiff penalties for offenders who denied any citizen "full and equal enjoyment of inns, public conveyances, . . . theaters, and other places of public amusement." Also punishable was denial of equal rights to serve on juries. After this act, Congress would pass no further legislation to secure Negro rights for another eighty years. Even the verbal thrust of the humanitarian, democratic revolution stopped at this point. A reaction had already set in, resulting in the shaving away of Federal protection of equal rights and opportunities for Negroes.

2. *"Reunion and Reaction:" Making a President and Unmaking a Revolution*

As the 1876 Presidental contest neared, each national party strove to heal its own internal wounds and bind together its discordant factions. Most Liberal Republican mavericks of 1872 had resumed their allegiance but insisted that the party cleanse itself of the stench of the Grant regime's corruption. Some party regulars were pushing the candidacy of "Plumed Knight" James G. Blaine, House Speaker for the past five years, whose presidential looks and manner made him appealing. Blaine's reputation, however, became tarnished when a House investigation tied him to a questionable connection with the Union Pacific.

At the Cincinnati convention, when an effort to renominate Grant collapsed, a drive to nominate Blaine was stymied by "Stalwart" professionals led by New Yorker Roscoe Conkling. Delegates then turned to name fifty-six-year-old Rutherford B. Hayes, currently in a second term as a reform governor of Ohio. Hayes's appeal stemmed from his record as a Union army officer and as a competent governor, unconnected with "the mess in Washington."

At their St. Louis convention the Democrats, anxious to regain the Presidency they had not held since Buchanan's day, managed to submerge their sharp differences on tariff and monetary policies. They chose as their candidate the wealthy New York lawyer Samuel J. Tilden, whose earlier labors in sending notorious Boss Tweed to prison had won Tilden election to the governor's chair where he further enhanced his reputation as a reformer. In their favor, the Democrats had economic distress, the Grant scandals, and a public clamor for change.

On November 7, when the election returns clicked over the telegraph wires, the New York *Tribune* headlined, "Tilden Elected." On the face of it, Tilden appeared to have captured 4,282,000 votes, giving him a margin of 250,000 over Hayes's 4,033,000 in the popular votes. If these returns held, Tilden would also have the edge in the electoral college vote, to be tallied in December. For some weeks reports from the South indicated active intimidation of prospective Negro voters by Red Shirts, Rifle Clubs, and other Pro-Democratic "Redeemer" outfits. Such action may have occurred in every Southern state, but it was especially noted in three—South Carolina, Louisiana, and Florida, where whites struggled to oust carpetbag regimes. Without these three states, Tilden had 184 undisputed electoral votes (185 being needed for election); Hayes had 166. One more vote would make Tilden President. But South Carolina's 7 electoral votes, plus Florida's 4 and Louisiana's 8 totaled 19. Leaders quickly noted that if these were determined to be Republican and one disputed Oregon vote held, Hayes would become President.

On November 8, the day after the election, sniffing victory, Republican national chairman Zachariah Chandler issued the bold claim: "Hayes has 185 electoral votes and is elected." Simultaneously he wired Southern Republican state chairmen to hold their states in line. As Republican chiefs hustled southward to bolster their party's claims, Democratic chairman Abram S. Hewitt countered by dispatching spokesmen for his party, too.

The three questionable states now became the target of both parties—each tugging to gain their votes and not scrupling about methods used to win. Threats, bribes, perjured testimony, jiggered vote tallies—all played a part on both sides. In each doubtful state, attention soon focused on the "returning" or "canvassing" boards whose job was to "review" the voting returns, scrutinize polling methods and ballots, and render a judgment giving the official state count. The boards, almost exclusively Republican in membership, proceeded to "review" by throwing out some ballots or even the whole vote of a district.

The result was that an apparent, original Tilden majority was converted in the process into a Hayes majority. For example, in Louisiana, Tilden's original 6,000-vote margin melted away and became a 4,000-vote edge for Hayes. In Florida, encouraged by "visiting statesmen" from Washington, the board seemed to have fabricated evidence that gave the state to Hayes. Because of massive dishonesty on both sides, a fair conclusion as to who rightly won these states is impossible to reach. How far Democratic intimidation at the polls was offset by Republican dishonesty in the tally leaves an almost insoluble riddle. Research suggests that making allowances on both sides, Tilden was entitled to Florida's 4 votes, Hayes to the others.

When Congress met in December, 1877, it wrestled with the dual question—how to count the electoral vote and which votes to count, the three doubtful states having submitted double sets of returns. An earlier Congressional joint rule of procedure provided that if either house objected to an electoral ballot it would not be counted except by a concurrent vote of both House and Senate together. The rule had lapsed. Republicans held a majority in the Senate, Democrats in the House. Naturally Republicans refused to reinstate it, since Democrats outnumbered Republicans in the combined houses. Instead, Republicans contended for the constitutional provision that the Vice President "shall in the presence of both houses open the certificates [of each state's returns] and the votes shall then be counted." This would in effect authorize the Republican Vice President to determine which returns were legitimate.

Democrats, of course, objected to such a proposal. Hewitt cautioned that stealing the election would rouse Democratic war veterans to arms in the North. Democrat Henry Watterson even threatened to march 100,000 Kentuckians to Washington to install Tilden as President. One historian estimated later that more Americans feared bloodshed in 1877 than in 1861. Republicans talked of calling out the army. Amid such talk Congress, with more Democrats than Republicans in support, agreed to a special electoral commission, composed of five members each from the House, the Senate, and the Supreme Court. The fifteen members would include seven Democrats, seven Republicans, and an independent from the Court. Unfortunately the intended independent, Justice David Davis resigned from the bench (having just been elected Senator from Illinois) the same day the electoral commission bill was approved. In his place Justice Joseph P. Bradley, a Republican, was selected. In February, 1877, when the contested returns from the three Southern states went before the commission, the latter in each instance voted 8–7 to accept the Hayes returns.

Democratic opposition to accepting Hayes, intense at first, had been melting noticeably, especially among Southern Congressmen, in the weeks since Congress had met in early December. Republicans came to realize the difference between Northern and Southern Democrats. While both wanted Tilden to become President, Northern Democrats saw this as the only goal. For Southerners, it was more important to achieve home rule and Federal troop removal than to have a Democrat in the White House. Playing on this Democratic cleavage, Hayes's men in Washington, notably James A. Garfield, made it clear to Southern leaders that Hayes's views, expressed in the campaign and afterward, were not far different from theirs. Hayes had said he wanted fair play for Southern whites and for Negroes justice and citizenship recognition. These latter goals, he believed, could be best achieved through reliable, upper-class whites in control of Southern governments. Indeed, Hayes seemed almost to echo what white Southerners had been urging for years. No matter how much most Southerners might disagree on other question, restoration of white supremacy brought them together in a united front. The ending of Federal troop interference and the recovery of home rule were basic to acceptance of Hayes by virtually all Southern Democrats. Republican leaders soon saw that they could trade home rule for getting Hayes in the White House. But they had to offer something in addition, since Tilden, too, would have granted home rule.

As historian C. Vann Woodward has made so clear, other forces operated to generate an amicable settlement in Hayes's favor. Even before 1875, prominent Southerners, mostly prewar Whigs, as noted earlier, had been seeking to develop a new industrialized, business-oriented South. To them Republican actions on Federal subsidies and spending were more appealing than those of Northern Democrats who battled for economy in government expenditures. With private investment in Southern economic ventures dried up by the panic, what was wanted by Southern politicians, reflecting Southern entrepreneurs' views, was Federal aid for river-harbor works and for building the levees, canals, and railroads to insure decent transportation and stimulate their section's economic prosperity.

Just as Hayes's managers became conscious of such Southern desires, so did Northern businessmen. Tom Scott of the Pennsylvania Railroad was already seeking Congressional aid for his Texas and Pacific line that would tie the lower South with the Far West through branch lines to New Orleans, Memphis, Vicksburg, and other points. An anti-Scott lobby under the Southern Pacific's Collis P. Huntington had been fighting the Scott plan. Gradually, as politicians negotiated during December and January, opposition softened. An arrangement was devised that would allow Huntington to build the western end of the rail line and Scott the eastern. Hayes's lieutenants in the capital, particularly Garfield, Murat Halstead, and William H. Smith, reported by mid-January that at least fifty Southern Congressmen were prepared to support Federal subsidies for the Texas and Pacific. The understanding which emerged called for Hayes's managers to promote Federal subsidies for additional Southern transportation projects in return for promises by Southern Congressmen not to oppose Hayes's selection, and to support Garfield for House Speaker in return for appointment of a Southerner to Hayes's cabinet. When this understanding became firm in late January, Congressional approval of the electoral commission plan followed.

The opening of state ballots then proceeded before Congress, meeting in joint sessions. Disputed returns were referred to the fifteen-man commission. After hearing arguments, the commission made its key decision on the Florida returns, where the Democrats had the strongest case. On February 9 it announced that it would not "go behind the returns," thereby giving Florida's votes to Hayes. In another two weeks the arbiters had resolved the disputes over Louisiana and South Carolina ballots by an 8–7 vote in favor of Hayes. The dispute over one Oregon electoral vote was similarly resolved. These decisions, assuming Congressional concurrence, would raise Hayes's electoral count to the 185 needed for victory.

At this point, balking Democrats threatened an extended filibuster to block Congressional approval and thereby stymie Hayes's inauguration.

New negotiations went over the same ground as the December-January talks, with added Southern participants, and culminated in the famed "Wormley Hotel Bargain." Therein Hayes Republicans again assured Southern Democrats that in return for abandoning the filibuster they could count on troop removal and home rule. On March 1, President Grant made it known that he was rejecting an appeal for troops by the tottering Radical regime in Louisiana.

Northern Democrats, incensed that Southern cohorts had sold out to the Republicans, staged a ranting protest in a wild, eighteen-hour session on March 1. They even pushed through a House resolution declaring Tilden the rightful next President. This frothy fury notwithstanding, Hayes came on from Columbus in a private rail car supplied by Tom Scott. On March 3 (the new President having religious scruples about oath-swearing on Sunday, March 4) he took the Presidential oath in a private ceremony. Some said the early oath-taking was to forestall possible violence. On Monday, March 5, he retook it publicly.

The Republicans' "Southern strategy" that fashioned the Compromise of 1877 was interpreted in varying ways, according to the outlook and interest of the interpreter. Some saw it as the natural upshot of the national mood of conciliation. Americans, having wearied of extremism and the brawling discord of the past two decades, longed for relief in moderation and peaceful harmony that only compromise and accommodation could bring. Even Tilden himself rejected violent protest, saying "it will not do to fight."

To some the Compromise appeared as a statesmanlike act engendering happy adjustment and good will between the sections of the now reunited nation. Some politicians took the pragmatic view that the Compromise insured practical, immediate objectives, both political and economic, which was after all what politics was all about. Southern Democrats thought of the Compromise as promising broad economic progress for the South. But other Southerners, of agrarian persuasion, feared that the deal presaged a coming Northern exploitation which would hold the South in economic dependence. Northern Democrats viewed the arrangement as a stab in the back for the party just as it was on the verge of recovering control in Washington. The resulting "Solid Democratic South" would be only marginally useful to the party in framing national legislation.

Indeed, a long-range political view suggests that the Compromise marked the beginning of a continuing flirtation between Southern Democrats and Northern Republicans, which on many subsequent occasions would operate as an effective coalition in determining the course and nature of Congressional legislation.

It was clear to Southerners at the time of making the Compromise, and over the years it became increasingly clear to the country at large, that Republicans in agreeing to home rule for Southern whites were surrendering the idealism that infused the party's birth twenty years earlier, and they were abandoning the cause of equal rights for Negroes that Radical Republicans had written into the Fourteenth and Fifteenth Amendments just a decade before. Old-time abolitionists Garrison and Wendell Phillips howled in protest, but their cries faded as echoes of a past out of tune with the times. Home rule, men knew full well, meant white supremacy. The Negro in the South would now have only such rights as "home rulers" chose to grant and must suffer such restrictions as they chose to impose—whether by private individual action, legislation, or constitutional evasion. The revolution, so nobly begun and stubbornly fought for, lay aborted—victim of a struggle for political place and economic favor. The natural extension of the Civil War's highest purpose lay abandoned.

3. Aftermath of the Compromise of 1877

Putting the provisions of the Compromise into effect did not go exactly according to its framers' formula. President Hayes did name ex-Confederate David M. Key of Tennessee as Postmaster General and, after some static from "Stalwarts," got him confirmed. On the troop withdrawal promise, Hayes stalled for a time. Twelve Southern Republican Congressmen threatened to bolt the party if the troop order were issued. And the Radical Republican elected on the face of the returns as governor of Louisiana in the election of 1876 captured more votes than Hayes in that state. For Hayes to abandon him would tacitly concede that Republicans had not carried Louisiana and thereby further weaken the position of Hayes, whom Democrats were already calling "His Fraudulency." Growing restive over the delay, Southern Democrats bombarded Hayes with repeated calls for troop withdrawal. Finally in April, six weeks after inauguration, Hayes dispatched the order. Actually, troops were not literally "removed from the South" but redeployed and not later called on for civil duty. Radical regimes in Louisiana and Florida folded quietly, yielding place to "Redeemer" regimes. Southern Democrats glowed even more when the President allowed roughly a third of Federal appointments in the South to go to Democrats. And Hayes's Memorial Day journey to Tennessee, where he decorated Confederate graves, was hailed as a goodwill gesture to help heal the nation.

Northern Democrats, seething over the sellout, waited for their chance to even the score with the arrangers of the Compromise. The opportunity came in October when Hayes called Congress into special session to get approval of the military appropriation bill that had stalled in the previous session. Southern Democrats went along with Northern colleagues in opposing Garfield, and the Speakership went to Pennsylvania Democrat Samuel J. Randall. The Northern Republican–Southern Democratic legislative combine now began to come apart at the seams. True, Randall appointed a railroad committee favorable to Scott's Texas and Pacific subsidy plan. But the bill reported by the committee lost on the House floor. Scott disgustedly gave up and sold his Texas and Pacific-Railroad to Jay Gould, who later made a deal with Huntington. Eventually the South got a railroad to the Pacific but not in the manner intended by the Compromise framers. But on Southern internal improvements the story was different. Many bills were introduced, few got out of committee, and most of these died at the hands of fuming, economy-minded Northern Democrats. Southern disillusionment grew larger.

Mounting agrarian radicalism in the South still further undermined the Compromise. A Southern-Western coalition in Congress pushed through the inflation-intended Bland-Allison Silver Act over a Hayes veto. Northern Republicans, especially business-oriented ones, fearful that this new alignment might overturn other Civil War economic legislation, now revived "bloody shirt" tactics against the South. In the midterm elections of 1878, most remaining Southern Republicans were trounced, and Northern Republicans became further upset. Outraged by the "bloody shirt" routine, House Democrats now staged a full-scale investigation of the "fraud" of Hayes's election. In retaliation, Senate Republicans mounted their own probe of the 1878 elections in the South and discovered that the "Redeemers" had disregarded the pledge implied in the 1877 Compromise to respect Negro rights. When Hayes then refused to go along with repeal of the remaining Reconstruction legislation on the books, the Compromise appeared shattered.

After a time, Southern conservatives, increasingly disillusioned with their brief alliance with radical agrarians, returned to a closer working arrangement with Republicans. Standing by the Civil War economic legislation, they aided Northern conservatives in fighting off reform in the economic field and in supporting the new industrial order that the Civil War era had done so much to establish.

In the matter of Negro rights, the Compromise proved more durable. Largely surrendering their earlier humanitarianism, most Republicans now fully abandoned insistence on Federal efforts to protect Negro rights and to prevent local interference with Negro efforts to enter the mainstream of American life. In 1883 the Supreme Court conferred legal blessing on this new attitude when Justice Bradley's decision in the Civil Rights Cases held that the Fourteenth Amendment did not prohibit private discrimination by individuals against other individuals in the field of public accommodations and that the Civil Rights Act of 1875 was therefore unconstitutional. Later Court decisions, notably *Plessy* v. *Ferguson*, decreeing the "separate but equal" doctrine, went further in placing judicial approval of legal segregation in schools.

The dream and promise of the incipient social revolution of the 1860's wilted rapidly. The bright hopes of the antislavery-Radical idealists of the Civil War era to carry the fine phrases of the Declaration of Independence into American practice faded. The aspirations of 4 million Negro Americans for full acceptance into American life atrophied. The revival of these dreams and hopes remained at least three generations away—to be revitalized by twentieth century Americans.

The Civil War generation had accomplished much. It had preserved the American nation. It had developed efficient organizations for pushing the country forward in economic development. It had kept alive the idea that popular self-government could work. It had renewed the belief that America, even with its limitations, should serve as an example of democracy for the world. It had erased the centuries-old stain of legal human bondage. If the men of that generation failed in their effort to build a new social order based on human decency, freedom, and justice, they had the satisfaction of knowing that they had at least tried to bring it off. They had kept alive the ideal of "liberty and justice for all" and passed it on for future generations of Americans in the century that followed to nurture and to fulfill.

Bibliographic Essay

Historical writers on the Civil War and Reconstruction era have for over a hundred years been pouring out an enormous, continuing deluge of books. The bibliography that follows is of necessity selective. Its aim is to aid the reader in choosing books that amplify topics treated briefly in the present work.

For convenience and ready use, this bibliography is divided into four main parts. Part I lists general works and periodicals spanning the full period. The second part provides titles of works relating to prewar developments, which make up this volume's first five chapters. Part III deals with books on the varied aspects of the war period, covered in the middle four chapters of this volume. The last part includes volumes on Reconstruction, the subject of the present book's five final chapters.

I

The best, most comprehensive, thorough, and readable account of the period from the Mexican War to Appomattox is the monumental eight-volume work by the late Allan Nevins. The first two volumes bear the title *The Ordeal of the Union* (1947); the second two, *The Emergence of Lincoln* (1950); and the final four, *The War for the Union* (1959, 1960, 1971). The superb Nevins volumes supersede the earlier, somewhat limited work of James Ford Rhodes, *A History of the United States from the Compromise of 1850* (7 vols., 1893–1906). The best single volume coverage is James G. Randall and David Donald, *The Civil War and Reconstruction* (2nd ed., 1961), which carries an unmatched critical bibliography. With differing emphases, Edward Channing, *The War for Southern Independence, 1949–1865* (1925), Arthur Cole, *The Irrepressible Conflict, 1850–1865* (1934), and Roy F. Nichols, *The Stakes of Power* (1961) provide briefer treatments, while Thomas J. Pressly gives a splendid historiographical analysis of *How Americans Interpret Their Civil War* (1954). Other good, concise works are A. Barker, *The Civil War in America* (1961), R. T. Cruden, *The War That Never Ended* (1973), T. H. O'Connor, *The Disunited States* (1972), R. H. Jones, *Disrupted Decades* (1973), and D. M. Potter, *Division and the Stresses of Reunion* (1973). Collections of contemporary documents and interpretive readings appear in C. Crowe, ed., *The Age of the Civil War and Reconstruction* (1966), R. W. Johannsen, ed., *Democracy on Trial, 1845–1877* (1966), J. Niven, ed., *Years of Turmoil: Civil War and Reconstruction* (1969), J. Silbey, ed., *National Development and Sectional Crisis* (1970), and I. Unger, ed., *Essays on the Civil War and Reconstruction* (1970). The scholarly quarterly, *Civil War History*, is devoted exclusively to the subject, and *Civil War Times Illustrated* (monthly) offers popular articles. *Civil War Books: A Critical Bibliography* (2 vols., 1967, 1968), edited by A. Nevins, J. I. Robertson, Jr., and B. I. Wiley, provides a comprehensive, annotated listing.

II

For the growth of the nation and its sections in the prewar years Frederick J. Turner, *The United States, 1830–1850* (1935) gives a concise picture. Economic aspects are explored in the following works: T. C. Cochran and W. Miller, *The Age of Enterprise* (1942), P. W. Gates, *The Farmer's Age: Agriculture, 1815–1860* (1960), G. R. Taylor, *The Transportation Revolution, 1815–1860* (1951), and D. C. North, *The Economic Growth of the United States, 1790–1869* (1961). R. Burlingame, *The March of the Iron Men* (1938) and J. A. Kouwenhoven, *Made in America* (1948) offer original, stimulating treatments of American inventive and technological ingenuity.

For changes taking place in the Northeast, see E. C. Kirkland, *Men, Cities and Transportation* (2 vols., 1948), S. E. Morison, *The Maritime History of Massachusetts, 1783–1860* (1921), C. F. Ware, *The Early New England Cotton Manufacture* (1931), J. Mirsky and A. Nevins, *The World of Eli Whitney* (1952), R. G. Albion, *The Rise of New York Port, 1815–1860* (1939), and S. H. Holbrook, *Yankee Exodus*. For the old Northwest, especially helpful are A. L. Kohlmeier, *The Old Northwest* (1938) and H. C. Hubbart, *The Older Middle West, 1840–1880* (1936).

Good brief treatments of the ante-bellum South appear in F. B. Simkins, *A History of the South* (1956), R. S. Cotterill, *The Old South* (1939), and W. E. Dodd, *The Cotton Kingdom* (1919). Fuller treatments are provided in U. B. Phillips, *Life and Labor in the Old South* (1929), C. S. Sydnor, *The Development of Southern Sectionalism, 1819–1848* (1948), A. O. Craven, *The Growth of Southern Nationalism, 1848–1861* (1953), C. Eaton, *The Growth of Southern Civilization* (1961), and E. Genovese, *The World the Slaveholders Made* (1969). For analyses of Southern attitudes and thought patterns, see W. J. Cash, *The Mind of the South* (1941), J. H. Franklin, *The Militant South* (1956), R. G. Osterweis, *Romanticism and Nationalism in the Old South* (1949), J. T. Carpenter, *The South as a Conscious Minority, 1789–1861* (1930), and C. Eaton, *Freedom of Thought in the Old South* (1940). Illuminating special studies include R. R. Russel, *Economic Aspects of Southern Nationalism, 1840–1861* (1934), F. L. Owsley, *Plain Folk of the Old South* (1949), A. O. Craven, *Edmund Ruffin, Southerner* (1932), B. Mitchell, *William Gregg, Factory Master of the Old South* (1928), and C. V. Woodward, *The Burden of Southern History* (1960).

On immigration and its impact on America, three good treatments are found in C. Wittke, *We Who Built America* (1939), O. Handlin, *The Uprooted* (1951), and M. A. Jones, *American Immigration* (1960). For the expansionist drive west to the Pacific, appropriate chapters in R. A. Billington's *Westward Expansion* (rev. ed., 1967) give a fine survey. For special aspects of the westward thrust, see N. A. Graebner, *Empire on the Pacific* (1955), A. K. Weinberg, *Manifest Destiny* (1935), C. G. Sellers, *James K. Polk, Continentalist* (1966), and O. A. Singletary, *The Mexican War* (1960).

The older, more mellow view of slavery in U. B. Phillips, *American Negro Slavery* (1918) has to be supplemented by K. M. Stampp's more realistically critical appraisal in *The Peculiar Institution* (1956) and the readings in A. Weinstein and F. A. Gattell, eds., *American Negro Slavery* (1968). Two other different and stimulating approaches are S. Elkins, *Slavery* (1959) and E. D. Genovese, *The*

Political Economy of Slavery (1966). J. H. Franklin, *From Slavery to Freedom* (3rd ed., 1967) gives the best overall history of the Negro in the United States. Comparative studies include F. Tannenbaum, *Slave and Citizen: The Negro in the Americas* (1947) and D. B. Davis, *The Problem of Slavery in Western Culture* (1966). Special aspects are well treated in H. Aptheker, *American Negro Slave Revolts* (1943), W. S. Jenkins, *Pro-Slavery Thought in the Old South*, and R. C. Wade, *Slavery in the Cities* (1964).

The general reform movements are splendidly covered in A. F. Tyler, *Freedom's Ferment* (1944), supplemented by C. S. Griffin, *Their Brother's Keeper* (1960). The antislavery movement receives full treatment in L. Filler, *The Crusade Against Slavery, 1830–1860* (1960), which supplants J. Macy, *The Antislavery Crusade* (1919). The role of the Midwest, and especially of Weld and Birney, is stressed in D. L. Dumond, *Antislavery* (1961), *Antislavery Origins of the Civil War* (1939), and in G. H. Barnes, *The Antislavery Impulse* (1933). Abolitionists are closely examined and ably defended in M. Duberman, ed., *The Antislavery Vanguard* (1965), B. Quarles, *Black Abolitionists* (1969), B. Fladeland, *James G. Birney*, R. B. Nye, *William Lloyd Garrison and the Humanitarian Reformers* (1955), B. Thomas, *Theodore Weld* (1950), and H. S. Commager, *Theodore Parker* (1936). Original treatments of special phases appear in L. Gara, *The Liberty Line: The Legend of the Underground Railroad* (1961), S. Campbell, *The Slavecatchers* (1970), and E. H. Berwanger, *The Frontier Against Slavery* (1967).

The flaring sectional clashes of the 1850's and the rising heat of controversy are vigorously and provocatively presented in the writings of A. O. Craven, notably *The Coming of the Civil War* (2nd ed., 1957), *The Repressible Conflict* (1939), and *Civil War in the Making* (1959). The decade is also surveyed in H. H. Sims, *A Decade of Sectional Controversy* (1942), D. M. Potter, *The South and the Sectional Conflict* (1968), and G. F. Milton, *Eve of Conflict* (1934). R. F. Nichols presents the full, colorful picture of what happened to the Democratic party during the time, in *Disruption of American Democracy* (1948), *The Democratic Machine, 1850–1854* (1923), and *Franklin Pierce* (2nd ed., 1958). E. B. Smith, *The Death of Slavery* (1967) provides a fast-paced narrative. Offering fresh analyses are J. H. Silbey, *The Shrine of Party: Congressional Voting Behavior, 1841–1852* (1967) and T. B. Alexander, *Sectional Stress and Party Strength* (1967).

The opening crisis is ably treated in H. Hamilton, *The Crisis and Compromise of 1850* (1964) and *Zachary Taylor* (1951). For an understanding of the Kansas issue, the reader should consult J. C. Malin, *The Nebraska Question, 1852–1854* (1953) and *John Brown and the Legend of Fifty-Six* (1942). Also useful is J. A. Rawley, *Race and Politics: "Bleeding Kansas" and the Coming of the Civil War* (1969).

For the beginnings of the Republican party, see A. W. Crandall, *The Early History of the Republican Party, 1854–1856* (1930), R. J. Bartlett, *John C. Frémont and the Republican Party* (1930), M. F. Holt, *Forging a Majority* (1969), E. Foner, *Free Soil, Free Labor, Free Men* (1970), and J. A. Isely, *Horace Greeley and the Republican Party* (1947). On expansionist diversions during the 1850's, W. O. Scroggs, *Filibusters and Financiers* (1916) and E. S. Wallace, *Destiny and Glory* (1957) offer colorful reading. The roles of individual leaders in the mounting crisis are fully examined in D. Donald, *Charles Sumner and the Coming of the*

Civil War (1960), D. E. Fehrenbacher, *Prelude to Greatness: Lincoln in the 1850's* (1962), G. M. Capers, *Stephen A. Douglas* (1959), A. J. Beveridge, *Abraham Lincoln, 1809–1858* (2 vols., 1928), C. Sandburg, *Abraham Lincoln: The Prairie Years* (2 vols., 1926), L. A. White, *Robert Barwell Rhett* (1931), A. D. Kirwan, *John J. Crittenden* (1962), and P. S. Klein, *President James Buchanan* (1962). R. A. Billington, *The Protestant Crusade* (1938) and P. S. Foner, *Business and Slavery* (1941) add new dimensions to the controversy.

III

On the election of 1860 and the subsequent crisis, R. H. Luthin, *The First Lincoln Campaign* (1944), O. Crenshaw, *The Slave States in the Election of 1860* (1945), and D. L. Dumond, *The Secession Movement, 1860–1861* (1931) provide general overall coverage. Penetrating analyses are offered in D. M. Potter, *Lincoln and His Party in the Secession Crisis* (1942), K. M. Stampp, *And the War Came* (1950), and P. G. Auchampaugh, *Buchanan and His Cabinet on the Eve of Secession* (1926). Efforts to resolve the crisis by compromise are ably treated in R. G. Gunderson, *Old Gentlemen's Convention: The Washington Peace Conference of 1861* (1961) and Mary Scrugham, *The Peaceable Americans of 1860–1861* (1921). For special aspects and emphases, see R. A. Wooster, *The Secession Conventions of the South* (1962), N. A. Graebner, ed., *Politics and the Crisis of 1860* (1961), G. H. Knoles, ed., *The Crisis of the Union* (1965), R. N. Current, *Lincoln and the First Shot* (1963), and W. A. Swanberg, *First Blood, The Story of Fort Sumter* (1957).

For overall treatment of the war, perhaps the most useful single volume is C. R. Fish, *The American Civil War* (1937). This should be supplemented by Bruce Catton's militarily oriented *This Hallowed Ground* (1956), G. F. Milton, *Conflict* (1941), and E. S. Miers, *The Great Rebellion* (1958). The reader should also consult J. Rawley, *Turning Points of the Civil War* (1966), W. B. Wood and J. S. Edmonds, *Military History of the Civil War* (1960), and J. B. Mitchell, *Decisive Battles of the Civil War* (1955).

On the North during the war E. D. Fite, *Social and Economic Conditions in the North during the Civil War* (1910) is an excellent starting point. Delving into special topics are M. Leech, *Reveille in Washington* (1941), F. A. Shannon, *Organization and Administration of the Union Army* (2 vols., 1928), E. P. Oberholtzer, *Jay Cooke: Financier of the Civil War* (2 vols., 1907), B. I. Wiley, *The Life of Billy Yank* (1952), and P. W. Gates, *Agriculture and the Civil War* (1965). Treating Northern opposition to the war, Wood Gray, *The Hidden Civil War* (1942) should be read together with F. L. Klement, *The Copperheads of the Middle West* (1960). B. A. Weisberger, *Reporters for the Union* (1953), T. Weber, *The Northern Railroads in the Civil War* (1952), E. W. Lonn, *Desertion during the Civil War* (1928), and W. B. Hesseltine, *Civil War Prisons* (1930) help illuminate particular aspects.

The best works dealing with Lincoln are J. G. Randall, *Lincoln the President* (4 vols., 1945–55; vol. IV completed by R. N. Current), Carl Sandburg, *Abraham Lincoln: The War Years* (4 vols., 1939), D. Donald, *Lincoln Reconsidered* (1956) and B. P. Thomas, *Abraham Lincoln* (1952). Virtually every phase of Lincoln's executive leadership has attracted attention and produced a book. Among the best studies are W. B. Hesseltine, *Lincoln and the War Governors* (1948), T. H. Williams, *Lincoln and the Radicals* (1941), R. S. Harper, *Lincoln and the Press* (1951), R. V. Bruce, *Lincoln and the Tools of War* (1956), J. G. Randall, *Constitutional Problems under Lincoln* (1926), J. Monaghan, *Diplomat in Carpet Slippers* (1945), and B. J. Hendrick, *Lincoln's War Cabinet* (1946).

On the Negro and the war, most useful studies are J. H. Franklin, *The Emancipation Proclamation* (1963), B. Quarles, *The Negro in the Civil War* (1953), D. T. Cornish, *The Sable Arm* (1956), J. M. McPherson, *The Negro's Civil War* (1965), J. M. McPherson, *The Struggle for Equality* (1964), and W. L. Rose, *Rehearsal for Reconstruction* (1964) on the Port Royal experiment.

Other special aspects of the Civil War are treated in M. E. Massey, *Bonnet Brigades: American Women and the Civil War* (1966), R. Andreano, ed., *The Economic Impact of the American Civil War* (1962), E. Wilson, *Patriotic Gore* (1962), G. M. Frederickson, *The Inner Civil War* (1965), P. W. Gates, *Agriculture and the Civil War* (1965), Harold Hyman, ed., *Heard Round the World* (1972), W. R. Brock, ed., *The Civil War* (1969), D. Donald, ed., *Why the North Won the Civil War* (1960).

Biographies of Northern Civil War leaders offer rich and varied fare. A cross section includes the following: M. B. Duberman, *Charles Francis Adams* (1961), F. H. Harrington, *Fighting Politician: Nathaniel P. Banks* (1948), H. L. Trefousse, *Ben Butler* (1957), T. G. and M. R. Belden, *So Fell the Angels* (1956) on Chase to be read in conjunction with D. Donald, ed., *Inside Lincoln's Cabinet: The Civil War Diaries of Salmon P. Chase* (1954), D. Lindsey, *"Sunset" Cox: Irrepressible Democrat* (1959), B. Quarles, *Frederick Douglass* (1948), C. A. Jellison, *Fessenden of Maine* (1962), G. J. Clarke, *George W. Julian* (1923), F. Brown, *Raymond of the Times* (1951), Glyndon G. Van Deusen, *William Seward* (1967), B. P. Thomas and H. M. Hyman, *Stanton* (1962), R. N. Current, *Old Thad Stevens* (1942), F. M. Brodie, *Thaddeus Stevens* (1959), S. Mitchell, *Horatio Seymour* (1938), R. S. West, Jr., *Gideon Welles* (1943) to be read in conjunction with H. K. Beale, ed., *Diary of Gideon Welles* (3 vols., 1960) and H. L. Trefousse, *Benjamin Franklin Wade* (1963).

The diplomatic phase of the war is dealt with in E. D. Adams, *Great Britain and the American Civil War* (2 vols., 1925), D. Jordan and E. J. Pratt, *Europe and the American Civil War* (1931), M. Duberman, *Charles Francis Adams* (1961), F. L. Owsley, *King Cotton Diplomacy* (1931), and J. M. Callahan, *Diplomatic History of the Southern Confederacy* (1968).

The story of the Confederacy is best surveyed in C. Eaton, *A History of the Southern Confederacy* (1954). It should be supplemented by E. M. Coulter, *The Confederate States of America* (1950), C. P. Roland, *The Confederacy* (1960) and C. Dowdey, *The Land They Fought For* (1955). Also useful are B. J. Hendrick, *Statesmen of the Lost Cause* (1939), R. Patrick, *Jefferson Davis and His Cabinet* (1944), R. S. Henry, *The Story of the Confederacy* (1931), and C. Dowdey, *Experiment in Rebellion* (1946).

Bell I. Wiley has helped fill out the Confederate side of the story in *The Life of Johnny Reb* (1943), *Southern Negroes, 1861–1865* (1938), *The Plain People of the Confederacy* (1943), and *The Road to Appomattox* (1956). Particularly good on special phases are F. L. Owsley, *State Rights in the Confederacy* (1925), C. M. Ransdell, *Behind the Lines in the Confederacy* (1944), F. E. Vandiver, *Plough-*

shares into Swords (1952), R. C. Black, III, *Railroads of the Confederacy* (1952), F. B. Simkins and J. W. Patton, *Women of the Confederacy* (1936), and R. C. Todd, *Confederate Finance* (1954). For a fascinating contemporary view, see M. G. Chesnut, *A Diary from Dixie,* ed., by B. A. Williams (1944). Illuminating biographies of Southern leaders include H. Strode, *Jefferson Davis, Confederate President* (1959), R. D. Meade, *Judah P. Benjamin* (1943), J. T. Durkin, *Stephen R. Mallory* (1954), L. B. Hill, *Joseph E. Brown* (1939), and D. S. Freeman's classic study of *R. S. Lee: A Biography* (4 vols., 1934–35).

For a vivid, first-hand introduction to the war's military phase, consult any of three documentary anthologies of eye witness accounts: P. M. Angle and E. S. Miers, eds., *Tragic Years* (2 vols., 1960), H. S. Commager, ed., *The Blue and the Gray* (2 vols., 1950), O. Eisensciml, R. Newman, and E. B. Long, eds., *The Civil War: The American Iliad* (2 vols., 1956). Surviving participants' narratives, written soon after the war, are available in *Battles and Leaders of the Civil War* (4 vols., 1887), which has been edited in a modern single volume edition by Ned Bradford.

A convenient, brief introduction is R. E. and T. N. Dupuy, *The Compact History of the Civil War* (1960). More extended and delightfully readable is Bruce Catton's "Centennial" trilogy, *The Coming Fury, Terrible Swift Sword,* and *Never Call Retreat* (1961–65), which enlarges his earlier Union-oriented *This Hallowed Ground* (1956). T. H. Williams, *Lincoln and His Generals* (1952) and F. E. Vandiver, *Rebel Brass* (1956) analyze high level command problems, while K. P. Williams, *Lincoln Finds a General* (5 vols., 1949–59) details Northern military operations. An outside view is given by British military analysts, J. C. F. Fuller, *The Generalship of Ulysses Grant,* G. F. R. Henderson, *Stonewall Jackson* (2 vols., 1919), B. Liddell Hart, *Sherman* (1929), and C. R. Ballard, *The Military Genius of Abraham Lincoln* (1926).

Bruce Catton gives a colorful, sprightly account of the Army of the Potomac in *Mr. Lincoln's Army* (1951), *Glory Road* (1952), and *A Stillness at Appomattox* (1954). D. S. Freeman does the same for the Army of Northern Virginia in his classic, *Lee's Lieutenants* (3 vols., 1942–44). Other major campaigns are covered in S. F. Horn, *The Army of the Tennessee* (1941), E. S. Miers, *The Web of Victory* (1955), Miers, *The General Who Marched to Hell* (1951), G. Tucker, *High Tide at Gettysburg* (1958), C. Dowdey, *Death of a Nation* (on Gettysburg) (1958), Tucker, *Chickamauga* (1961), E. J. Stackpole, *Chancellorsville* (1958), E. Steere, *The Wilderness Campaign* (1960), and Dowdey, *Lee's Last Campaign* (1960). Worthwhile military biographies include for the Federals: W. W. Hassler, Jr., *General George B. McClellan* (1957), Lloyd Lewis, *Sherman* (1932), and *Captain Sam Grant* (1950), T. H. Williams, *McClellan, Sherman and Grant* (1962), and B. Catton, *Grant Moves South* (1960); and for the Confederates: T. H. Williams, *Beauregard* (1955), F. E. Vandiver, *Mighty Stonewall* (1957), and C. P. Roland, *Albert Sidney Johnston* (1964). The best of the generals' own recollections appear in the *Personal Memoirs of U. S. Grant* (2 vols., 1885–86) and W. T. Sherman, *Memoirs* (2 vols., 1886). For naval warfare, see V. C. Jones, *The Civil War at Sea* (3 vols., 1960–62), J. M. Merrill, *The Rebel Shore* (1957), R. S. West, Jr., *Mr. Lincoln's Navy* (1957), and W. M. Robinson, Jr., *Confederate Privateers* (1938).

IV

Recent interpretations of Reconstruction in J. H. Franklin, *Reconstruction after the Civil War* (1961), K. M. Stampp, *The Era of Reconstruction* (1965), Rembert W. Patrick, *The Reconstruction of the Nation* (1967), A. O. Craven, *Reconstruction: The Ending of the Civil War* (1969), and M. Perman, *Reunion Without Compromise: The South and Reconstruction* (1973) have substantially modified the earlier picture presented in W. A. Dunning, *Reconstruction: Political and Economic, 1865–1877* (1907), W. L. Fleming, *The Sequel to Appomattox* (1919), and E. M. Coulter, *The South during Reconstruction, 1865–1877* (1947). W. E. B. DuBois, *Black Reconstruction* (1935) offered a new view giving greater stress to Negro achievements, followed by J. S. Allen's Marxist-oriented *Reconstruction: The Battle for Democracy* (1937). More popularized accounts offering the traditional view are C. G. Bowers, *The Tragic Era* (1929), G. F. Milton, *The Age of Hate* (1930), R. S. Henry, *The Story of Reconstruction* (1938), and with modifications H. Carter, *The Angry Scar* (1959). For social developments see A. Nevins, *The Emergence of Modern America, 1865–1878* (1934).

Focusing on the Johnson-Radicals struggle, English scholar W. R. Brock, *An American Crisis* (1963) offers an ideological view in contrast to H. K. Beale's economically oriented *The Critical Year* (1930). Other stimulating interpretations are offered in K. M. Stampp and L. Litwack, eds., *Reconstruction* (1969), E. L. McKitrick, *Andrew Johnson and Reconstruction* (1960), H. M. Hyman, ed., *New Frontiers of the American Reconstruction* (1966), L. and J. H. Cox, *Politics, Principles and Prejudice* (1963), and D. Donald, *The Politics of Reconstruction* (1965).

Economic phases are examined in I. Unger, *The Greenback Era* (1964), R. P. Sharkey, *Money, Class and Party* (1959), R. Andreano, ed., *The Economic Impact of the Civil War* (1962), and W. T. K. Nugent, *The Money Question during Reconstruction* (1967). J. E. Sefton ably explores a long neglected area in *The United States Army and Reconstruction* (1967).

Studies dealing with individual Southern states are numerous. Among the best of them are T. B. Alexander, *Political Reconstruction in Tennessee* (1950), F. B Simkins and R. H. Woody, *South Carolina during Reconstruction* (1932), J. W. Garner, *Reconstruction in Mississippi* (1901), R. W. Shugg, *Origins of the Class Struggle in Louisiana* (1939). On the Ku Klux Klan, see S. Horn, *The Invisible Empire* (1939) and A. Trelease, *White Terror* (1971).

Useful studies on special topics include G. R. Bentley, *A History of the Freedmen's Bureau* (1955), J. B. James, *The Framing of the Fourteenth Amendment* (1956), H. M. Hyman, *The Era of the Oath* (1954), O. A. Singletary, *The Negro Militia and Reconstruction* (1957), T. B. Wilson, *The Black Codes of the South* (1966), J. T. Dorris, *Pardon and Amnesty under Lincoln and Johnson* (1953), J. M. McPherson, *The Struggle for Equality* (1964), W. C. Gillette, *The Right to Vote* (Fifteenth Amendment) (1965), M. R. Dearing, *Veterans in Politics* (GAR) (1952), P. H. Buck, *The Road to Reunion* (1937).

On the Negro, the best survey is R. Cruden, *The Negro in Reconstruction* (1969). This should be supplemented by V. L. Wharton, *The Negro in Mississippi, 1865–1890* (1947), J. Williamson, *After Slavery: The Negro in South Carolina during Reconstruction* (1965), Booker T. Washington, *Up from Slavery* (1901), John T. Lynch, *The Facts of Reconstruction* (1913), A. A. Taylor, *The Negro in Ten-*

nessee from 1865 to 1880 (1941), and S. D. Smith, *The Negro in Congress, 1870–1901* (1940). See also O. Singletary, *Negro Militia and Reconstruction* (1957), W. E. B. DuBois, *The Souls of Black Folk* (1961), and C. H. Wesley, *Negro Labor in the United States, 1850–1925* (1927).

Among biographies the following provide a cross section of Reconstruction figures: B. P. Thomas and H. M. Hyman, *Stanton* (1962), H. L. Trefousse, *Ben Butler* (1957), W. B. Hesseltine, *Ulysses S. Grant, Politician* (1935), F. M. Brodie, *Thaddeus Stevens* (1959), M. M. Krug, *Lyman Trumbull* (1965), A. Nevins, *Hamilton Fish: The Inner History of the Grant Administration* (1937), J. A. Carpenter, *Sword and Olive Branch: Oliver Otis Howard* (1964), and the second volume of David Donald's splendid life of Charles Sumner (1971). The overly sympathetic biographies of Andrew Johnson by L. P. Stryker (1929) and R. W. Winston (1928) need to be read in conjunction with the McKitrick volume previously cited.

Among the best anthologies of source materials are H. M. Hyman, ed., *The Radical Republicans and Reconstruction, 1861–1870* (1967), H. Wish, ed., *Reconstruction in the South* (1965), and J. P. Shenton, Ed., *The Reconstruction* (1963).

On the critical ending of the Reconstruction era, C. V. Woodward, *Reunion and Reaction* (1951) has substantially changed the older view in P. L. Haworth, *The Hayes-Tilden Disputed Election of 1876* (1906). For the aftermath, see Woodward, *The Origins of the New South* (1951) and *The Strange Career of Jim Crow* (2nd ed., 1966), V. P. DeSantis, *Republicans Face the Southern Question* (1959), and S. P. Hirshon, *Farewell to the Bloody Shirt* (1962).

Index

ABCDEFGHIJ–VB–79876543